FAULT LINES
IN THE FAITH

FAULT LINES IN THE FAITH

HOW EVENTS OF 1979 SHAPED THE ISLAMIC WORLD

IQBAL S. HASNAIN

First published by
Rupa Publications India Pvt. Ltd 2023
7/16, Ansari Road, Daryaganj
New Delhi 110002

Sales centres:
Bengaluru Chennai
Hyderabad Jaipur Kathmandu
Kolkata Mumbai Prayagraj

Copyright © Iqbal Syed Hasnain 2023

The views and opinions expressed in this book are the author's own and the facts are as reported by him which have been verified to the extent possible, and the publishers are not in any way liable for the same.

All rights reserved.
No part of this publication may be reproduced, transmitted, or stored in a retrieval system, in any form or by any means, electronic, mechanical, photocopying, recording or otherwise, without the prior permission of the publisher.

P-ISBN: 978-93-5702-900-1
E-ISBN: 978-93-5702-941-4

First impression 2023

10 9 8 7 6 5 4 3 2 1

The moral right of the author has been asserted.

Printed in India

This book is sold subject to the condition that it shall not, by way of trade or otherwise, be lent, resold, hired out, or otherwise circulated, without the publisher's prior consent, in any form of binding or cover other than that in which it is published.

CONTENTS

Foreword vii
Preface xi

Prologue 1

1. Wahhabism as Ideological Source of Global Jihad 25
2. Sectarian Fault Lines and the Future of the Middle East 60
3. Rise of the Shia Crescent in the Middle East 80
4. Saudi Arabia and Iran: A Tale of Two Rival States 107
5. Radicalization of Muslim Youth in Europe and America 135
6. The Internet of Jihadi Mobilization 170
7. Evolution and Expansion of the Islamic State in Iraq and Syria 194
8. Reviving Sufi Traditions to Restore Peace in the Islamic World 227

Conclusion 263
Acknowledgements 277
Index 279

FOREWORD

Our views and knowledge of contemporary Islam are not only gained through scholarship in this regard but shaped by important events in its modern history. Prof. Iqbal S. Hasnain is addressing a deeply significant issue in this well-written book, focussing on a major turning point in modern Islamic history. To comprehend his project, it is essential to contextualize it within the philosophy of the history of Islam. Unlike the Western understanding of history, which views history as a linear, progressive advancement with each period surpassing its predecessors, Islamic history, as argued by scholars such as Abdur Rahman Ibn Khaldun, follows a cyclical, ascending trajectory. Each cycle in Islamic history represents a higher level than the previous one, with a pattern of advancement, stability, collapse and subsequent rebirth. Understanding the progress of this history necessitates identifying the turning points that mark the end of one cycle and the beginning of a new one.

In the 1970s, a new cycle commenced, as evidenced by three significant events explored by Prof. Hasnain. These events, occurring in 1979, shaped the course of Islamic history in subsequent years. Notably, another event took place concurrently, although its momentum had started two years earlier: the Camp David Accords between Egypt and Israel, initiated in 1977 when the president of Egypt, Anwar Sadat, visited Israel. This historical development had profound repercussions on the regional system in the Arab and Islamic worlds.

During this period, two main powers vied for leadership in the Arab and Islamic world: nationalism and Islamism. Nationalism found its expression in Arab republics such as Egypt, Algeria, Iraq, Syria, Yemen, Pakistan and Indonesia, while Islamism was associated with traditional systems in Saudi Arabia and other Arab and Muslim monarchies. President Sadat's visit to Israel marked the decline of Arab nationalism, paving the way for the emergence of Islamist ideologies. The success of Islamist ideology coincided with the rise of Islamic movements in Egypt and other countries, gaining strength and influence within society.

Within this context, three pivotal turning points shaped the Islamic world. First, the Islamic Revolution divided the Islamic world along sectarian lines, fundamentally altering the political and state-level dynamics. This event led to the establishment of a new state based on Shia Islam, which distinctively separated Muslims into Shia and Sunni factions. Before this, no other state, including Saudi Arabia or Sudan, proclaimed itself a Sunni state. They referred to their governments as Islamic states without emphasizing sectarian divisions. Additionally, the events of 1979 included the Juhayman incident in Mecca that gave rise to the Sahwa movement in Saudi Arabia. Sahwa represented a fusion between the ideologies of the Muslim Brotherhood and Salafism, significantly influencing the Saudi political landscape. Lastly, the Soviet invasion of Afghanistan was the occasion that created the globalization of Islamic jihad, as Islamic movements shifted from pursuing national causes to international ones. This globalized trend subsequently led to the emergence of violent extremist groups in various regions, such as al-Qaeda, ISIS, and Boko Haram.

The Islamic Revolution and its subsequent spread triggered a wave of affiliated movements linked to the revolution's ideology. The resulting sectarian divisions, particularly between Shia and Sunni, intensified conflicts in countries like Afghanistan, Pakistan, Iraq, Syria, Lebanon, Yemen and Nigeria. Consequently, the events of 1979 divided the Islamic world along sectarian lines and instigated a revolutionized Islamic movement, which increasingly sought political power.

These events also gave rise to the global phenomenon of jihadist terrorism, as witnessed in groups like ISIS and al-Qaeda.

Although some of these movements may have waned in recent years, their impact will persist for generations. The intellectual and epistemological legacy left by these events has fostered a sectarian mindset, and a global perspective within the Muslim community, deviating from the traditional focus on reforming local contexts. Moreover, the politicization of Islam, driven by the aspiration to establish an Islamic state, has led to an imagined utopia.

In an academic manner, Prof. Hasnain has conducted an in-depth investigation into three significant events that occurred in 1979 that had a profound impact on the history of the Islamic world in subsequent years. Using rigorous scholarly research methods, he has examined each event, drawing from immediate authentic resources to construct a comprehensive and clear understanding of the occurrences. Prof. Hasnain has employed a scientific methodology to analyse the development, causes and consequences of each of these major events of 1979. His meticulous analysis provides a thorough examination, interpretation and assessment of the repercussions of these events in various Islamic countries and across different subject areas, shedding light on their influence on the development and progression of Islamic societies.

The title of Prof. Hasnain's work holds significant meaning, as it highlights the Muslim world's inability to halt its current trajectory and regain control for sustainable development. This is essential for societies to achieve their goals and address pertinent issues that affect both society and state in the Islamic world as a whole. The present situation is steering Muslim societies in different directions, resulting in a loss of control and damage to the societal fabric, which, in turn, has been destabilizing many states, particularly in the Middle East. This region is grappling with fundamental, violent and unstable problems that impede its progress and often lead to a near collapse of the state apparatus.

I extend my gratitude to Prof. Hasnain for his valuable contribution, appreciating the significance of his work. I encourage readers to delve deeper into his research and explore additional studies that adopt Prof. Hasnain's approach, investigating various issues that have arisen in the Muslim world as a consequence of these three pivotal developments.

Nasr M. Arif, PhD
Visiting Professor, St Andrews University, UK
Professor of Political Sciences, Cairo University, Egypt

PREFACE

The fault lines in the faith began in 1979—a defining year with some major events, which became catalysts for change in the Middle East, and in the entire Muslim world. The Kingdom of Saudi Arabia reaffirmed its loyalty to the fundamentalist ideology of Wahhabi Salafism after a radical Islamist group questioned the moral legitimacy of the ruling family, and accused it of economic and moral corruption. The Europeans hailed the Islamic Revolution as a 'liberation event', while the United States of America (USA or US) looked the other way. The literal abandonment of Afghanistan by the Americans after the Soviet retreat left hundreds and thousands of young radical Islamist fighters stranded and ready to become suicide bombers under the leadership of Osama bin Laden. It was an unintended consequence of the American support to Afghanistan.

Unlike Christianity and Judaism—two great monotheistic religions—Islam got mired in the cycle of global terrorism, driven by the radical Salafi ideology. According to the global database, as many as 5,704 Muslims were involved in small and big terrorist acts between 1979 and 2017.[1] This book attempts to find some reasons for this uptick in jihadi terrorism and its direct connection to a fundamentalist ideology among the ethnically and culturally diverse Muslim communities in the world.

The book opens with a prologue which describes three apocalyptic events that occurred in 1979 and that shaped the political and religious discourse of the Middle East, unleashing a wave of political Islam globally.

---

[1] Fondapol, *Islamic Terrorist Attacks In The World (1979-2019)*, November 2019, https://tinyurl.com/tr2xbjy3. Accessed on 20 September 2023.

The Islamic Revolution of Iran in 1979 sent shock waves across the Sunni Arab world. The Kingdom of Saudi Arabia (also referred to as Saudi Arabia or the Kingdom) fast-tracked the enforcement of the Wahhabi–Salafi puritanical Islam to counter the revival of Shiite Islam among the Muslim communities around the world. Wahhabism underscores an intense hatred for Shias and Sufi Sunni Muslims, who encourage paying obeisance to saints and show tolerance for other faiths.

In December 1989, the Soviet army withdrew from Afghanistan, leaving a physically ravaged and ethnically divided nation behind them. Afghanistan is a layered, complex society with multiple ethnic strands that defy simplistic narrations. Its population is composed of many ethnic groups. The majority of the people, however, are Pashtuns, followed by Tajiks, Hazaras, Uzbeks and a sizable Shia population. Once the Soviets withdrew from Afghanistan, the US lost interest in the region and abandoned it without realizing that Afghanistan was not Vietnam or Korea, which became normal nations after the war. The ethnic and religious complexities of Afghanistan became apparent in the intense rivalry between the tribal warlords and mujahideen groups. Every group was pitching for power and was freely using weapons to settle scores. According to Ahmed Rashid, journalist and foreign policy expert, there was no international effort or funding to revive the economy of Afghanistan after the war. Little help came by for the five million refugees eager to return home; there was no diplomatic pressure to force the mujahideen to come to a political compromise. The Central Intelligence Agency (CIA) handed over the charge of its Afghan policy to its allies in the region, Pakistan and Saudi Arabia.

Pakistani army leadership and the Inter-Services Intelligence (ISI) with its strong colonial impulse saw an opportunity to intervene in Afghanistan through the Taliban. The Pakistani army selected Mohammad Omar, known as Mullah Omar, born in a poor Pashtun family outside Kandahar, as their leader. He had fought against the Soviets and had permanently lost an eye. The ISI generals gave military training to all Taliban fighters while Saudi funds were used to purchase army vehicles mounted with guns. At the same time, children of millions of Afghan refugees were taught the puritanical Wahhabi Islam in madrasas. The Pakistani ISI military officers and Taliban leaders catalogued a minimum agenda: to restore peace, disarm the warlords, enforce the Sharia law and cleanse the society of its ills. Pakistan persuaded the United Arab Emirates (UAE) and Saudi Arabia to support the agenda through monetary help and by recognizing Taliban as the official and legitimate government of Afghanistan.

Taliban's senior leadership was fully controlled by the jihadi philosophy of al-Qaeda; Mullah Omar had invited Osama bin Laden to Kandahar in late 1996. The CIA had already reported bin Laden's involvement in the anti-American campaigns. They were not happy with his involvement in the Afghan government. The Taliban government gave full facilities and protection to al-Qaeda for opening terrorist training camps. A large number of Arabs and Pakistani terror groups, who were involved in the Kashmir, Chechen, Bosnian and Philippines insurgencies, received their training in Afghanistan.

Between 1996 and 2001, al-Qaeda camps in Afghanistan had trained about 30,000 terrorists from around the world. A robust supply chain of suicide bombers and terrorist attackers was established in the training camps spread across the region. When the US tried to destroy these camps, Pakistani ISI misguided the CIA and continued to inform the occupants of the training camps in advance of the attacks. The Americans ended up hitting only empty cabins. By 2000, there were clear indications that the al-Qaeda and the Taliban government had created an international army of Islamic terrorists for carrying out various terrorist missions. Many analysts, including Ahmed Rashid, cautioned the Americans about the dangers of the emerging situation. But there was no perceptible change in the US policy towards the growing Internet of Wahhabi Salafism, which was the ideological backbone of global Islamic terrorism.

It is beyond anybody's comprehension, why the smart strategic thinkers of the US, including those from its National Security Council

(NSC), did not flag Afghanistan as a failed country populated with rancid Wahhabi terrorist groups, like the al-Qaeda, who strongly hate Americans and Western values. In fact, they were already attacking the American targets in the region and would soon emerge as a serious threat to the US. If the famed think tank had already cautioned the US authorities, the million-dollar question remains why the US president and the Congress did not take any cognizance or tangible steps to stop the ensuing attacks on the US embassies in East Africa, the USS Cole bombing in Yemen or the calamitous September 11 attacks commonly known as 9/11.

The first chapter analyses how Wahhabism works as an ideological source of global jihad. Its core literature is based on the writings of the fourteenth century cleric Taqi al-Din Ahmad Ibn Taymiyyah, which was later expanded and institutionalized by the Islamic scholar and theologian from Najd, Muhammad ibn Abd al-Wahhab, during the eighteenth century. The chapter throws light on the early history of Saudi Arabia from a religious and political angle and explains how a pact made between Abd al-Wahhab and Ibn Saud, founder of the Kingdom of Saudi Arabia, mutually helped them to achieve their larger ends eventually.

They had initially faced various impediments from the oasis settlements as they tried to spread the ideology of Wahhabism. The visionary and ambitious chieftain of Diriyah, Ibn Saud himself, had first argued against the ideology. However, he later got convinced by it on seeing it as a religious and political tool to overwhelm the settlements of Diriyah. Slowly it got traction among the Arabs, and Ibn Saud emerged as a leader who could take the Ottoman rulers head-on and capture the Hijaz region, a big money-spinner in those days. The first Saudi state was thus formed in Diriyah oasis. The Ottoman Empire, which was ruling the entire Arabian Peninsula, smelled the rat and soon dispatched a bigger force under the command of Ibrahim Pasha, and hanged the Al Saud ruler and his followers who were preaching Wahhabism. The remaining leadership was driven out of the region and they took refuge in Kuwait.

The chapter goes on to explain how Abd al-Aziz ibn Abd al-Rahman of the Al Saud family later took help from the Ikhwan group and other mercenaries to return and recapture the Arabian Peninsula. The British at that time were in competition with the Ottoman Empire for political supremacy in the Arabian Peninsula. The British supported the Saudi forces and they soon established authority over the Arabian Peninsula.

The Second World War brought the US to the European war theatre as leader of the alliance. President Roosevelt developed a special relationship with Saudi Arabia and assumed the position of the ruling family's mentor and protector, which continues to the present day. The relationship, however, ran into rough weather after the 9/11 terrorist attacks on the US. Despite the CIA and Federal Bureau of Investigation (FBI) establishing direct links of Saudi citizens and officers in the conspiracy and execution of 9/11 attacks, the US administration always protected them from interrogation and legal proceedings.

The chapter discusses how the Wahhabi–Salafi Islam has been influencing American Muslims during the last 40 years, how the successive presidents of the country have conveniently ignored its threat and have never bothered to warn Saudi Arabia despite the American experts cautioning them many times.

It is maintained that, in the twenty-first century, Muslims globally are facing the consequence of a decision taken by Saudi Arabia in 1979—to promote the strident Wahhabi Islam by marginalizing a more tolerant and broadminded strain of Sufi Sunni Islam that always respected other faiths. The current Saudi leadership under Crown Prince Mohammed bin Salman (popularly known as MBS), however, is trying to reduce the damage by introducing some measures to moderate Wahhabism including by restricting the religious leadership of the kingdom and cutting down on the funding given to them.

It also cites an example adopted by the North African country of Morocco in purging Wahhabis from various religious institutions of the country. The religious leadership under the guidance of the

Moroccan king is showing the world that Islam can be restored with an emphasis on its core values of tolerance and respect for other faiths, if the authorities willed so. If so, art, culture, music, science and education, with full participation of women, would flourish in Muslim societies around the world as they did once, about a century ago.

The second chapter talks about the sectarian fault lines of the Muslim world and how it shapes the future of the Middle East. Sectarianism had entered a new phase with the Islamic Revolution in 1979. Nonetheless, the defining moment of the historic schism (Sunni–Shia) in the Muslim world was the Battle of Karbala, which took place in Iraq in the year 680. After Karbala, followers of the fourth caliph, Ali ibn Abi Talib, converted their camp as a theological movement, and Islam fractured into two sects: Sunni and Shia. The chapter provides a cursory glance into the history of Shia Iran and how Shah Ismail, founder of the Safavid dynasty in 1501, declared Shiism as the official religion of Iran. The Safavid dynasty ruled Iran between 1501 and 1722. The Sunni Ottoman and the Shia Safavid had a strong rivalry leading to a continuous turf war in the heart of the Middle East. This was the beginning of a major sectarian divide, which slowly widened as both Ottomans and Safavids fought many wars. For a short time, Safavids also controlled Iraq and brought a large section of the population into the Shia fold, largely by coercion and persuasion.

The state of Iraq was created by a British mandate in 1921 and granted independence as a nation in 1932. Nevertheless, Iraq did exist as a group of provinces for well over a millennium under different rules including the Abbasid, Mongol and Ottoman. Iraqi Arabs always were proud of their Arab identity, and stood for Iraqi nationalism even as they kept their Sunni and Shia identities separate. All three types of nationalist identities existed simultaneously.

The House of Saud had warned against the unintended consequence of the US invasion of Iraq as it would further the democracy and empower the Shia majority in Iraq. The Sunni Arab monarchies of the Peninsula strongly detested such an eventuality in the centre of the Middle East. The US administration was blissfully unaware of the sectarian fault lines of the Islamic world and thought, in their wisdom, that removal of the tyrannical dictator Saddam Hussein would solve all the problems of Iraq. The US administrator installed the first Shiite-led government in Iraq which would naturally be allied to Iran. Undoubtedly, the Islamic Republic of Iran was the biggest beneficiary of the US intervention in Iraq. For the first time, Iran had a friendly government in its Western neighbourhood. All the important religious places of Shiite Islam were located in Iraq. After a long gap, the Shias of Iran and other countries got free access into the shrines in Karbala and Najaf.

Jihadists associated with al-Qaeda and its derivatives like Jamaat al-Tawhid wal-Jihad, under the leadership of Abu Musab al-Zarqawi, however, were not playing mute witness to these developments. They organized guerrilla Sunni groups in towns across the Euphrates river valley. The objective was to develop an anti-Shia narrative in the Sunni neighbourhoods and attract former army officers retired by the US administrators. A perception was created among the Sunni Arab communities across Middle East that the US invasion was primarily meant to weaken Sunni Islam and empower the 'heretic' Shias. The sectarianism got a further boost when President Barack Obama believed that it was imperative for the US to engage with Iran to keep them away from achieving the nuclear threshold. The US–Iran nuclear agreement enhanced the sectarian feelings in the region. Sectarianism became a giant prism: people began to view their neighbours through it and governments used it to size up their rivals in the region. The conflict in Syria, Yemen and Iraq assumed great undertones of proxy sectarian wars between the Shia and Sunni nations of the region.

The chapter looks into the sectarian angles of the changing political equations between the major economies of the Middle East such as Saudi Arabia and Qatar, and how Israel was changing the matrix of the Middle East by using sectarianism as a tool to bring all the Arab monarchies against Iran. The Israel strategy worked very well in that they could make the world put the question of Palestinian homeland on the backburner and annex the West Bank territories further. The sectarianism in the Middle East is not showing any sign of a downturn; instead it is all set to widen further and put the future of 1.6 billion Muslims in jeopardy.

The rise of the 'Shia Crescent' in the Middle East is the discussion of the third chapter. It begins with a metaphor used by Jordan's King Abdullah II in 2004 on the interventionist policies of the Islamic Republic of Iran. He has rightly foreseen the disruption of the balance of power in the region with the rise of Iran. Since the US invasion of Iraq in 2003, Iran's influence has been growing steadily in the region. The two regional powers—Saudi Arabia and Iran—continue to assert their regional hegemony by using their interpretation of Islam. The US president, at the behest of Israel and Saudi Arabia, had imposed economic sanctions on Iran with extreme severity. Indeed, the animosity is very real on both sides. But, it is often overwhelmed by Arab nationalism, as was seen during the anti-Iran demonstrations by Shias in Iraq in the early 2020.

The Israeli treaty with Egypt in 1979 had profoundly impacted the regional groupings. The then president of Syria, Hafez al-Assad, had felt isolated and had developed a strategic relationship with Iran which was tradable. At one point, Syria negotiated with Israel for the Golan Heights and promised to improve relations with the US, and in exchange, agreed to trash relations with Iran. From the beginning of the Syrian civil war, Iran had arranged access to Hezbollah fighters from Lebanon and kept Saudi Arabia from meddling with Syria. For Iran, the Syrian war was important, as it was against a radical Sunni uprising that saw Shias as infidels deserving to be annihilated. As Iran's regional and sectarian enemy, Yemen, like Syria, is strategic towards Iran, because of the Bab-el-Mandeb Strait and the long border it shares with Saudi Arabia. Iran's support to the Houthis in Yemen constitutes a threat to the Saudi national security. At the same time, the unrelenting bombing by Saudi air force on Yemeni cities has created a humanitarian crisis in Yemen. The United Nations

(UN) and the US Congress expressed their anguish over the issue and requested the US president to ask Saudi to stop bombing and start a dialogue with Houthis to resolve that which had become a nightmare of civil society.

Iran, under the Joint Comprehensive Plan of Action (JCPOA), was in total compliance with the 2015 agreement, made between Iran and the P5+1 countries along with the European Union. The International Atomic Energy Agency (IAEA) in its technical reports also categorically stated that Iran was in full compliance with the agreement. The US president in a bizarre move, however, decided to withdraw from JCPOA. In November 2018, the US sanctions also came back into effect, forcing Iran to dramatically alter its policies, including its support for militia groups in the region and its development of ballistic missiles. All security experts in the US and European countries unanimously criticized President Donald Trump's immature and weird action. The then US ambassador to the UN, Nikki Haley, tried to manufacture a case against staying in the JCPOA. She argued that there were many sites in Iran which were left uninspected. It was, however, trashed by the IAEA and the European allies.

President Vladimir Putin's direct intervention in Syria brought Iran and Russia on the same page as a powerful counterforce to the Saudi–US bloc. The single best organized bloc of states like Turkey, Qatar and Russia has gathered around Iran. It is marching steadily ahead, motivated by clear strategic goals, powerful ideological backing and a long experience of supporting resistance forces in the Middle East. Iran is currently supporting proxies in many conflict zones in the region. The US withdrawal from the Middle East and Russian entry to the scene has empowered Iran regionally.

Jared Kushner, chief adviser to the US president on Middle East affairs, has brought Israel close to the Saudi-led Sunni block of Arab nations. The UAE and Bahrain have already signed an agreement with Israel to establish diplomatic relations. For the first time, all Arab nations seem to be ready to abandon the Palestinian cause.

The false pretext of peace-making is put up by the US, to control the interventionist ambitions of Iran and bring all important oil-producing Arab countries under the Israeli tent and its intrusive surveillance programme.

The secret normalization agreement of 'Abraham Accords' is a cause for major concern. Under it, Israel will monitor the sea, airports, communication networks as well as the bank accounts in Emirates. The 70-year old Israeli–Palestinian conflict, the main concern of Arab nations, has gone out of their radar. Nevertheless, Iran has taken a central role in defending the rights of Palestinians, and Israel has pitched it as its chief adversary in the Middle East. Israel will help in gathering intelligence and developing military strategy for the Arab nations. Bahrain's Sunni rulers have always feared the Shiite majority in the country. Israel's intelligence surveillance will help them in governance. Another long-term enemy of Israel is the Hamas, the militant group that runs Gaza. It is an offshoot of the Muslim Brotherhood, one of the main and common enemies of the Arab monarchies. Mossad, Israel's intelligence agency, will get complete access to intelligence gatherings of the Arab monarchies in the Gulf region.

The complex and layered relation between the Kingdom of Saudi Arabia and the Islamic Republic of Iran is primarily about the leadership in the Middle East region. It is about dominating its politics, economy, ideology and geopolitics, which has been going on in one form or the other for the last several decades.

Chapter four looks into the genesis of the rivalry between Saudi Arabia and Iran since the Islamic Revolution. The US–Saudi economic and military alliance since the 1930s is one of the consistent factors in the American foreign policy in spite of the fact that the Arab country is governed by a repressive monarchy. It is known to the world that Saudi Arabia's Wahhabi ideology is a major contributing factor in the spread of extremism among the Muslim communities around the world. This rigid ideology demonizes other faiths and promotes intense intolerance towards all sects of Islam other than

Wahhabi–Salafis. It also sanctions violence towards the followers of other faiths, which is forbidden in the traditional Sufi Sunni Islam.

Saudi Arabia led a tacit alliance of Sunni Arab countries in Middle East and its tension with the Islamic Republic of Iran basically boiled down to two issues: the fight for political and economic leadership, and the battle for religious or ideological dominance as they represented two rival branches of Islam. A vast majority of Muslims are Sunnis, amounting to around 80 per cent, and they are spread across the world. The countries with major Shia populations are Iran, Iraq, Azerbaijan and Bahrain. They are also present in countries like Yemen, Syria, Lebanon, Kuwait and Qatar in substantial numbers.

The Arab Spring of 2011 was an important milestone in the history of Saudi–Iran rivalry. It has profoundly transformed the political landscape of the Middle East. One of its important consequences was that the people in Arab countries like Bahrain, Yemen, Syria and Lebanon got fully polarized and the Shia population in these countries started demonstrations against the ruling Sunni elites.

Hussein Badreddin al-Houthi and his brother Abdul Malik al-Houthi hail from Yemen's northern coffee-growing Saada province. They are leaders of the Zaydi Shia movement. They operate in the mountainous northwest of Yemen. The Houthi leadership has forged a personal and organizational relationship with the tribal clans, most of whom are Zaydi Shias. They have been fighting the central government since 2004, when the movement was founded to strengthen the rights of the Zaydi sect, which represent 30 to 40 per cent of the Yemeni population. The Houthi movement came into being basically to fight the discrimination against the tribes of northern region by the Yemeni government. Yemen never had sectarian issues in the past and there was no animosity between the Shia and the Sunni sects. During the Houthi uprising following the Arab Spring, Saudi Arabia launched an aerial attack on the protesters. Subsequently, Iran entered the scene, and eventually, contours of the conflict changed in favour of the Houthi fighters. Riyadh feared that

Houthis under the guidance of Hezbollah and Iran, would emerge into a deadly fighting force on its southern border.

After sustained Saudi air bombardments and over 10,000 civilian casualties, the Houthi militia was capable of firing ballistic missiles reaching up to the Riyadh airport. It is no secret that Houthis were using Iranian missiles to hit the high-value Saudi targets. Tehran is actively engaged in providing trained fighters from Afghanistan, Pakistan and some Shia Arab countries to Yemen. Crown Prince MBS was strongly counseled by the Americans not to resort to counter attacks or escalate the conflict with the poor Arab fellow nation by any means. The UAE has withdrawn from the coalition with Saudi Arabia in the Yemen conflict. The US is trying to enforce a cease-fire and bring all the factions to a negotiating table.

The US president and the Israeli team have convinced the crown prince that the biggest threat in the Middle East is from Iran and its proxies and not from the Zionist state of Israel. The Palestinian issue has frozen in time and the Arab solidarity is no longer sustainable on this issue. The Saudi-endorsed Middle East plan under the US leadership has advised the Arab GCC (Gulf Cooperation Council) monarchies to establish a diplomatic relationship with Israel against Iran. The US withdrawal from the Middle East has scared the monarchies and they are looking for a security alternative. For the first time, the Israeli secret intelligence agency, Mossad, will work closely with the security establishments of the Arab monarchies and advise them on various potential threats. The Saudi foreign policy, under the crown prince, is misguided if it takes much solace from the US support for Saudi's regional policies in the Middle East. The Saudi surrender to Israel along with the smaller Sunni Arab nations on US's advice is sure to have long-term negative consequences. Iran is not worried about this 'unholy alliance'. On the contrary, it has emerged as an important member of a new bloc led by Russia and accompanied by countries like Turkey, China and Qatar.

It is the matrix of radicalization among the Muslim youth in the US and Europe that is analysed in chapter five. After shedding some light into the history of Muslim migration to the US and other Western countries, it goes on to explain the different ways of radicalization adopted by the international jihadi outfits, inspired by the Wahhabi-Salafi ideology, globally promoted by Saudi Arabia. It starts with the Muslim migration to Europe as early as in the year 710, when the Arabs and North African Berbers conquered the Iberian Peninsula, where they founded a series of dynasties over a period of several centuries. The Muslim cultures that arose under these conditions were marginalized during the Christian renaissance that followed.

The large flow of immigration after the First World War brought many Muslims to Europe later. At one level, the leftist political parties in Spain are romanticizing the Islamic past of Spain. Nevertheless, a great resentment was seen among the orthodox Christians against any attempts to bring the past glory of Islam back to Spain. The Islamic orthodoxy, driven by Wahhabi Salafism has overwhelmed Europe's decaying Christianity. The Christian supremacists fear that there are thousands of empty churches in different parts of the country just waiting to be converted into mosques and Muslim prayer halls.

France has an estimated six million Muslims in a country that holds fast to the idea of state secularism. The transformation of French Muslim communities to Wahhabi Salafism was completed in the last 45 years, as it became the dominant discourse in all mosques, funded by the Muslim World League (MWL) of Saudi Arabia. They pumped millions of dollars into the construction of mosques, training of imams and distribution of Wahhabi literature. Their focus was on the suburban communities as they lived separately with no social and cultural interaction with the mainstream French societies. Their identity was based exclusively on Islam they rejected all French social values as anti-Islamic.

Since 2013, at least 1,700 young French men and women have joined the Islamic State of Iraq and Syria (ISIS). They were behind the attacks France faced in 2015 and 2016. The French State, despite its neutrality, took several initiatives to integrate the Muslim immigrants to the national mainstream. President Macron's present plan is to put the brakes on the foreign funding to the Muslim community in order to disentangle the Muslim organizations in France from other countries. Another initiative is to train the imams at home. The training would be in cultural values and not in religious texts in order to foster a generation of 'made in France' imams. The Salafi imams would be replaced in mosques and moderate Sufi Sunni imams would be installed to change the religious narrative.

The current population of Muslims in Britain is around 1.8 million. The Salafi teachings and radicalization of youth are widespread in all the mosques. The main organization responsible for spreading Salafism in Britain is the Society for the Revival of the Prophetic Ways. They spread Salafism among the youth through Islamic 'study circles', mosques, community centres and universities across Britain. All terrorist attacks from 2016 to 2018 were directly linked to the jihadi groups that staunchly follow Salafism. The ideology has penetrated deeply into the psyche of the young generation of British Muslims, which has manifested as terror attacks at various places in the country from time to time, killing hundreds of innocent people on the streets.

The Muslim Students Association (MSA) was started in 1963 in the US and Canada on a number of university campuses. The MSA, in the initial years, worked with students in universities and with the leadership of communities. By 2020, more than 80 per cent of the American mosques were attached with Sunday schools, and community centres had been widely using Wahhabi–Salafi literature to advocate fundamentalist ideology. The Council on American–Islamic Relations (CAIR) is the main ideological agency of Wahhabism in America. The Salafi control over mosques implies control of property, buildings, appointments, training of imams and content of preaching at the mosques. The literature distributed among the believers comes directly from the Ministry of Islamic Affairs, Dawah, and Guidance (MOIA) in Riyadh.

The Islamic Society of North America (ISNA) is the largest body of Muslims in North America. Every year, it holds a large convention in any of the major US cities. Both CAIR and ISNA maintain close relations with the Saudi government. They receive huge funds regularly through Saudi charities, like Muslim World League (MWL) and the World Assembly of Muslim Youth (WAMY); at one point, they were the main funders of al-Qaeda.

A third and fourth generation of Muslim youth, irrespective of their ethnicities and colour, attend the Wahhabi–Salafi mosques and become rigidly conservative. They keep their world view within a narrow ideological bandwidth. Their Friday sermons or *khutbah* are always loaded with strong Wahhabi messages. The rhetoric to a large extent is based on real-time events like the Israeli occupation of Palestine or the US invasion of Iraq. The simultaneous alienation from the pervasive Western culture, and the isolation and restrictions imposed by the community they live in, encourage them to be glued to the Internet and social media platforms. It makes them extremely vulnerable to the self-radicalization processes devised by the Wahhabi–Salafi organizations and their online literature.

The Islamist jihadis use all the modern communication technologies and Internet platforms to leverage their Wahhabi–Salafi goals. The famous *New York Times* columnist Thomas Friedman used the metaphor of the 'flat world'[2] to describe the globalization driven by information and communication technology. Islamic terrorist organizations like al-Qaeda, ISIS and al-Shabaab are some of the major beneficiaries of global connectivity. They use fast connectivity to spread encrypted messages across the world and raise millions of dollars through online crowd-funding. Contrary to popular perception, most young people radicalized online are not devout Muslims. Online radicalization occurs in all economic classes. The common denominator seems to be that everyone who is radicalized and recruited online agrees with the Wahhabi–Salafi ideology and their anti-West narratives.

---

[2]Friedman, Thomas, *The World Is Flat: A Brief History of the Twenty-First Century*, Farrar, Straus and Giroux, 2005.

The US National Security Council should internally debate on the appropriate strategy to counter the radical Salafi ideology, which basically triggers the violent Islamist extremism among the Muslim communities. Their recruitment needs to be stopped by changing their narrow-minded Wahhabi–Salafi narrative of Islam and also by ideologically discrediting these groups. All the big and small Muslim organizations should be taken on board and officers of the National Security Council should convince them that no extremist ideology would be considered sustainable any more.

The US security and counter-terrorism agencies need to first do something about regulating the appointment of imams in the mosques across the country. Steps should be taken to sensitize them towards a peaceful co-existence in a pluralistic society as they once did before the hard push of Salafism by Saudi Arabia. The US Congress should legislate to the effect that no foreign funding be allowed to the Islamic extremist organizations in the country; countries like France have taken similar initiatives in recent years. Measures can also be taken to strengthen the fabric of local communities to resist extremist ideas from influencing the young generation via different sources.

Chapter six describes how the Islamist groups have been smartly using social media platforms, including by creating 'cyber armies', to recruit and radicalize a large number of millennial Muslims. The Islamic State (IS) brought cyber jihad to a whole new level—from using static websites, chat forums and online magazines, to making intelligent use of interactive and fast-paced social media platforms. ISIS, which branched out from the al-Qaeda tent, used social media apps and other advanced tools to propagate their ideology and to execute their missions.

Several studies on the process of radicalization have suggested that radical online content by itself does not recruit or radicalize people. Rather, it tends to complement offline efforts to radicalize or makes the job easier for recruiters.

The Internet and social media platforms offer a world of possibilities even to a common user. It is cost-effective and user-friendly. One can hide behind fake identities, and thus, anonymously spread messages. These messages can reach a large target group. They can be one-to-one or one-to-many with a high degree of interactivity. The next generation of computers with the help of artificial intelligence is sure to open a world of new possibilities for the jihadi organizations in realizing their destructive ends. The chapter observes that the dichotomy that exists between the Western and the Islamic cultures can cause Muslim teenagers in Western countries to feel isolated and disconnected from their peer groups, which would eventually make them more vulnerable to online radicalization and recruitment by different terror outfits.

The rise and fall of the Islamic State is analysed in the seventh chapter. From its birth in the hands of its founder and patriarch Abu Musab al-Zarqawi under the auspices of the al-Qaeda leadership, the outfit grew into becoming one of the largest and most powerful extremist organizations in the world. The section explains how Islamic terror outfits attracted thousands of jihadi fighters from different parts of the world to its training camps in Afghanistan, and how it slowly evolved from the al-Qaeda tent to have its own identity and character to the extent of establishing a caliphate of its own.

It was the US invasion of Iraq in 2003 that expedited the growth of the organization. It unleashed a new social and sectarian chaos in Iraq. Zarqawi and his forces escalated sectarianism by attacking Shiite groups and the US forces. Sectarianism got a real boost when the Coalition Provisional Authority (CPA) decided to dissolve the entire military, security and intelligence services of the earlier regime. This one decision gave a big opening to Zarqawi and his associates. Sacked soldiers of Saddam's Baathist force joined the insurgency under the loose ISIS leadership, which got structured only later. Zarqawi had his focus on the immediate creation of the Islamic State as the base for the caliphate. He brought all the Sunnis on a single platform by spreading the message that the greatest threat to Sunnis in Iraq were Shiites. Zarqawi even spoke about the genocidal 'final solution' doctrine against Shias and cleverly used social media platforms to spread his extremist ideas.

Zarqawi was killed during a special operation raid undertaken by the US in October 2006. A new emir was appointed to lead the outfit after his death. The al-Qaeda in Iraq (AQI) was renamed as the Islamic State in Iraq (ISI). The intended Islamic state would include Iraq's existing Sunni majority provinces of Baghdad, Anbar, Kirkuk, Saladin and parts of Babil. The ISI formation statement named Abu Omar al-Baghdadi as the caliph. However, he too was soon killed by the US forces along with Abu Hamza al-Muhajir, next in line after Zarqawi. He was replaced by another prominent ISI leader, Abu Bakr al-Baghdadi.

Under the leadership of Abu Bakr al-Baghdadi, the Islamic State saw the greatest expansion between 2011 and 2014. All the Sunni tribal leadership came under the control of the Islamic State and they thwarted all attempts by the Shia government and sought reconciliation with the Sunni communities. In 2007, the city of Damascus in Syria became a major transit port for the foreign fighters joining the Iraq insurgency. But later, as the dynamics of Syrian insurgency shaped against Bashar al-Assad, a large number of foreign fighters stayed back in Syria and established ISIS. In 2013, there was a free flow of jihadists between Iraq and Syria. By June 2014, ISIS fighters had captured the cities of Samara and Mosul. Panic ran high among the US-trained new Iraqi army. The fall of Mosul changed the balance of power among Iraq's three main communities: Sunni, Shia and Kurds. The Iraq–Syria border no longer existed, as ISIS forces became more powerful, drawing weapons, fighters and money from the conquered areas of Iraq.

Abu Bakr al-Baghdadi declared himself as the caliph of ISIS and he conceived its administrative structure like a pyramid with him as chief of the state at the top. Many important positions were given to former senior army officers of the Baath party. The monthly income of the state at one point was US\$3 million making it the wealthiest terrorist organization in the world. Sharia law was followed strictly in the state, under which harsh punishments were given to offenders.

It structurally always remained a jihadist organization, undergirded by the ideology of Wahhabi Salafism.

It has been alleged that President Obama's inept handling of the expanding footprints of ISIS gave full opportunity to Abu Bakr al-Baghdadi to establish the caliphate and capture a large swathe of area in Syria and Iraq. President Obama had finally decided in 2015 to provide air power and military advisers to help the Kurds in their battle against the Islamic State. This was indeed a game changer: the US could decimate ISIS caliphate without putting its boots on the ground. In 2016, President Trump inherited the policies from the Obama administration that were working effectively both in Syria and Iraq.

The Syrian Democratic Forces (SDF), an alliance of Kurdish and Arab fighters backed by US air cover defeated ISIS caliphate, which once covered large areas in Iraq and Syria. The SDF fighters with the US support recaptured almost 95 per cent of its land and took thousands of Arab and foreign fighters in custody. By 2017, the SDF had secured all the cities in the Euphrates river valley except some small pockets. Although the physical caliphate of ISIS, spread across Syria and Iraq, has been destroyed, it continues to exist virtually as an ideology.

The importance of reclaiming and promoting a peaceful, tolerant and progressive tradition of Islam, represented by Sufi Sunni Islam, is the focus of the eighth and last chapter. It proposes the Sufi traditions of Islam as an alternative to the Wahhabi–Salafi ideology that has, for the last several decades, been wreaking havoc in the world with its violent and bigoted ideology. The chapter describes how Sufi Sunni Islam flourished in different parts of the world for centuries, as it is an ideology that considers peace and love as the fundamental philosophy of human life. Sufism, throughout history, has drawn people to its fold through simplicity, sincerity, broadmindedness and compassion. Sufis have built bridges of understanding, amity and conciliation between different faiths, cultures and sects.

Prophet Mohammad's companions were inclined towards the

deepest possible expression and fulfilment of their love for God. The guidance that forms the basis of Sufi practices is found in the teachings of Quran and Hadith. For example, the practice of silently remembering the Divine was taught by the Prophet himself to his companions. The famous *miraj*, or the night journey of the Prophet, has long been inspiring to serious followers of Islam and mystics as a metaphor for a spiritual journey. The Sufi aspirants strive to transcend the physical limitations of space and time to draw closer to the Divine. There are many examples to demonstrate that there was a strong mystical element in the life of Prophet Mohammad. The Sufi Sunni tradition of Islam had produced a flourishing intellectual culture throughout the Islamic world between the thirteenth and sixteenth centuries, which is considered to be the 'Golden Age' of Islam.

The fourteenth century cleric Ibn Taymiyyah was the first Islamic scholar to attack the 'devotional Islam' practised by the Sufis. Later in the eighteenth century, another scholar, Muhammad ibn Abd al-Wahhab, got inspired by his teachings and expanded it further to enforce them among the Saudi settlements after making an agreement with the rulers of the land. His teachings later came to be known as Wahhabism. In fact, it was a form of Salafism, which argues that going back to the old and 'purest' form of Islam, as it was during the time of Prophet Mohammed, was the only way to protect it. Abd al-Wahhab blamed the traditional Sunni ulamas for moving away from the original principles of Quran.

With the help of the authorities and massive financial support from the Saudi government Wahhabi Salafism was propagated aggressively in Arabia and exported extensively to other countries. Thus, Wahhabi Salafism has been destroying the soft nuances of Islam, thereby transforming it into the jihadi brand of faith abhorred and feared by people across the globe.

Sufism continued to be a crucial part of global Islamic life until the twentieth century, when its historical influence upon Islamic civilization began to be undermined by the influx of Wahhabi Salafism driven by Saudi Arabia.

Turkey and Persia together have been the centre of many Sufi lineages and orders in the past. Sufi poets and philosophers like Jalal ad-Din Muhammad Rumi have greatly helped in spreading Islam in central and South Asia. Sufism was also the guiding principle of the Ottoman Empire. When, in the eighteenth century, Abd al-Wahhab rebooted Islam with puritan rigidities and branded Sufis as heretics, it was the Ottoman rulers of the Arabian Peninsula, who came to their rescue. The Wahhabis made all efforts to establish the new Wahhabi Islam as the real and the only true Islam.

The Wahhabi Salafists did not recognize the old Sufi Sunni traditions of Islam, which accommodated metaphysics, ethical disciplines, devotional practices, music, poetry and mystical experiences. They found it incompatible with the values that they conceived as Islamic. The Salafi followers always strived to purge Islam of beliefs and practices for which they believed there existed no backing of Quran and Hadith. During the fourteenth and fifteenth centuries, many Syrian and Indian scholars like Shah Waliullah combined orthodox Sufism with the Salafi spirit. Most of the founders and the early leaders of Tablighi Jamaat also had strong connections with different Sufi orders. However, the movement firmly rejected Sufism as it existed in South Asia, especially the veneration of saints. The Tablighi Jamaat also, over the years, played a crucial role in taking the ultra-conservative Wahhabi–Salafi strain of Islam to the Muslim communities globally.

The Islamic Society of North America (ISNA), the largest Muslim organization in the US has been strongly associated with Wahhabi Salafism since 1979. The eighth chapter suggests the US National Security Council to involve the ISNA leadership to take measures to moderate the extremist narrative of Wahhabi–Salafi Islam preached at the mosques and cultural centres across the country. The authorities have also been urged to initiate steps to promote the progressive Sufi Sunni traditions of Islam across the country, as an alternative to the Wahhabi–Salafi ideology. The chapter suggests that the US congress needs to also pass legislation to stop foreign funding to the fundamental Salafi outfits in the country as proposed by President Macron in France. It argued that the US, as a sovereign nation, has every right to do so in the interest of national security and world peace.

PROLOGUE

The year 1979 witnessed three apocalyptic events in the Middle East that shaped the contemporary Muslim World. They were important historical pivots to which most of the modern Islamic extremism and acts of terrorism could be linked. The first of such acts was the Iranian Revolution (also called as Islamic Revolution of Iran) led by Ayatollah Khomeini (1902–1989). He arrived in Tehran by a chartered plane from Paris along with his aides and journalists on the early morning of 1 February 1979. Khomeini was given a rousing welcome by an estimated crowd of over 3 million people, who had gathered along his way. He immediately appointed Mehdi Bazargan, leader of the Liberation Movement of Iran, as the prime minister of the interim government. For the first time in the Middle East, a monarchy was removed not by a military coup (as it had happened earlier in Egypt and Iraq) but by the masses, inspired by Islamic religious fervour of Shiism. At that time, in the Kingdom of Saudi Arabia, the ailing King Khalid and his half-brother, Crown Prince Fahad, took it in stride as the anti-royalist coup that had happened earlier in Cairo and Baghdad.

Saudi Arabia recognized the Khomeini regime. The deputy prime minister, Prince Abdullah bin Abdulaziz Al Saud, said in an interview with the *Gulf News* that the Holy Quran was the constitution of their two countries, and thus their relationship was no longer determined by material interests or geopolitics. Perhaps the Saudi leadership underestimated the long-term consequences of the Islamic Revolution in Iran. Tehran and Tel Aviv under the Shah's regime used to be strong allies. Iran supplied Israel with oil and had lots of trade agreements between them. All these ended with the revolution of 1979. Although the Islamic Republic of Iran is a Muslim country, Shia

Muslims and Persians considered themselves culturally superior to Arabs. Furthermore, the religious revolution had also brought to the fore the age-old Sunni–Shia rivalry in the Middle East. Ironically, the Wahhabi–Salafi dominated Sunni Muslims of Saudi Arabia consider Shia Muslims as apostates.

The second apocalyptic event took place in November 1979—the seizure of the Grand Mosque in Mecca by Juhayman al-Otaybi, a Saudi militant, inspired by Wahhabi Salafism. He was a member of an influential family from Najd and former personnel in the Saudi Arabian Armed Forces. He recruited a group of men and trained them first to seize the Grand Mosque and eventually overthrow the Saudi royal regime. He had chosen the first of Muharram, the first month of the Islamic calendar, for the act, when hundreds of believers converged to circumambulate the Holy Kaaba after the dawn prayers.

According to the attackers, 'The ruling al-Saud family had lost its legitimacy because it was corrupt, ostentatious and had destroyed Islamic basic values by aggressive policy of Westernizing the Saudi society.'[1] Al-Otaybi was largely inspired by the fourteenth century Islamist scholar Ibn Taymiyyah (1263–1328), and the eighteenth century Islamist theologian and scholar Muhammad ibn Abd al-Wahhab (1703–1792).

With his huge religious standing, Abd al-Wahhab pushed the boundaries of Ibn Taymiyyah's ideology. He extensively researched on Taymiyyah's works and extracted his core beliefs in order to drill them once again into his contemporary Muslim society. During the time of Abd al-Wahhab, the Arabian Peninsula did not have any unified state organization. His first priority was to unite the Arab Muslims in their 'initial purity' by implementing Ibn Taymiyyah's ideology. He started discussions with the chiefs of various settlements in the region. He convinced them that simply fighting on trivial issues would not bring them any dividend; the best thing to do was to return to the teachings of the Holy Quran and the Prophet's

---

[1] Lewis, Bernard, *The Middle East Mosaic*, Modern Library Paper, 2001, p. 466.

Sunnah, and make them attractive to all the communities across settlements. He articulated the views written in his book *Kitab Al-Tawhid* (Book on Monotheism) in which he underscored all the prevalent deviations from the kind of Islam that he believed was the right one. He opposed obeisance at the graves of saints for blessings. He maintained that venerating the cult of saints was like worshipping idols and strongly denounced Sufism—a flexible, tolerant and open form of Islam. In 1744, Abd al-Wahhab made a historic agreement with Ibn Saud, an ambitious chieftain of Diriyah province in Najd, the central region of the Arabian Peninsula. The agreement was a game changer for Abd al-Wahhab to legitimize his teachings and unleash an extremely puritanical narrative of Islam. Various Muslim settlements in the region were united in bringing back the early mythical days of Islam when it was assumed to be 'uncorrupted'. This is called Salafi Islam. For the first time on a large scale, the Muslim communities of the Arabian Peninsula started marginalizing Sufism, a religious idea which believes in syncretism and tolerance of other religions.

Ever since the formation of the kingdom in 1932, the Saudi royal family had been working in harmony with the Wahhabi clerics to systematically push the ideology among the communities. Nonetheless, the real game changer was the discovery of oil in the eastern province of the kingdom in 1938 and the subsequent glut of petrodollars that helped them operate independently with huge funds at their disposal. The Al Saud's extended family members and succeeding rulers had an ostentatious lifestyle with luxurious palaces and yachts built or bought for them. Whereas, the religious establishment had total freedom to fund mosques, schools and Islamic centres globally and to promote the Wahhabi–Salafi strain of Islam, pushing the tolerant stream of Sufi Islam to the periphery. The strict Wahhabi teachings—aggressively advocated along with a generous financial package—found many takers throughout the Muslim world, with a vast majority of Sunni followers being lured to the fundamentalist ideology and the path of extremism.

The third apocalyptic event of the year 1979 occurred in the month of December when the Soviet Union invaded Afghanistan and the US administration led by Ronald Reagan decided to defeat the Soviet Union by arming the Islamists in Afghanistan. The group who fought the American war consisted of Afghanis, mujahideens (fighters converged in Pakistan from the Arab and Muslim world), Taliban (young students from Pakistani madrasas) and mercenaries. The American CIA made enormous funds available to the jihadi groups through the Pakistani ISI so as to bleed the Soviet Union using Islamists. This US project was called Operation Cyclone[2], the longest and most expensive covert operation the CIA ever undertook. The funding rose to US$630 million per year in 1987. The Pakistan government received more than US$20 billion to train and arm the Afghan resistance groups. The support proved vital to the mujahideen efforts against the Soviets. During this time, Arab volunteers, strongly subscribing to the Wahhabi–Salafi ideology, came to Pakistan in large numbers to build support groups. Even Saudi Arabia's leadership poured millions of dollars into it. Osama bin Laden, scion of the famous and fabulously rich bin Laden family of Saudi Arabia, landed in Pakistan with a large group of his Arab followers. Soon, jihadi volunteers from Yemen and Syria joined the holy war against the Soviet Union. The US-built Stinger anti-aircraft missiles and other light weaponry were brought and distributed to the fighters through the Pakistani ISI. The corrupt Pakistani army generals swindled huge amounts of US funds and sold weaponry, including the Stinger missiles and AK-47s, in the open market of Karachi, Quetta and Peshawar.

The Soviet invasion also caused the migration of around 4 million ordinary Afghans, displaced internally and across the border, into Pakistan. They moved into the border regions and settled in the sprawling refugee camps along the Durand Line, the border

---

[2]Algar, Hamid, *Wahhabism: A Critical Essay*, Islamic Publications International, New York, 2002.

between Pakistan and Afghanistan. The young boys were admitted to thousands of madrasas, financially supported by Saudi Arabia's Wahhabi–Salafi establishments. They were largely given hate lessons against Sufi Islam and Shiism. One of the by-products of the US decision to support mujahideen in Afghanistan was the emergence of a new generation of student community (*taliban*), who were also taught in their early years about the Islamic sanction and benefits of the Supreme Sacrifice by different means, including suicide bombing. The students who graduated from these madrasas were well armed to spread the extremist version of Islam. When the Soviet Union decided to withdraw from Afghanistan in 1989, the power vacuum was filled by the warring groups of former warlords. This triggered a civil war that totally devastated the Afghan countryside. Smartly, the security establishment of the Pakistani government thought it to be the right moment to increase its influence in Afghanistan. They termed this as 'strategic depth', which would be highly crucial given the possibility of India trying to push them from the eastern border. After the initial military training, the Pakistan establishment pushed the Afghan Taliban from their madrasas, arming them with weapons and tanks. The friendly Saudi Arabia provided them with funds to purchase pickup trucks. A new army of Taliban, backed by the Pakistan army, entered Afghanistan and quelled the warring factions of warlords and established a Taliban-led Islamic government, based on the strict Sharia law. It was a model originally proposed by Ibn Taymiyyah, the fourteenth century Islamic scholar, and revived and institutionalized by Ibn Abd al-Wahhab in Saudi Arabia, after signing a pact with the Ibn Saud family in 1744.

Both Pakistan and Saudi Arabia recognized the Mullah Omar government as the legitimate administration of Afghanistan. The US intelligence agencies were also complicit in endorsing this failed nation with a fundamentalist character, without comprehending its long-term consequences. Soon, the Kabul government implemented Sharia law. All women were put under strict face veil, women's education was banned and they were removed from government jobs throughout Afghanistan. After installing the Taliban-led government, the US administration declared this Afghanistan project as 'mission accomplished' and behaved as if they had nothing to do with a country in which they had poured billions of dollars to arm a breed of ultra fundamentalist jihadi fighters. The US intelligence or administration traditionally never had a post-military-intervention strategy. Years later, they repeated the same mistake after the Iraq invasion, and left the country without any post-invasion governance plan in place. The result was profoundly devastating as a full-blown sectarian conflict was unleashed, which facilitated the eventual founding of ISIS, making the world witness a second wave of global jihadi terrorism by the followers of the Wahhabi–Salafi ideology.

Wahhabi–Salafi Creed of Islam

The 1980s and '90s were crucial decades when the Kingdom of Saudi Arabia took to an aggressive promotion of the Wahhabi–Salafi version of Islam. They did this by globally financing Islamic centres (Sunday schools), mosques and private schools in the US and most of the major European countries, including the United Kingdom (UK), Belgium, Spain, France and Germany. This global drive publicly radicalized young Muslims attending high schools and professional colleges, by using the Wahhabi English translation of the Quran and the Hadiths. Islamic professors from Saudi Arabia were brought to address Muslim students in various universities. This was also the period when the national security apparatus of the US administration supported the Wahhabi–Salafi creed of Islam, aggressively pursued by Saudi Arabia in the US, without properly understanding the history of Islam or the implications of such an act. The Taliban-led government of Afghanistan once hosted more than 100,000 radicals from around the world under the leadership of Osama bin Laden, who, in due course, became enormously powerful with the followers. It helped him set up many training centres across Afghanistan. A Frankenstein was created by the US by dispensing billions of dollars and modern weaponry to jihadi groups during the war in Afghanistan. The al-Qaeda under the leadership of Osama bin Laden enjoyed a safe haven under the Mullah Omar government and started recruiting educated professionals and willing terrorists from the US and European countries. The Pakistani ISI actively supported the al-Qaeda's nefarious designs as they saw a window of opportunity to rule Afghanistan by proxy forces and thus bleed India in Kashmir with the help of willing jihadists. The Pakistani president at the time, General Muhammad Zia ul-Haq, brought sweeping changes in his country by implementing a Wahhabi curriculum in the madrasas and introducing Salafi reforms in the mosques to thereby methodically marginalize Sufi Islam. In the Indian-held Kashmir, the jihadis were pushed through the Line of Control (LoC) to disturb the social and cultural fabric of Kashmir. Many Hindu Kashmiri Pandits were killed or forced to migrate out of the Valley, while many dargahs of Sufi saints, frequented by the moderate Sufi Muslims, were bombed. The powerful Council on Foreign Relations (CFR), which plays a behind-the-scenes role in the formulation of the US foreign policy, confirmed that the terror groups Lashkar-e-Taiba and Jaish-e-Mohammed were created by the ISI for bleeding Kashmir with the tacit approval of the CIA.[3]

The jihadi tourism experienced a sudden uptick, both at Karachi and Peshawar airports, when they were used as international transit points for extremists who were visiting Kabul and Kandahar to listen to bin Laden and his key advisers.[4] Regular brainstorming sessions were held by the senior operatives of the al-Qaeda to unleash attacks across the world. The meetings were conducted in a highly secretive and professional manner. The participants attending such meetings were not directly flying to Karachi or Peshawar airports but were

---

[3]Rashid, Ahmed, *Descent into Chaos: The U.S. and the Disaster in Pakistan, Afghanistan, and Central Asia*, Penguin Books, 2009.
[4]Rashid, Ahmed, *Taliban: Militant Islam, Oil and Fundamentalism in Central Asia*, Yale University Press, 2010.

taking circuitous routes, as they would first travel from Frankfurt to Bangkok and then to Karachi, before they were taken to Kandahar or Kabul by road. The Kosovo Liberation Army (KLA) was also hand in glove with al-Qaeda. Drug trafficking was another business that the al-Qaeda was fully involved in. It pushed drugs across the world via India and Kosovo.

The ISI secretly kept a tab on the CIA operatives in Pakistan and Afghanistan and shared critical information with bin Laden. At the same time, details regarding bin Laden's hideouts and al-Qaeda training camps were not shared with the CIA. The ISI often provided fake information and misled the Americans. In time, ISI emerged as the biggest beneficiary of the whole deal, both financially and militarily, by arming and strengthening the jihadis. The Pakistani military establishment, led by the ISI, fully protected bin Laden and his followers, and doubled the jihadi activities in Kashmir to make it an almost independent state. The American operatives in the Afghanistan–Pakistan jihadi theatre eventually went out of the equation.

First Gulf War

In August 1990, Saddam Hussein invaded Kuwait by marching his armed forces into the neighbouring state. President George H.W. Bush saw this as a threat to US interests in the Middle East and created a global consensus by involving the United Nations and many European nations to liberate Kuwait from the Iraqi forces. The military operation was named 'Operation Desert Storm' and under the US command, the forces landed in Saudi Arabia to launch ground and air attacks on Iraq to liberate Kuwait. In January 1991, an operation was launched and the Iraqi forces were expelled from Kuwait. The entire operation was completed in three days. However, the US forces landing in Saudi Arabia and launching an attack on a fellow Arab country didn't go well with bin Laden and his extremist outfit.

Bin Laden, as a believer of Wahhabi Salafism, considered non-Muslims as infidels and the presence of the US forces in the Holy Land as blasphemous. Bin Laden's anger intensified against the US administration, notwithstanding the aid he received from the US military advisers when he had to fight against the Soviet Union occupation in Afghanistan. The CIA channelized US dollars to all the jihadi groups, including the al-Qaeda, in purchasing weapons and arming the Arab fighters. The simmering Palestinian issue and the blatant US support to Israeli occupations came into his mind frequently and it made him increasingly uncomfortable with the US. Meanwhile, the Americans had also intervened in Somalia in the early 1990s, apparently 'to restore order' and end the in-fighting between the local militia there.

Rise of Osama as a Jihadi Icon

By 1995–96, bin Laden had gained international popularity as a jihadi icon, which soon made him a darling of the global media. His persona was merchandized globally, and Muslim youth in South Asia and elsewhere hailed him as their role model and as an inspiring figure.

He discussed time and again with his core group how to punish the Americans and their 'evil empire'. He was fully aware of the might of the American military and was smart enough not to confront it directly. He conceived a unique strategy to hit the American assets in the Arab region and test their response to it. He masterminded a well-planned suicide attack by ramming a car fully laden with explosives into the US air force housing complex at al-Khobar in Saudi Arabia on 25 June 1996. In this attack, more than 19 US servicemen were killed. It sent a strong message to the Saudi royal family to the effect that foreign forces would not be tolerated in the Holy Land.

The US intelligence agencies, like the CIA and the FBI, began to suspect the role of bin Laden and his al-Qaeda in the attacks at the Al-Khobar tower. This was the time when the US agencies were also waking up to the reality that the jihadi organization, al-Qaeda or 'the base' that he had built during the Afghan war to expel the Soviet Union, had not only continued to exist but had also grown exponentially by then. Till then, the US intelligence was constantly misled by the ISI about the strength of the al-Qaeda. After the Afghan operation, bin Laden was seen going back and forth between Kabul and Khartoum in Sudan. He had started a construction business in Sudan mainly to build roads. In 1993, a low-intensity bomb was detonated in the basement of the World Trade Center in New York City. The US administration began to put pressure on the Sudanese government to expel bin Laden. In 1996, he arrived in Kabul by a chartered flight with a group of 200 followers. With special privileges, he was treated as the official guest of the Pakistani-backed Taliban government. He soon acquired enormous power and the Taliban ruler Mullah Omar, considered him as his spiritual mentor. The US administration also exerted pressure on Saudi Arabia to hand him over to the US, which was strongly resisted by the Taliban government.

In 1998, bin Laden issued a fatwa against the Americans to overthrow the Saudi government. In the same year, the al-Qaeda carried out simultaneous attacks on the US embassies in Nairobi, Kenya and Tanzania, killing more than 200 people and wounding about 10,000 more. For the first time, the American public and the media—both print and electronic—recognized the unprecedented danger posed by al-Qaeda and its leaders Osama bin Laden and Ayman al-Zawahiri.

The US intelligence agencies fully woke up to the reality that the attacks on its embassies in Africa were the handiwork of al-Qaeda and Osama bin Laden. The elephant in the room was, of course, Osama bin Laden. President Bill Clinton ordered a retaliatory strike across Afghanistan against the training camps managed by bin Laden. The US army launched 70 cruise missiles. They hit targets, but bin Laden and all the top leaders of the al-Qaeda escaped unhurt, as the ISI had tipped them well in advance. The bin Laden core group had already started preparation for spectacular attacks on the US symbols of money, power and democracy. At this time, Khalid Sheikh Mohammad, who had graduated from an American university with a degree in agricultural sciences, gave some striking ideas to bin Laden. In one of the brainstorming sessions, he proposed hijacking passenger planes from both East and West coasts of America and crashing them into the iconic structures of the US.

Bin Laden first rejected the idea and commented that it would be too big a project, in which a large number of people would be involved and hence the news was likely to be leaked. Nonetheless, he went on to adopt the idea and decided to select a few targets and hit them by crashing passenger planes into them. It was in early 1999 that bin Laden summoned Khalid Sheikh Mohammad to Kandahar and gave permission to him to go ahead with the plot. In a subsequent brainstorming, a suggestion was put on the table to attack the US nuclear facilities, but this was quickly dropped as the collateral damage would have involved a large US Muslim population too. That said, Khalid Mohammad started his operations from a safe house in Pakistan under the protection of the ISI. He organized the money and logistics. The task of selecting the crew was given to Imam Fazazi of the al-Quds Mosque of Hamburg who would identify potential team members for training and meetings with bin Laden in Afghanistan.

Into the scene came Mohamed Atta, who was the leader of the 9/11 attackers. When he arrived in Germany in 1992 to study urban planning at the Technical University of Hamburg, he was deeply religious but not fanatically inclined. While in Hamburg, he used to visit the al-Quds Mosque, the centre of the team selection, to offer Friday prayers. The imam of the mosque was a strong adherent of the fundamentalist Wahhabi–Salafi Islam. He was given the responsibility by Khalid Mohammad to select young Saudi nationals who were excelling academically and subscribed to the fundamentalist ideology. The imam, through his contacts with other imams in the major cities of Western countries, selected suitable candidates and encouraged all of them to first visit Hamburg and then Afghanistan to meet bin

Laden. Bin Laden himself systematically trained them using lectures, videos and other interactive programmes. They were shown videos of American atrocities on Arabs. In one brainstorming session at the Kandahar camp, bin Laden insisted that all attackers be nationals of Saudi Arabia as it would be easier for them to get a US visa. They were asked to get admitted to a flying school in Florida to get a commercial license. The funds were channelled through banks in Dubai and Bangkok and into the US.

On 11 September 2001, the world was shocked, and only then it realized that the US embassy attacks in the East African countries were merely a prelude to a far more devastating strike against the US. On that fateful day, 19 al-Qaeda Saudi nationals deftly exploited the weakness in the American airport security system and hijacked four US airliners that were bound for the West Coast from its East Coast cities. Two airliners flew into the twin towers of the World Trade Center and a third crashed into a Pentagon building near Arlington in Virginia. The fourth airliner, bound for the Capitol Hill, was downed in Pennsylvania. In the event, 6,000 people were killed and more than 10,000 were wounded. For the first time in the history of the US, non-state actors had attacked the American symbols of power.

US Response to 9/11

On 20 September 2001, President George W. Bush addressed a joint session of the Congress. This was the first address after the 9/11 attacks which set the agenda of the US against Islamic terrorism. Unfortunately, it felt short of identifying the Wahhabi–Salafi creed of Islam, which, since 1979, had been unabashedly pushed by the Kingdom of Saudi Arabia. That was also the year marked by the seizure of the Grand Mosque of Mecca by a group of Wahhabi–Salafi radicals. Earlier, many American scholars had voiced their concerns about Saudi Arabia unleashing a Frankenstein in the form of a rigid Wahhabi–Salafi Islam, which encourages Muslims to hate other faiths and legitimize the killing of innocent people of other faiths.

In his address, President Bush spoke directly to Muslims throughout the World. He said:

> We respect your faith. It is practised freely by many millions of Americans, by millions more in countries that America counts as friends. Its teachings are good and peaceful, and those who commit evil in the name of Allah blaspheme the name of Allah. The terrorists are traitors to their own faith, trying in effect, to hijack Islam itself. The enemy of America is not our many Muslim friends; it is not our many Arab friends. Our enemy is a radical network of terrorists.[5]

The American Islamic scholars and security strategists had voiced their concerns about 'Desert Islam' or the Wahhabi-Salafi creed that had been unleashed by Saudi Arabia. It is no rocket science to understand that 'radical terrorist networks' follow the radical Wahhabi-Salafi ideology which promotes hatred against other faiths and extreme rigidity in its practices. None other than the US's close ally, the Kingdom of Saudi Arabia, spread this radical Islam after the Grand Mosque seizure and the consequent agreement made by the Salafis with the ruling Saudi royal family. The larger Islamic world, which believes in the Sufi Sunni traditions, wished that President Bush should have instead said that any country that spreads radical, jihadi Wahhabi Salafism is the enemy of America.

As a sovereign country, the US has a right to ban Wahhabi Salafism from Muslim practices in its land as done by the Islamic government of Morocco.

The 9/11 Commission Report, on page 373 states: 'Many Americans see Saudi Arabia as an enemy, not as an embattled ally. They perceive an autocratic government that oppresses women, dominated by a wealthy and indolent elite. Saudi contacts with

---

[5]'Address to a Joint Session of Congress and the American People', *The White House: President George W. Bush*, 20 September 2001, https://tinyurl.com/yc6df2ze. Accessed on 22 September 2023. Press release.

American politicians are frequently invoked as accusations in partisan political arguments. Americans are often appalled by the intolerance, anti-Semitism, and anti-American arguments taught in schools and preached in mosques.'[6] On 7 October 2001, America struck back by launching the Operation Enduring Freedom (OEF), the US-led international effort to hit the Taliban regime in Afghanistan. Relentless air bombing was carried out on the training camps of the al-Qaeda.[7] The northern forces opposing the Taliban regime of Mullah Omar were encouraged to proceed to capture Kabul. In the operation, hundreds and thousands of Taliban fighters were killed. Some of them moved to Pakistan to escape the war. The ISI again played a dubious role, and provided a safe passage to the senior al-Qaeda leaders, including Osama bin Laden and Ayman al-Zawahiri, to Pakistan. The ISI misled the CIA suggesting that the leadership had moved to the mountains of Tora Bora and it would not be easy to trace them. In reality, they were given large bungalows near Abbottabad in Pakistan to live with their large families with all material comforts.

After 9/11, the bin Laden-backed terrorists unravelled in various forms both in the Western and Muslim worlds. They engaged in direct clashes with all other major religions like Christianity, Hinduism and Judaism. A war within the Muslim society against Sufism and its symbols, like the graves of revered saints (*mazar*), also touched its peak. Saudi Arabia's religious department, with the help of enormous funds, could construct hundreds and thousands of mosques around the world and stack them with the Wahhabi interpretation of the Quranic verses and the sayings of the Prophet. An exponential growth of the extremist creed of Islam was also seen among the Western, Asian and African Muslim communities. Even the dress code prescribed by the Wahhabi Islam for men and women is openly

---

[6]National Commission on Terrorist Attacks, *The 9/11 Commission Report*, https://tinyurl.com/yat5jrc6. Accessed on 22 September 2023.

[7]'1999–2021, Timeline: US War in Afghanistan', *Council on Foreign Relations*, https://www.cfr.org/timeline/us-war-afghanistan. Accessed on 04 September 2023.

visible in all the major cities of the world. The isolated attacks by youths called as 'lone wolves', radicalized by the Internet or the neighbourhood mosques, are even now a concern for the global communities. Such incidents have continued to be reported from across the globe, including the US, France, Germany, England, India, Morocco, Indonesia and Egypt... The list is long.

Second Gulf War

In the year 2003, the US army invaded Iraq with its full military might on the pretext of Saddam Hussein having developed weapons of mass destruction.[8] This was termed the Second Gulf War. The main objective of the campaign was to bring down a brutal ruler and bring about regime change, a favourite tagline of the US security establishment. The Americans were successful in removing Saddam Hussein from power and empowering the demographic majority of the Shias. Nevertheless, it also led to the unleashing of the worst sectarian divide in the history of Islam.

For nearly a decade, Iraq became a laboratory for terrorists to hone techniques that could be shared globally. The terrorist tradecraft innovated in Iraq includes a widespread campaign of suicide attacks, sophisticated efforts to spread jihadi propaganda via video recordings of terrorist activities and development of jihadi bulletin boards and websites, besides the extensive use of improvised explosive devices.

Between 2003 and 2005, actors in Iraq executed suicide attacks with increasing frequency before replicating and perfecting their tactics in the neighbouring states of Afghanistan and Pakistan. Iraq became the place where the Islamists perfected the use of car bombs and Vehicle-Borne Improvised Explosive Devices or VBIEDs. The number of vehicle-borne attacks in Iraq increased exponentially

---

[8] '2003–2011, Timeline: The Iraq War', *Council on Foreign Relations*, http://tinyurl.com/2ubjz6tp. Accessed on 04 September 2023.

before ISIS firmly took hold of the terrorist activities in Iraq and neighbouring Syria.

In the year 2004, the aim of the al-Qaeda in Iraq was to remove the Western occupation and replace it with the Wahhabi Sunni Islamist regime. ISIS in Iraq was originally headed by Abu Musab al-Zarqawi, a close follower of Osama bin Laden. He was driven by sadism, a thirst for fame and a vague apocalyptic ideology. He was killed in an air strike in 2006. The next person to take the leadership was an Egyptian called Abu Ayyub al-Masri, who also died in a US–Iraq operation. For some time then, ISIS was without a leader. Nevertheless, in 2011, Abu Bakr al-Baghdadi emerged from the cadre and took full control of the outfit. He led the sectarian war against Iraqi Shias and the Bashar al-Assad forces in Syria. In 2013, a group named ISIS was founded.[9] At one time, they controlled a large area, both in Iraq and Syria. The group focussed on creating an Islamic state with Sharia law as was originally conceived by Ibn Taymiyyah in the thirteenth century and transformed by Ibn Abd al-Wahhab as a mass movement during the eighteenth century.

In 2014, ISIS fighters took control of the Sunni-dominated areas of Fallujah, Mosul and Tikrit in Iraq and the towns along the river Euphrates in Syria. The supporters of Saddam Hussein dominated these towns and the US occupation forces terminated all members of these regions from the services—rather foolishly, I may add. They were frustrated and ready to take revenge on the new Shia administration installed by the American forces. A full-blown sectarian war started with suicide bombers blowing vehicles at checkpoints in and around Baghdad and other towns of Iraq. The ISIS implemented strict Sharia laws in their controlled areas.

The US administration raised new security forces for the region. The majority of the officers, who were earlier part of the Iraqi army, now joined ISIS and formed a strong fighting force under

---

[9]Lister, Charles. R., *The Syrian Jihad: Al-Qaeda, The Islamic State and The Evolution of an Insurgency*, Pentagon Press, USA, 2015.

the command of al-Baghdadi. They were experienced and smart. Soon, they killed thousands of new Iraqi army recruits and occupied large areas of Iraq. But the Kurdish forces—northern Iraq being a Kurdish autonomous region—gave a tough fight to ISIS and kept it at a distance from their towns. The Yazidi community living in some pockets in northern Iraq were slaughtered, raped and taken into slavery by ISIS forces, who termed them heretics belonging to some strange sect of Christianity. The escalating brutality of ISIS in Iraq and Syria reached its peak by the end of 2016. The global media reports literally shook the civilized world; the IT-savvy members of ISIS used social media platforms to propagate their heinous crimes and to recruit large number of youths to its fold. Interestingly, the al-Qaeda formally broke with ISIS group under al-Baghdadi as the al-Qaeda argued that killing innocent people by violent means would alienate the Muslim world. The orgy of heinous crimes committed by ISIS continued unabated till 2017. They slaughtered US journalists and international aid workers. They used public-viewing platforms to upload a series of videos showing the beheading of enemies. Between November 2015 and May 2017, the world also experienced a large number of terrorist attacks by jihadis. The major centres targeted were in France (Paris, Toulouse, Nice), Belgium (Brussels), Spain (Madrid train bombings, Barcelona), USA (California, New York, Boston, Florida), UK (Manchester, London) and Germany (Berlin). In all these attacks, young and educated Muslims were involved. They were either radicalized by social media platforms and Internet websites that focussed on the Wahhabi-Salafi Islam or inspired by ISIS.

Racism Versus Islamism

The year 2018 saw the emergence of white supremacist attacks in the Western world. A synagogue in Pittsburgh, US; a Friday congregation in a Christchurch mosque in New Zealand; and another mosque in Oslo, Norway were attacked. After Donald Trump won the contentious 2016 US presidential elections regardless of his controversial tweets and speeches, his actions further inspired and emboldened the violent bigots. The conservative US media continued to amplify President Trump's racist rhetoric against the Democrats, liberals and Latino immigrants at the southern US border. He described them as a caravan of drug peddlers and criminals invading the southern states of America. By 2019, the white nationalists had become much more vocal and public. The groups that had a history of violence, now began to feel that they had state sanction to commit violence. The radicalization process, tactics and narratives used by the white supremacists were actually similar to those employed by ISIS terrorists. In reality, extremism is an architecture of beliefs, be it in the West or East.

On the surface, white nationalists and ISIS recruits would not have much in common. One group embraces a racist anti-immigrant ideology and is mobilized by a fear that the coloured people will soon be the majority. The other group believes in migration to non-Islamic nations to increase numbers and to kill 'the infidels' in order to reduce their numbers and create a caliphate where Sharia law can be enforced. Both have used information technology to leverage their divisive ideology on social media platforms and both have strikingly similar tactics and narratives, and believe that they are in the midst of an existential crisis that threatens their way of life and the only way to ensure self-preservation is to use violence.

ISIS, at the height of its powers, controlled a taxable population of six to eight million people, oilfields and refineries, vast granaries, lucrative smuggling routes and huge stockpiles of arms, ammunition and sophisticated military hardware. Its economic capital was Mosul, Iraq's second-largest city. The ISIS was the most powerful, wealthiest and the best-equipped jihadi force with educated and computer-savvy fighters. Its success sent shockwaves throughout the Islamic world. Its blitzkrieg campaign and the re-establishment of an Islamic caliphate, announced from the pulpit of the 950-year-old al-Nuri mosque in Mosul by its leader Abu Bakr al-Baghdadi, attracted the attention of the world.

The Fall of ISIS

Soon, ISIS caliphate in Iraq and Syria was destroyed, but not the group's ideology.[10] At the start of 2018, ISIS barely held a small desert terrain in Iraq's Anbar province and a few small villages along the Euphrates riverbank in Syria. Nonetheless, small enclaves had been cleared, and women and children lodged in little camps were released by the joint US–Kurdish forces. At that time, the Iraqi government was struggling—it is even now—with rampant poverty and sectarian divisions. Billions of US dollars are still needed to rebuild the cities and other infrastructure destroyed since 2003, first by the US invasion and then by sectarian conflict. The ISIS fighters continue to pop up in Egypt, Afghanistan, Pakistan, Bangladesh and Philippines. Many of them are also sighted in Yemen, where they take advantage of the chaos, civil war and a weak and practically non-existent government.

The militant group is slowly resurging in Afghanistan and is known as the Islamic State Khorasan (IS-K). 17 August 2019 Kabul bombing on Saturday, 17 August 2019, at a Shia wedding reception is now the group's reassertion of their growing footprints in the non-Arab Afghanistan. The IS-K officially began its operations in 2015. Its name invokes the Khorasan province, a medieval region that encompasses parts of Afghanistan, Iran and Central Asia. The ISIS was able to establish a base in this region owing to former Pakistani and Afghan Taliban members. They had pledged allegiance to ISIS caliph Abu Bakr al-Baghdadi in 2014. The group included local Taliban sympathizers and Pakistani Taliban drifters, who hold their sway in eastern Afghanistan. In line with their ideological orientation, they frequently carry out brutal attacks on women and Shiite communities. The number of ISIS fighters in Afghanistan has grown indigenously and their numbers also include migrants from Syria after the collapse of the caliphate. They are mostly located in

---

[10] Awan, Imran, 'Cyber Extremism: ISIS and the Power of Social Media', *Society*, Vol. 54, 15 March 2017, pp. 138–149.

the Nangarhar province in eastern Afghanistan. According to the United Nations, their reach has grown further after the attack at the wedding reception in Kabul. Time and again, ISIS has demonstrated that they are the most stringent followers of the Wahhabi–Salafi ideology in letter and spirit than either the Taliban or al-Qaeda.

President Donald Trump's special ambassador, Zilmay Khalizad, has signed an agreement with the Taliban in February 2020, to completely withdraw the American troops from Afghanistan in phases. The leadership of the Taliban has long hammered a schedule for the gradual withdrawal of the US-led army from Afghanistan. The Taliban leadership who are engaged in talks with the US forces are the ones who, during their rule, had enforced the strict Sharia law, which included banning of music and films on television, enforcing public executions of adulterers and deliberate destruction of archeological sites. Today, by contrast they are trying to project the image of a changed regime. But with only one woman member in their delegation, they are presenting a false picture of liberalism. The Taliban is shrewdly attempting to fog the American negotiating team, putting out an image that it has changed and adopted a tolerant tradition of Sufi Islam and does not adhere to the Wahhabi–Salafi stream of Islam anymore. These efforts are made primarily by leveraging social media. Taliban's cultural commission employs Facebook and Twitter (now X) to broadcast its propaganda in multiple languages. It spreads fake news on WhatsApp, Viber and Telegram. The main objective is to manipulate the global perception of Taliban and reassure the Afghan middle class of its stability. They skilfully spin narratives by depicting themselves as patriots. The ultra-conservative Wahhabi–Salafi movement of the fourteenth century manifesting itself through the twenty-first-century technology is indeed a smart option. The Taliban, in return, offers some significant concessions to the graceful exit of American forces. In reality, the Taliban still follows the ultra-conservative Wahhabi–Salafi ideology. But today, they have a better understanding of how to market it as a moderate entity to a gullible world. The lower cadres of Taliban and al-Qaeda are clearly raised in the Wahhabi–Salafi ideology and their hatred towards the mazars of Shiite saints and towards Sufism in general is visibly visceral.

The latest attempt at a peace deal, however, may prove to be disastrous for the Americans. The Taliban leadership has little control on their foot soldiers and the hardliners, whether they belong to Taliban, al-Qaeda or ISIS. All of them believe that, one day, they will come together and create a formidable Islamic State in Khorasan.

Meanwhile, with President Trump approving the withdrawal of American forces from northern Syria, thereby allowing Turkish forces to enter the country, history might repeat in Syria in a similar fashion. It is a recipe for chaos and future uncertainties. The Kurdish-led Syrian militia (Syrian Democratic Front or SDF) was the main ground force that defeated ISIS in Syria. Without American backing, the Kurds have been dealt a huge blow in terms of any future deal-making either with Turkey or the Syrian administration. Upfront, all the sleeper cells of ISIS in the region are taking advantage of the withdrawal of the SDF–American forces. A reactivation of turmoil has been reflected in the Turkish invasion of northern Syria. With ISIS all set to return to the region, the Middle East and Afghanistan once again stand to pay a huge price for the flawed policies of the American administration.

Amidst all this mess, Israel has consistently raised the pitch against the nuclearization of Iran, seemingly to widen the fault lines between the Sunnis and Shias of the Middle East. Israel leadership understands that Saudi Arabia and Egypt will have to be on their side of the equation if they want to live in peace. In reality, Israel has no dispute with Iran. But Tehran, like the rest of the world, articulates the untold sufferings of Palestinians people under Israeli occupation. Who can forget the brutality Israel unleashed by bombing schools and apartment blocks where hundreds and thousands of innocent Palestinians lost their lives? Benjamin Netanyahu, the Israeli leader pretending as a friend of the Arabs, described the Iran nuclear deal as a 'stunning, historic mistake', thereby smartly steering the sectarian divide of the region to his advantage.

The new and young Saudi leadership should understand that most of us have a firewall in our brain that keeps us safe from bad ideas. Israel sees a sectarian divide between Saudi Arabia and Iran as a huge crack in the wall. They are relentlessly attacking the Iran nuclear deal and pushing the two-nation solution for the Israeli–Palestinian conflict to the dustbin.

It is time to realize that the growing ISIS ideology in the Middle East and beyond is a real existential threat to all the Muslim countries across the world. If the Middle Eastern countries continue with the sectarian turf wars as we see in Yemen, Syria, Iraq, Lebanon and Libya, ISIS groups would soon emerge as an authority and enforce the strictest of Sharia laws to create a Salafi Islamic state wherever possible. Quite literally, ISIS has stemmed from the al-Qaeda and Salafist ideology. It rejects the notion of nationalism and secularism and aims to replace monarchies with a pan-Islamic caliphate.

Tens of thousands of foreign Muslims had migrated to ISIS in its heydays. The recruits hail from France, the UK, Belgium, Germany, Holland, Australia, India, Pakistan, Indonesia and the US. Analysts have been puzzling over the organization's attraction with the third and fourth generations of Muslims in Europe and the US besides some fresh converts. The Muslim communities in Western countries live together but separately. The third and fourth generations of Muslims are torn between two extreme cultures. At school and from friends, they learn liberal socio-cultural values whereas at home they are forced to follow the Salafi Islamic ways and values. They are restricted from meeting their Western friends and attending weekend parties, where girls and boys mix freely. Most of the time during weekends and holidays, they are forced to spend time at home which is restrictive and gets monotonous for them. The bland social environment at home compels them to spend lots of time on the Internet. The young, impressionable minds react strongly; they are hooked to jihadist websites and other social media platforms. Slowly they start communicating through encrypted apps that often camouflage group identities. Meanwhile, some reject their parents' choices and follow the so-called liberal Western values and become a part of the mainstream.

The ISIS social media teams have recruited hundreds and thousands of smart, educated and tech-savvy youths from the US and European countries for round-the-clock propaganda. The lone wolf militants, committing heinous crimes as had happened at Dallas, Texas and Chattanooga are not part of any big conspiracy. Instead, they are bored Muslim youths indoctrinated by some extremely intolerant ideologies who have romanticized the description of 'heaven' as a reward for 'jihad'. The Arab–American youth Mohammad Abdulazeez of Chattanooga, wrote in his last blog entry that the world for him was a 'prison of monotony and routine'. In short, what happened was that the virus of an anti-pluralistic, misogynistic Islam that had come out of Saudi Arabia post-1979, had multiplied and mutated, picking up new elements from its hosts globally. As a result, a virulent jihadism evolved through subtle changes in its genome and transformed into the al-Qaeda and ISIS of today.

Emergence of Moderate Islam in Saudi Arabia

The good news is that the powerful crown prince of Saudi Arabia, MBS, has been on a mission since 2017 to bring subtle changes to Saudi's Wahhabi Islam. He has curbed the authority of the feared Saudi religious police who could earlier arrest a woman for not covering every inch of her skin. He has also made it permissible for women to drive cars and travel without a male escort. He said in an interview to the *The New York Times* columnist Thomas Friedman that he was not 'reinterpreting Islam' but only 'restoring Islam to its origins'.[11] He suggested that Saudi Arabia changed for the worse in 1979 when Islam became politicized through events like the rise of Ayatollah Khomeini in Iran and the fundamentalist takeover of the Grand Mosque in Mecca.

---

[11] Friedman, Thomas L, 'Saudi Arabia's Arab Spring, at Last', *The New York Times*, 23 November 2017, http://tinyurl.com/4epsvys7. Accessed on 4 September 2023.

In March 2018, during a 60-minute interview, Crown Prince MBS said that, before 1979, Saudi Arabia was like the rest of the Gulf countries—women were driving cars, there were musical theatres, mixing was normal between men and women and there was respect for Christians and Jews. In fact, in the 1950s, Saudi women would move freely without hijabs. They would wear skirts, walk with men in public and attend concerts. In essence, Saudi Arabia was functioning like any other country in the world until the events of 1979.

In short, even as the foggy past lingers on, there are some silver linings—at least, far in the horizon—as the Taliban is now negotiating with the US, as ISIS is making efforts to build new images on social media, and as the Saudi royalty is busily taking reformative steps to offer more freedom to its citizens.

Paradigm Shift in US's Middle East Policy

For many decades, US foreign policy in the Middle East centred around Israeli–Palestinian conflict. All the US presidents always maintained a bipartisan approach and a special relationship with Israel. The last four US presidents—two Republican and two Democratic—positioned themselves as honest brokers in the Israeli–Palestinian conflict and always argued for two state solutions. Richard Haass in his article published in *Foreign Affairs* in 2020 stated that, 'President Trump has disrupted and unmade US foreign policy in Middle East by bringing Israel and Arab monarchies on one page against Iran.'[12] Trump has tragically isolated poor and weak Palestinians by trashing a two-state solution, has recognized Israel's annexation of Golan Heights, Jerusalem as the capital of Israel and has also set the stage for Israel's annexation of the occupied West Bank.

---

[12]Hass, Richard, 'Present at the Disruption: How Trump Unmade U.S. Foreign Policy', *Foreign Affairs*, Vol. September/October 2020, 11 August 2020, http://tinyurl.com/2dhz8prx. Accessed on 4 September 2023.

1

WAHHABISM AS IDEOLOGICAL SOURCE OF GLOBAL JIHAD

Wahhabism is primarily a theological movement emerging from Sunni Islam since the end of the eighteenth century and its theoretical underpinnings can be traced back to Salafism. The word Salafi derives from the Arabic term *al-salaf al-salih*, which means 'the pious predecessors', who are believed to be the first two or three generations of Muslims whom Salafis seek to follow. The fourteenth century Islamic scholar Taqi ad-Din Ahmad ibn Taymiyyah (1263–1328), had said that the downfall of the Abbasid dynasty of Baghdad in 1258, by the invasion of Mongols, was the natural culmination of the decadence of the Islamic values.[13]

The undercurrent of Salafism among Muslim societies in the Middle East gained traction during the second half of the nineteenth century, when Muslim lands were colonized by Western countries. Salafi reformists quickly blamed the believers for moving away from the fundamental faith, citing it as a reason for their downfall. They argued that there was no option but to return to the old and 'pure' ways of Islam. Salafism has sought to purify Islam of the Western influences and what they call 'digressions' from the real faith including Shiism, Sufism and other non-Salafi forms of Sunni Islam. The core literature was based on the writings of Ibn Taymiyyah and

---

[13]Ibn Taymiyyah, Sheikh ul-Islam, commentary by Dr. Mohammad Khaili Harras, *Sharah Al-Aqeedat-il-Wastiyah: Text on the Fundamental Beliefs of Islam and Rejection of False Concepts of its Opponents.*, Dar-us-Salam Publications, Saudi Arabia, 1989.

his disciples. They emphasized the restoration of Islamic doctrines in their pure form within the literal framework of the Quran and Sunnah. Salafism focusses on eliminating idolatry (*shirk*) and affirming God's oneness (*tawhid*). They claim themselves to be the true followers of Islam. Those who revere saints or pray at their tombs are considered apostates who have lost their religion. Salafis restrict the freedom of women and prefer to keep them confined within the four walls, often depriving them of even formal education.

The eighteenth century reformist movement called Wahhabism, led by Muhammad ibn Abd al-Wahhab (1703–1792) in Saudi Arabia, was actually an extension of the original Salafist concept proposed by Ibn Taymiyyah even a few centuries before Abd al-Wahhab. Wahhabism proclaims tawhid or monotheism as its primary doctrine. The perceived moral decline and political weakness of the Muslim community in Arabia provided traction to the movement. The tolerant Hanafi Sufi Sunni Islam was the base of the Ottoman Empire. In order to counter the popular and devotional narratives of Islam, Ibn Saud, founder of the first Saudi State, joined hands with the religious scholar Abd al-Wahhab, through a treaty signed in 1744. It triggered a socio-political and religious movement and eventually dislodged the Ottoman rule from Saudi Arabia. This movement reasserted the fundamental monotheism and reliance on a literal interpretation of the Holy Quran and the Hadith, the reported traditions of Prophet Mohammad. Their campaign, termed as 'jihad', among other things involved the destruction of tombs and shrines of Sufi saints, which flourished and expanded during the medieval centuries.

Wahhabism emphasizes the strict application of Sharia laws. It is vehemently opposed to the Western influences and the artistic and mystical traditions of Islam. The Kingdom of Saudi Arabia provided Wahhabi movement with a state, which included the holy cities of Mecca and Medina, increasing its acceptance in the Muslim world. The Wahhabi influence on the Muslim culture and thinking rose phenomenally following the tripling of oil prices during the early 1970s. Since then, the Saudi government has been spending billions of dollars to promote Wahhabism throughout the world by constructing mosques and setting up madrasas and Islamic centres that preach stringent Wahhabi doctrines. As a consequence, local interpretation of Islam that was not as strict as the Wahhabi version and was loosely based on the Sufi Islamic traditions, got slowly marginalized and completely replaced by a rigid version of jihadi Islam.

All Wahhabis are Salafists, but not all Salafists are Wahhabis. However, both the terms are often used interchangeably. From a theological perspective, Wahhabism and Salafism share the same doctrines. The two pillars of these ideologies are an extreme puritanical outlook and a craving for returning to the mythical early days of Islam, when it was assumed to not have been 'corrupted' by external influences. The Salafis and Wahhabis also share a disdain for all developments subsequent to the first few generations of Muslims after the Prophet's time (al-salaf al-salih), a rejection of Sufism and a dismissal of adherence to the Hanbali Sunni schools of Islamic jurisprudence.

However, In a critical essay on Wahhabism, Hamid Algar, Professor of Islamic studies at the University of California, identifies two ways to distinguish the Salafis from Wahhabis: 'A reliance on attempts at persuasion rather than coercion in order to rally other Muslims to their cause; and an informed awareness of the political and socio-economic crisis confronting the Muslim world.'[14]

Saud–Wahhab Alliance in 1744

Wahhabism as an Islamic puritanical doctrine of reforms and renewal is attributed to Abd al-Wahhab, who allied himself with the House of Saud, the ruling royal family of Saudi Arabia, in 1744 through a pact. It has since been the official ideology of the kingdom with Holy Quran serving as its constitution.

---

[14] Algar, Hamid, *Wahhabism: A Critical Essay*, Islamic Publication International, New York, 2002.

To understand the phenomenon of the twenty-first-century Islamic extremism, one has to delve deep into the layered history of the Arabian Peninsula and its link with the Wahhabi ideology, which is the bedrock of the modern Kingdom of Saudi Arabia.

Abd al-Wahhab was born in 1703 in the Banu Tamim tribe of the desolate and poor region of Najd, central part of present-day Saudi Arabia. His father was a jurist associated with the Hanbali School of Sunni jurisprudence, known for its conservativeness and strict interpretation of Islam.

The young Abd al-Wahhab travelled to the province of Hijaz, where he received his training in law, theology and Sufism, in the holy cities of Mecca and Medina.

During his stay in Medina, he was introduced to the teachings of Ibn Taymiyyah (1263–1328), the famous scholar who had fought against the Crusaders and believed that the foundation of Islam was the Quran and the sword. These teachings had a profound influence on the young Abd al-Wahhab, who later took these to their extremes. Ibn Taymiyyah was uncompromising on the Sufis–Sunni and Shia sects of Muslims, and called them heretics.

Abd al-Wahhab during his travels to Iran, Iraq and Syria came to see Muslims in those regions constructing tombs for revered persons and paying their obeisance at the mazars of saints and imams. In Medina also, he often observed Muslims worshipping at the tomb of the Prophet Mohammad. According to him, these practices seriously compromised the oneness of God. What upset him was the fact that, in Mecca and Medina, the homeland of the Prophet, such practices were rampant. He believed that these were deviations from the true Islamic path, leading to the moral decay of the community. He was convinced that all Muslims needed to return to the original and 'unadulterated' ways of Islam, as it was believed to be practised during the couple of centuries following the Prophet's death. Abd al-Wahhab called for an *ijtihad*, which required all the post-Prophet developments, practices and interpretations of the faith be reviewed in the light of the present day using only Quran and Sunnah for guidance. He thus justified the war against his Muslim brothers, who he believed were practicing shirk, as permissible and obligatory for every Muslim.

He upheld the argument that attributing a partner to Allah was nothing less than polytheism and clearly against the guidelines of the Quran and hence an unforgivable sin. Abd al-Wahhab had become hugely controversial in the Najd region with his puritanical interpretation of Islam and the upsetting of the established practices of venerating saints. His father and brother disowned him and counseled him to disown his ideology. Attempts were even made to assassinate him. After the death of his father in 1740, he moved to the small market town of Diriyah, ruled by the local chieftain Muhammad Ibn Saud. Abd al-Wahhab sought a meeting with the chieftain, but he was reluctant to have an audience with the controversial cleric. The fiefdom of Ibn Saud was very poor with meagre revenue. He drew influence in the local settlement by owning a few water holes in the neighborhood. It was the wife of Ibn Saud who prompted her husband to meet Abd al-Wahhab and listen to what he had to say. Ibn Saud was sceptical in the beginning about Wahhab's proposals on the interpretation of Islam. Nonetheless, he liked the suggestion of sharing *zakat* (religious duty of almsgiving) with the ruler. Finally, content of the alliance were discussed and approved by them, in which religious authority and administrative powers were clearly defined. As per the deal, Abd al-Wahhab and his descendants would have the sole authority on religious matters of the land and Ibn Saud and his descendants would control administration of the monarchy as it evolved subsequently.

The epoch-making alliance[15] would give Ibn Saud an extra source of religious legitimacy and an additional monetary benefit by way of zakat. In turn, Abd al-Wahhab would be given by the ruler complete protection for his life and a solid platform to propagate

---

[15] Alrebh, Abdullah F., 'A Wahhabi Ethic in Saudi Arabia', *Sociology of Islam*, Vol. 5. No. 4, 2017, pp. 278–302.

his interpretation of Islam. It also guaranteed him total authority to wage jihad against those who opposed his teachings. It was a win-win alliance for both the leaders. While it enabled Ibn Saud to push the boundaries of his small fiefdom to conquer newer areas in the Arabian Peninsula, the unique alliance provided Abd al-Wahhab with an opportunity to change the narrative of Islam through a fundamental interpretation of the Quran and the Sunnah. In hindsight, it seems that neither of them would have been successful in fulfilling their aspirations without this alliance.

The Saud–Wahhab alliance started off with a recruitment drive for fighters from the settlement populations. As expected, there was opposition from several quarters as people were opposed to Wahhabism or any changes in their traditional Islamic practices, which they had been following for centuries. The duo applied strong tactics and compelled people to accept the rule of the new Al Saud emir. Those who resisted were subjected to persecutions, raid and murder. Once the alliance began to gain traction in the local settlements, they raised a dedicated fighting force in the region with an ideology that bore a clear signature of Ibn Abd al-Wahhab. Seemingly, 'Wahhabism achieved the ultimate religious symbiosis between Bedouin nomads and local settlements by blending puritanical Islam with an obsession to ritual specialization'.[16]

By 1792, the alliance under the leadership of Ibn Saud's son, Abdul Aziz, could capture the provinces of Riyadh, Kharj and Qasim. The newly conquered settlements would get a Wahhabi judge as representative of their new ruler, but the emir allowed chieftains of the earlier settlements to remain in power as long as they were willing to pay the zakat as a token of their submission. They brought the central and southern regions of the Arabian Peninsula under their firm control and planned to capture the Shia Muslim enclaves like Hasa, which according to the Wahhabi interpretation belonged to *ahl al-Bida*

---

[16]Al-Rasheed, Madawi, *A History of Saudi Arabia*, Cambridge University Press, 2002, pp. 19–20.

(innovators of faith). By 1797, Hasa, Qatif, Qatar and Bahrain however, had been completely under the control of the Saudi emir.

Ottomans and the First Saudi State

The newly empowered Al Saud rulers turned their attention to Hijaz, a big money-spinner by way of the annual Hajj pilgrimage. The Hijaz province, seat of the two holiest cities of Islam—Mecca and Medina, had been part of the Ottoman Empire since 1517.[17]

The Ottoman Sultan had also assumed the title of protector of the two holy sanctuaries, signifying his religious role as the protector of Islam. The Al Saud ruler charged the Ottomans with a series of violations of Islamic principles including corruption, use of alcohol, veneration of imams and saints' tombs, which he decreed un-Islamic and against the directive of Prophet Mohammad. During the same period, writings of the medieval Hanbali scholar Ibn Taymiyyah were also incorporated into the main body of the Wahhabi traditions. Ibn Taymiyyah's views provided the necessary ideological support to allow a revolution against the unfaithful ruler on the basis of his failure to fulfill his responsibility to Islam.

The Saudi Wahhabi fighters, who faced strong resistance from the region, captured Hijaz by 1803. After the conquest, the Saudi forces attacked Mesopotamia and destroyed the Shia shrines in Karbala and massacred thousands of Shia inhabitants there. However, in the same year, the Al Saud ruler Abdul Aziz was assassinated by Shia activists as a revenge for the Karbala attack. The most important reason for the expansion of Saudi campaign in the settlement populations of Najd was believed to be Wahhabism, an ideology that motivated them to fight fiercely in the path of faith.

Unfortunately, the new Saudi Wahhabi state was short-lived. The Ottoman Empire dispatched a bigger force in 1811 under the

---

[17]Wynbrandt, James, *A Brief History of Saudi Arabia*, Infobase Publishing Co., 2014.

command of Ibrahim Pasha. The Beduin forces of Saudi were no match for the experienced and well-equipped Ottoman forces. The Saudi fighters either were killed or surrendered on 11 September 1818 after the Ibn Saud base camp in Diriyah was completely destroyed. Members of the Wahhabi ulama and the Saudi emir, Abdullah bin Saud, were executed by the order of the Ottoman Sultan.

Years later, along with the weakening of the Turkish caliphate, the Ottoman control on the Arabian Peninsula also began to grow shaky. By 1824, Turki bin Abdullah, son of former emir Abdullah bin Saud, got an opportunity to revive the formidable alliance of Saudi Wahhabi fighters and reassert control over the region. Turki bin Abdullah was a strict Wahhabist, but he restricted his attack to smaller regions which were economically inconsequential. He didn't venture to attack Hijaz, where the Ottoman forces were still in control with the annual Hajj pilgrimage bringing thousands of Muslims from foreign countries. The revenue generated annually by the Hajj was substantial for the Ottoman Governor and the local folks who used to earn a living by renting their premises to the visitors during the pilgrim season.

Turki bin Abdullah was, however, assassinated at the end of an internal family feud in 1834 and Turki's son Faysal, assumed office as the new emir of the group. In 1837, Faysal refused to accept the sovereignty of the Ottoman Empire over Hijaz and as a result he was captured and imprisoned in Cairo. Khalid, a member of the Al Saud family was appointed by the Ottomans to rule southern Najd, only to be assassinated by another member of the family soon. Intense family feuds and internal bickering jeopardized the Al Saud authority over the Arabian Peninsula, particularly in the economically important region of Hijaz. The Rashidi emirate, rival to Ibn Saud, emerged stronger in the Najd area, which soon overwhelmed the Al Saud family and exiled them to Kuwait in 1893.

The modern history of Saudi Arabia actually began in Kuwait, when Abd al-Aziz ibn Abd al-Rehman of the Al Saud family, popularly known as Ibn Saud, smartly devised a strategy during his exile in Kuwait, to recapture Riyadh with the help of religious activists called *Ikhwan* (tribal fighters). He attacked Riyadh using mercenaries and the Ikhwan force and, to his big surprise, captured it without many casualties. Ibn Saud was appointed ruler of Riyadh. He began his campaign to reclaim his family's lost territories from the bin Rashid forces.

The Ottomans supported bin Rashid's forces by providing them with funds and equipment to fight against Ibn Saud. Slowly, the Ottoman Empire was losing its firepower and control over the territories in the Arabian Peninsula. The British seemingly supported Saudi forces as the empire at that time was in competition with the Muslim Ottoman Empire for political supremacy in the Middle East. The campaign of Ibn Saud, under the patronage of the British Empire, established authority over a large part of the Arabian Peninsula. In May 1913, the Ottomans and Saudi Emir Ibn Saud signed a treaty that enabled him to rule over Najd as its governor.

Anglo-Saudi Treaty

The conquest of Al Hasa province posed two major challenges to Ibn Saud. First, the eastern region was dominated by Shia Muslims and the challenge was to incorporate them into the Saudi state. Ibn Saud entered into an agreement with Shia ulamas in Hasa, to maintain their religious freedom, as long as they pledged allegiance to him. This agreement was never to be fulfilled by the dominant Wahhabis, associated with the Ibn Saud regime, as they considered Shias as heretics. Ibn Saud also had lots of trouble with the Ikhwan supporters, who were fiercely opposed to any understanding with Shias and accused him of diluting the Wahhabi doctrines. The British also found fault with Ibn Saud for signing a treaty with the Ottoman Empire in 1913 to regain his authority over Najd.

The onset of the First World War, however, was a real blessing for Ibn Saud and his associates as the weakened Ottoman Empire was looking for a chance to pull out from the messy Arabian Peninsula. A second treaty was signed by Ibn Saud and the Ottomans in 1914. It gave the Al Saud family its right of succession as rulers of Najd in exchange of military support to Ottomans. However, in December 1915, Ibn Saud violated his treaty with Ottomans and signed the Anglo-Saudi Treaty, which envisaged military protection from the British to Ibn Saud for all his territories. In addition, Ibn Saud was also provided money and arms to fight his old rivals, the bin Rashidis.

The end of the First World War did not end the battle for Arabian Peninsula as the Bedouin forces, Ibn Saud and bin Rashid consolidated their control over their respective territories. After long-drawn battles between various players in the region, Ibn Saud's forces entered the prized Hijaz region and captured the holy cities of Mecca and Medina in 1925. By the early 1926, with support from the American and British forces, Ibn Saud proclaimed himself as the King of Hijaz and the Sultan of Najd and set the foundation for the modern Saudi Kingdom.

The British government signed another treaty with Ibn Saud in 1927. It recognized the complete independence of the Saudi Wahhabi emirate and Ibn Saud's right to choose his successors. As per the treaty, Ibn Saud would maintain a friendly relationship with the British-protected emirates in the region. The newly formed Saudi Kingdom with the help of the British air force crushed the Ikhwan fighters in 1929. This further solidified Ibn Saud's position as a ruler in the Arabian Peninsula and removed all potential rivals from the kingdom.

Modern Kingdom of Saudi Arabia

King Abdulaziz bin Abdul Rahman Al Saud established the Kingdom of Saudi Arabia in 1932 after crushing all pockets of resistance on the peninsula.[18] Within a year, he had signed a concession agreement with

---

[18]Ibid; 174–180.

the Standard Oil Company of California, today known as Chevron, to conduct oil exploration in the Shia-dominated eastern region of the Kingdom. This was a soft entry of the Americans into the region for oil exploration and economic development. Later, the Reform Church, a Christian mission based in Bahrain, advised the king to have more engagement with the Americans. For the first time, the medical wing of the Church entered the kingdom to treat army personnel and provide modern medical treatment to the king himself. The ruling Saudi family came to know that the Americans were different from the class-conscious British; informal and more likable in social dispositions, which was closer to the basic Islamic doctrine of equality (*musawat*).[19] The Americans were instantly liked by the ordinary Arabs. The US assistant secretary of state, George McGhee, held secret meetings with King Abdulaziz and subsequently signed an agreement with the Americans. As per the deal, the US would safeguard the kingdom from communist expansions and attacks from the British-backed Hashemite kingdom in Jordan and Iraq. In order to please the American administration, the King even agreed to extend the exclusive rights of oil concession to the American companies, not allowing the British counterparts to share the booty. The kingdom also allowed the Americans to build the first air force base at Dammam to safeguard its security.

The Second World War brought the US into the European war theatre as leader of the Allied forces. The Roosevelt administration began to realize that oil was going to be important during and after the war. In 1943, a special relationship between the US and Saudi Arabia started to evolve. President Roosevelt declared: 'The defence of Saudi Arabia is vital to the defence of the US.' It surprised many Americans, who had never even heard of a place like Saudi Arabia. Roosevelt's Secretary of the Navy, William Knox, told the Congress in March 1944, that the war had made the US administration extremely

---

[19]Jordan, Ann T, *The Making of a Modern Kingdom: Globalization and Change in Saudi Arabia*, Waveland Press, Inc, 2011.

conscious of its steady supply of oil. He also maintained that in the post-war scenario, the US was going to look for oil resources beyond its own territory, as it was important for the safety and security of the US. That was precisely the reason for the US administration to be deeply involved in the desert kingdom of Saudi Arabia.

The Standard Oil Company, California, struck oil in 1943 and it took a few years for the oil revenue to flow. In early years, the king used to take loans from the oil companies for the state expenditure. President Roosevelt met King Abdulaziz aboard the US cruiser, USS Quincy, on Egypt's Great Bitter Lake in February 1945. Since then, a strategic relationship has existed between the US and Saudi Arabia. The US provided security to the ruling Saudi monarchy and in turn, the Saudis allowed the American oil company to operate in the kingdom. In 1950, Bechtel, a US company based in California, built a 1000-mile pipeline to transport oil from the Ghawar oilfield, in eastern Saudi Arabia to the Mediterranean Sea, for the American and Western buyers. The pipeline passed through Jordan and the Syrian Golan Heights to Sidon in Lebanon.

The 1973 Israel–Arab conflict however, led to the Saudi boycott of oil supplies to the Western nations. This led to the quadrupling of the oil price, from US$3 to US$12 per barrel. Saudi Arabia's oil earnings went from US$8.5 billion to US$35 billion in a year. Saudi Arabia suddenly came on the radar of the Washington military–industrial complex. The US corporations getting orders for construction of palaces, malls and military hardware were on the shopping list of the Saudi royal families. Since 1950s, the US Army Corps of Engineers has been playing a vital role in the military and civil construction of Saudi Arabia. Over the years, the US–Saudi engagement had its primary focus on the security relationship and the kingdom became the US's largest customer of military hardware. Seemingly, sales ran into hundreds of billions of US dollars and it continues to scale up due to the changing technology.

Challenges in US–Saudi Alliance

The historically close relationship between the US and Saudi Arabia prompted the Americans to play the religious card in combating the Soviet Union, in partnership with the Saudis and Pakistanis, during the Cold War. One of the lessons Americans had learned from the Vietnam debacle was to not use American boots on the ground, and instead, use proxies to fight enemies in foreign lands. Against the Soviet Union, Saudis were natural partners because they were always anti-communist, as communism was said to be against religion, and Pakistanis were mostly Wahhabi Sunnis, averse to communism and allied to the US.

Ever since the modern US–Saudi relationship started in 1945, both the countries have been moving in alliance to protect their mutual interests on various fronts. It was primarily based on an 'oil for security' formula, by which Saudi Arabia would ensure supply of oil to the US for a politically and economically viable price and the US in turn would work towards ensuring the internal and external security of the Kingdom of Saudi Arabia. Nevertheless, there have been changes in this 'oil for security' formula which had shaped the alliance for many years, especially after the discovery of shale gas. Nonetheless, the US continues to give importance to Saudi Arabia, who is the largest producer of crude oil, as part of controlling the oil price in the global market.

With regard to the security part of the formula, the US has increasingly shifted its strategic interest to Asia as part of its new East Asian foreign policy programme called 'Pivot to Asia,' which was started by President Obama and continued by the Trump administration. Other interests of the US during the last forty years have included isolation of the Islamic Republic of Iran and sale of military hardware to Saudi Arabia for billions of dollars, annually.[20]

---

[20] Rauf, Imam Feisal Abdul, *What's Right with Islam is What's Right with America*, Harper One, 2004.

The lowest point in the US–Saudi relationship however, was following the 9/11 terrorist attack. The majority of the attackers and planners were Saudi nationals and members of the transnational Wahhabi-Salafi movement—the ideology fostered by the Saudi government domestically and internationally through a network of Sunday schools and madrasas, attached to the mosques.

Saudi Arabia's attempts to forge a strong relationship with the US following the anti-American Islamic Revolution in Iran was partly hypocritical as its real intent was to counter the Shiite ideology. The American policy makers at that time even devised a policy to pitch the Sunni Islam of Saudi Arabia against the Shia Islam of Iran. Ironically, it was the same intolerant ideology propagated by the Saudi regime that with the silent support of the US would, down the years, deeply radicalize the Muslim communities across the globe. Organizations like the al-Qaeda and its affiliates are only products of this centuries-old Saudi strategy that pushed Wahhabi Salafism as the mainstream narrative of Islam. The Gulf War of 1990–91 was the highpoint of the Saudi–American cooperation. Using the military and civilian infrastructure of Saudi Arabia, built over 70 years, half a million US forces defeated Saddam Hussein in Kuwait and restored the status quo in the Persian Gulf.

The banned Ikhwan group, which deeply adhered to the Wahhabi–Salafi jihadism, felt humiliated by the American attack on an Arab country and an Arab nationalist leader, Saddam Hussein. Arab intellectuals and followers of Ikhwan believed that the Saudi administration should not have been allowed to use its 'holy land' to launch a war against a fellow-Arab nation. For the first time, followers of Sunni Islam started a narrative against America and Western forces. The political cost of confronting Salafi jihadism, both ideologically and organizationally, was too high for the kingdom, even if it willed so. It would have entailed the formidable task of redefining Salafism at home, which was tightly entwined with the idea of jihad, and thus potentially disruptive to the very foundation of Wahhabism, which has been central to the Saudi regime since the eighteenth century.

The geopolitical interests however, necessitated a continued cooperation of Saudi Arabia and the US even after the 9/11 crisis.[21] But, in reality, the Washington think tank specializing in the Middle East was, for the first time, recognizing the need to confront the violent Salafi jihadism that undergirded all the anti-American and anti-west narratives among the Muslim communities across the world.

The president of Rockefeller Brothers Fund, Stephen Heintz, was devastated by the 9/11 attack on Twin Towers by the Arabs, majority of whom were Saudi nationals. The attack was planned and executed under the direct leadership of Osama bin Laden, scion of the famous Saudi bin Laden family, having close links with the Saudi ruling family. The bin Laden family owns one of the largest construction companies, which has constructed all the palaces and important buildings in the Kingdom. In late 2001, Rockefeller Brothers Fund convened a board retreat at its Pocantico Center, north of New York City, to consider new approaches to the Middle East at a time when the US was focussed on threats from al-Qaeda. One of the special invitees was Seyyed Hossein Nasr, an Iranian professor at George Washington University, Washington DC. During the session, Stephen Heintz was convinced by Professor Nasr about the geostrategic importance of Iran and the nuances of its relationship with the Sunni Arabs of the region.

The Rockefeller Fund decided to create the Iran Project in cooperation with the United Nations Association of the USA, a Washington DC based non-profit think tank that promotes UN activities. The Iran Project recruited many former career diplomats who had earlier served the republican administrations. The UN Foundation President William Luers contacted Iranian diplomat Javad Zarif through Iran's mission in New York. In early 2002, the Iran Project set up a meeting with the Tehran-based Institute for Political

---

[21]Alyas, Fatimah, US–Saudi Arabia Relations, *Council on Foreign Relation*, 2018, https://www.cfr.org/backgrounder/us-saudi-arabia-relations. Accessed on 2 September 2023.

and International Studies, a think tank with close government ties. It was mentored and hosted by the Stockholm International Peace Research Institute, outside Stockholm. The first meeting was held between Iranians and American participants. The Iranians came with talking points and, after a couple of days' deliberations, the meeting was concluded without any agreement. The initial objective was to develop a road map for future engagements between Washington and Tehran.

The Americans involved in the Iran Project were keeping the White House and the State Department in the loop. The secret meetings in the European capitals were suspended in 2005, when the hardliner Mahmoud Ahmadinejad won Iran's presidency. The American group kept its relationship with Javad Zarif at a low key during the hardliner's regime. However, the election of President Rouhani and the choice of Javad Zarif as the foreign minister in 2013, helped jump-start the negotiations. After 20 months of dogged discussions and 17 days of daily marathon meetings, the US team led by John Kerry, then secretary of state and the Iran group led by Javad Zarif and other important stakeholders, finally inked a deal on 14 July 2015 in Vienna.[22] The agreement was to restrict the nuclear capabilities of Iran for the next 15 years. Both critics and supporters of the deal have strong arguments. Many, including the Republican Congressmen, presidential hopefuls like Donald Trump and a few Democratic Party leaders saw a lot of holes in the deal. Apparently, regional Arab nations, led by Saudi Arabia and Israel, were most vocal in opposing the deal fearing Iran would use its oil wealth to ramp up support for its Shia militant proxies. Murdered Saudi analyst, Jamal Khashoggi, had very succinctly put that Iran with sanctions was a pain in the neck, but if sanctions wee removed it would emerge as a regional power and reshape the politics of the Middle East.[23]

---

[22]Zackary, and Kali Robinson, 'What is the Status of the Iran Nuclear Agreement', *Council on Foreign Relations*, 2020.
[23]Hubbard, Ben, 'Arab World Split Over Iran Nuclear Deal', *The New York Times*, 14 July 2015, https://tinyurl.com/5n7c69ft. Accessed on 21 September 2023.

On the flip side, the Iran-US deal appears to restrict Iran's military capabilities, but it also enormously improves its economic power by removal of the UN sanctions which link its economy with the rest of the world. Apparently, it looks like peace will return to the Arabian Peninsula. The analysts however, also feel that the nuclear proliferation race would get a fresh push from major players like Saudi Arabia and Israel.

The Israeli prime minister, Benjamin Netanyahu, was upset over the deal and issued a statement saying that the agreement was a 'stunning historic mistake'. He also said that he would do whatever he could to block Iran's nuclear ambitions. John Boehner, speaker of the US Congress, also rejected the deal and said it was unacceptable. Nevertheless, President Obama made it clear in his remarks that the deal was not based on trust but on verification. It is the best option for the US and its allies and for the world to integrate Iran with the rest of the world.

The Iran nuclear deal has brought Saudi Arabia and Israel closer, as the popular saying goes—the enemy's enemy is a friend. Saudi Arabia is currently engaged with the Houthi insurgency in Yemen. That the Houthis are backed by Iran is no secret. Saudi Arabia has money power and Israel has technology. They will collaborate and develop an Arab nuclear bomb for Saudi Arabia. It will suit the regional strategy of Israel to put the powerful Arab states against Iran and fully take away pressure from the Palestine-Israel conflict. Today, Jewish leadership is in a celebratory mode, as for the first time, the geopolitics of the Middle East has taken a full circle in favour of Israel.

Strategic partnership between Israel and Saudi Arabia will flourish in the years to come and scientists will soon start working on the Arab nuclear bomb project with the financial support of Saudi Arabia. The US strategy has checkmated the Arabs and brought Iran, a Shiite power, to the fore by signing a nuclear deal that will provide international legitimacy to Iran's peaceful nuclear programs. The Americans have thus permanently removed US boots from the

Middle East by using the Iran–Arab fault lines for leveraging their strategy in the Middle East.

Saudi Arabia and its regional allies see Iran as a driver of most of the region's violence for its support to Bashar al-Assad in Syria, Hezbollah in Lebanon and the Shiite militias in Iraq. Arab analysts view the subtle change in the US attitude towards Iran, reflected in the nuclear deal, as a major policy shift in the Middle East post 9/11. The American policy czars have created a new dynamic between the Sunni–Shia forces in the region by outsourcing to Iran the task of fighting ISIS in Syria, Yemen and Iraq.

Saudi Arabia ineffectively tried to use its political leverage with the Bush administration to not invade Iraq in 2003 as the kingdom was aware of its far-reaching implications. It knew well that a full-fledged sectarian conflict would be unleashed in the country once the Saddam Hussein regime fell. It was quite apprehensive of Shiites, who accounted for more than 60 per cent of the country's population, asserting their control over the new administration. The new Shiite regime of Iraq, it feared, would have Iran as their natural ally and then Iranians would also be controlling power in more than one Arab capital in the region. The insurgency in the Shia-dominated eastern part of Saudi Arabia, Bahrain and the Houthi–Zaydi movement in Yemen, getting a moral boost from such a development was another concern of the Kingdom.

Ideological Source of Global Jihad

In 1962, Saudi Arabia founded the Muslim World League, an international non-governmental organization, aimed at propagating Islam. MWL, in due course, however, became the primary tool for disseminating the Wahhabi version of the religion in different parts of the world. Its offices were opened in all places where Muslims inhabited in large numbers. The Saudi ministry of religion printed and distributed the Wahhabi translation of the Quran and a number of other textbooks and literature by Wahhabi intellectuals to the Muslims communities across the globe. A whole new generation of Muslims, with an intolerant, sectarian understanding of Islam and a negative outlook of other faiths, soon began to grow across continents.

In due course, globalization integrated the world economy, flattened the world in global communications and diminished the significance of national borders and many regional and international organizations came into being influencing the world order. The twenty-first century also witnessed a spike in national security threats from various non-state actors and an unprecedented rise in the number of religious extremist organizations like al-Qaeda. The modern state of Saudi Arabia under the leadership of the Al Saud family and its ministry of religious affairs, led by the descendants of Muhammad ibn Abd al-Wahhab, went on with their efforts to establish a Wahhabi version of Salafi Islam around the world.

Muhammad Abd al-Salam Faraj, the Egyptian radical Islamist, who was executed in 1982 for his role in coordinating the assassination of Egyptian President Anwar Sadat had said: 'The establishment of an Islamic State is an obligation for all Muslims. If such a state cannot be established without war, then war is mandatory on each Muslim.'[24] His followers maintained that jihad was an individual duty and there was no need to ask permission from parents even to leave one's house to wage jihad. They considered jihad mandatory on each individual like the daily prayers, fasting, zakat and the Hajj.

In 1998 the al-Qaeda leader Osama bin Laden and his deputy Ayman al-Zawahiri declared jihad against the Americans and their allies and declared it incumbent upon every Muslim to fight for liberating the al-Aqsa Mosque from Israeli control. In a series of suicide-bomb attacks directly executed under the supervision of bin Laden, they first attacked the American embassies in Kenya and Tanzania killing as many as 213 people and leaving around 4,000 wounded. That was the arrival of al-Qaeda as a terrorist organization

---

[24]Faraj, Abd al-Salam, *The Neglected Duty*, Johannes Jansen (trans.), Macmillan, New York, 1986.

at the global platform, conveying a strong message to America and its allies. The Bill Clinton administration of the US retaliated by attacking the training camps of al-Qaeda in Afghanistan. But, seemingly, the US administration had underestimated the outfit and its capabilities to strike the US mainland.[25]

The organization had drawn a detailed blueprint to carry out attacks on some of the famous landmarks in the US including the World Trade Center, Pentagon and Capitol Hill in Washington DC. The objective of the terrorist organization was to attack the great American symbols of power. Through the attack, the al-Qaeda wanted to convey an unambiguous message to the world and to the US in particular, that Islam cannot easily be cowed and it was capable of strong retaliations, if needed.

On 11 September 2001 a 19-member suicide squad of Arab descent, acting as pilots, hijacked six passenger jets, bound to the West Coast from the East Coast, with large quantity of aviation fuels. The evil plan of al-Qaeda was flawlessly executed, in which jetliners were used as weapons to kill people. Two planes crashed into the Twin Towers and killed more than 3,000 innocent Americans. More than hundred people were killed in the attack on the Pentagon but, fortunately, the plane intended to strike another target crashed far off from Washington DC.

The world later witnessed terrorist attacks in many countries including Indonesia, Turkey, Spain and the UK. After the American invasion of Iraq in 2003, The al-Qaeda and its affiliates globalized the assembly line of suicide bombers and all of them invariably believed in the idea of an Islamic state ruled by a caliph based on Sharia laws.

Former secretary of state, Hillary Clinton has famously deplored Saudi Arabia's blatant support for the 'radical schools and mosques

---

[25] Abdel Aziz, Ghada Ahmed, 'The Saudi–US Alliance Challenges and Resilience, 2011: 2019', *Review of Economics and Political Science*, Vol. 8, No. 3, 2023, pp. 208–225.

around the world that have set many smart young educated university graduates and professionals on a path towards extremism.'[26] She has called the Saudis the world's biggest funders of terrorism.

Farah Pandith, an American of Indian–Kashmiri descent, who served as the first American envoy to various Muslim countries, under the US secretary of state, after visiting more than 80 countries, observed that the Saudi money power has totally destroyed the tolerant Sufi Sunni traditions of Islam.[27] She was right that the tolerant Sufi Islam traditions, nurtured over centuries in Muslim countries around the world have been taken over by an intolerant Wahhabi strain of Salafi Islam. And the world is facing its consequences in different ways. Muslim youths in Western societies are using vans, cars and trucks as weapons to kill and terrorize innocent fellow countrymen. Time and again, the role of mosques with Saudi-funded imams has been proven in radicalizing innocent career-loving youths from middle-class Muslim families in many countries. Practically all journalists and television commentators are blaming Saudi Arabia for the jihadist violence. Fareed Zakaria, a famous Indian-American TV commentator has observed that Saudi Arabia has created a 'monster in the World of Islam'. Now, it has almost become public knowledge that Saudi Arabia has been smartly exporting to the world a rigid, bigoted, patriarchal and an extremely fundamentalist ideology, which is fuelling global Islamic extremism for the last few decades. William McCants,[28] member of the Project on US Relations with the Islamic World of the Brookings Institution, a Washington-based premier think tank, wrote that Saudi Arabia promotes a very toxic form of

---

[26]Shane, Scott, 'Saudis and Extremism: "Both the Arsonists and the Firefighters"', *The New York Times*, 2016, https://tinyurl.com/8twucnma. Accessed on 3 September 2023.

[27]Pandith, Farah, *How We Win: How Cutting-Edge Entrepreneurs, Political Visionaries, Enlightened Business Leaders, and Social Media Mavens Can Defeat the Extremist Threat*, Custom House, 2019.

[28]McCants, William, *The Man Who Runs Al-Qaeda*, Atlantic, USA, 2011, https://tinyurl.com/s5443c2y. Accessed on 4 September 2023.

Islam that promotes believers to attack non-believers and provides religious cover for violent jihadism. The reach of Saudis has been stunning, touching nearly every country with small and large Muslim population, from the Gothenburg Mosque in Sweden to the King Faisal Mosque in Chad, from the King Fahad Mosque in Los Angeles, to the Seoul Central mosque in South Korea. All these mosques were either constructed by support from the members of the Saudi royal families or Saudi charities and Saudi-funded organizations like the World Muslim League and the World Assembly of Muslim Youth. How Saudi influence plays out often depends greatly on the political, social and economic conditions of the respective country.

In parts of Africa and Southeast Asia, the Saudi teachings have visibly influenced the cultural behaviour of Muslim communities, collectively driving them towards a distressingly conservative direction. Women there strictly cover their heads with hijab, men grow beards without a moustache and wear trousers and pyjamas above the ankle. In many places women cover every inch of their skin with black robes except a slit for the eyes. Among the Muslim immigrant communities in North America and Europe, the first and second generation have been completely radicalized by Saudi Islam. In many countries of South Asia like India, Bangladesh, Sri Lanka, Pakistan and Afghanistan, the Salafis have become completely hostile to Shias and Sufi Sunni Muslims.

The suicide bombers are attacking Sufi shrines and Shia mosques, killing hundreds and thousands of fellow Muslims in Afghanistan, Mali and Pakistan. In the US and in many Western European countries like Britain, France and Sweden, the Saudi version of Sunni Islam is denigrating the Jewish and Christian faiths while Muslims encourage their kids to attend home learning schools for fear of getting mixed with the Western culture from an early age.

A senior Islamic cleric in Turkey, Mehmet Gormez, said in an interview: 'The Wahhabi teaching is undermining the pluralism, tolerance and openness to science and learning, that has long been the tradition in Islam.'[29] The Islamic State has adopted all books of Abd al-Wahhab, the eighteenth-century founder of the fundamentalist Salafi Islam, termed Wahhabism, to their madrasa curricula. Even the Imam of the Grand Mosque of Mecca proudly says that the Islamic State leaders 'draw their ideas and inspiration from Wahhabism,' which is followed in Saudi Arabia.

The American Islamic experts in Washington DC and diplomats specializing in Islam and the Middle East know well that Wahhabi worldview is systematically funded by Saudi Arabia, by paying for the religious textbooks, mosque constructions, TV stations and the training of imams.[30] The extremist narrative of Wahhabi–Salafi Islam has completely changed the Muslims during the last five decades. The million dollar question is why does Saudi Arabia unleash an ideology that much of the world finds repugnant? An answer to this question may be found in the historic alliance the founders of the Arabian Kingdom had made with a religious scholar, who was looking for administrative support to spread an ideology around the country a few centuries ago. That alliance, which was mutually beneficial, still undergirds the foundation of Saudi Arabia.

The Salafi scholar Ibn Abd al-Wahhab received military protection for his movement, and in return, the Saudi ruling family earned the endorsement of an Islamist cleric. Wahhab's version of Islam was the first of two historical accidents that would define the Saudi influence on the world centuries later. Akbar Ahmed, Ibn Khaldun Professor at the American University, USA, defines Wahhabism as 'a tribal, desert Islam'.[31] It was shaped by an austere desert ecosystem—xenophobic, fiercely opposed to shrines and tombs, disapproving of art and music and hugely different from

---

[29]Shane, Scott, 'Saudis and Extremism: "Both the Arsonists and the Firefighters"', *The New York Times*, 2016.
[30]Dillon, Michael R., *Wahhabism: Is it a Factor in the Spread of Global Terrorism?*, 2009, Naval Postgraduate School, Monterey, California, USA, Master's thesis.
[31]Ahmed, Akbar, *Journey into Islam: The Crisis of Globalization*, Brookings Press, 2007.

the cosmopolitan Islam of Baghdad, Beirut and Cairo. The second historical accident came in 1938, when the American oil prospectors discovered the largest oil reserves in Saudi Arabia. The oil revenue generated by the Arabian-American Oil Company (ARAMCO), helped the kingdom amass a fabulous amount of wealth. But it also froze in space and time a rigid socio-religious order that gave the conservative establishment (the monarchy) an extravagant budget to export its severe strain of Islam.

Interestingly, the credibility of Saudi religious teachers and imams is very high among the global Muslims as they are perceived to be highly knowledgeable in Islam, because they come from the land of Prophet Mohammad. When Saudi imams arrive in any non-Arab Muslim country, wearing the traditional robes, carrying checkbooks and quoting from the Quran and the Hadith, they receive a kind of rock-star reception. The awestruck Muslim communities look up to them for guidance in the multicultural societies. They preach separatism and a non-accommodative attitude with other faiths and cultures. Advising to spread the Wahhabi-Salafi interpretation of Islam they also encourage conversion of non-believers to the Muslim fold.

The 1979 Islamic Revolution brought to power a radical Shiite government in Iran, symbolically challenging the Wahhabi government of Saudi Arabia. The declaration of the Islamic Republic of Iran is one of the defining moments in the modern history of the Middle East, as the competition between two main branches of Islam—Sunni and Shia—got escalated. Saudi perceived the rise of Shia Iran as a major threat to its leadership in the Islamic world. Since then, the Saudi establishment has been redoubling its efforts in exporting Wahhabism, with a strong anti-Shia narrative, to other countries.

When the Grand Mosque of Mecca was stormed by a group of over 500 Ikhwan extremists in 1979, they were publicly calling Saudi rulers puppets of the West and traitors to Islam. The rebels were soon defeated, but the leading clerics agreed to back the monarchy only after getting an assurance of support for a crackdown on the immodest ways of the kingdom and an aggressive export of Wahhabism abroad.

The US and Afghanistan

Throughout the 1980s, Saudi Arabia and the US worked closely together to defeat the Soviet Union in Afghanistan. President Ronald Reagan even invited members of the Afghan Islamic party, headed by Gulbuddin Hekmatyar, a jihadist with anti-West DNA to the Oval Office. However, after 9/11, all the Afghan mujahideen joined the Taliban force to defeat the Americans. The US spent more than US$50 million between 1986 and 1992 to arm the Afghan mujahideen and the foreign jihadists, operating from Afghanistan. Bin Laden along with hundreds of Ikhwan volunteers from Saudi Arabia and Yemen camped in Pakistan and Afghanistan to fight the Soviet occupation in Afghanistan. Inadvertently, the Americans have been supporting the Islamic jihadists including bin Laden, who believed and practised an extremely rigid brand of Wahhabi Islam. It was only one of the repeated ironies of history that the Americans had to spend millions of dollars later, to fight an ideology that they themselves had once financed and helped flourish.

The American support to the Islamic jihadis forced the Soviet forces to withdraw from Afghanistan on 15 May 1988. It can be argued that the Soviet defeat, with financial and technological support from the Reagan administration, significantly empowered the non-state Islamic jihadists actors in Afghanistan.

The new jihadi brigade, drawn from different ethnicities and geographies, inspired by the Wahhabi–Salafi ideology, soon come under the big umbrella of al-Qaeda leadership in Afghanistan and Pakistan. Thus the US created a huge monster, which would pose serious challenges to it in the years to come. The Reagan administration, after the Soviet troops' withdrawal, thought that the mission was 'accomplished' in Afghanistan and withdrew its patronage shortly as the administration was not interested in pushing democracy in the post-Soviet Afghanistan. A similar mistake was committed by the George W. Bush administration in Iraq years later, after a forceful regime-change was brought about in the Arab country.

The power vacuum created by the withdrawal of the Soviet troops, soon turned Afghanistan into a battlefield of various warring groups, totally ravaging the country. The Pakistani military establishment and its intelligence agency ISI found an opportunity in the emerging situation and began to act cleverly by pushing radicalized young students of Salafi madrasas (Taliban) into Afghanistan. They were Afghani-descent students, enrolled in various madrasas in the refugee camps close to the Pakistan–Afghanistan international border. These students, who got trained by the Pakistani military officers and provided with tanks, pickup trucks and artillery guns, under the aegis of the Pakistani military officers in the 1990s, were the real game changers in Afghanistan. The Mullah Omar government in Kabul was installed under the direct supervision of the ISI and the Pakistan military operatives. The new Taliban government in Kabul was immediately recognized by Pakistan and Saudi Arabia. Afghanistan thus became a 'client state' of Pakistan and a nursery for the jihadists to be pushed into different parts of the world, including Indian Kashmir. Mullah Omar believed in the Wahhabi strain of Islam. The Saudi government was delighted with the new development and offered billions of dollars in aid to the Mullah Omar government. It also paid liberal grants to the Pakistani government for supporting the neighbouring Wahhabi regime. Pakistan commentators described the country's move in Afghanistan as a 'strategic depth' in the face of a possible attack from India on its eastern border.

In May 1996, Sudan came under strong diplomatic pressure from the US administration to expel bin Laden immediately from the country. The Saudi-born jihadist[32] was operating a construction

---

[32]Gartenstein-Ross, Daveed, and Nathaniel Barr, 'How Al-Qaeda works: "The Jihadist Group's Evolving Organizational Design"', *Hudson Institute*, 2018, http://tinyurl.com/2swazd33. Accessed on 5 September 2023.

company in Sudan as a cover for his anti-American activities from its capital city Khartoum. From there, however, bin Laden flew in a chartered plane to Afghanistan, where he was received as a special guest of the government. As a token of gift to the fellow brothers, he paid around US$3 million to the Mullah Omar government. In exchange, Kabul provided him with full security and land to set up training camps for the jihadis. It was geography familiar to Laden, where he had fought with the mujahideen during the Soviets' occupation. He infused fresh energy into the jihadi forces and intensified his writings and speeches against Americans and the west.

Laden's charisma attracted over 30,000 jihadis to his various camps from Europe and the Muslim world. They were comfortably housed in the sprawling facilities constructed all over Afghanistan. Bin Laden openly turned against Saudis in 1990 when the US troops attacked Iraq from the Saudi air-base. He described the Saudi royal family as apostates and from then on became fiercely anti-American.

Initially, al-Qaeda attacked the soft military targets in Saudi Arabia and slowly emerged as a powerful leader and the mentor to Mullah Omar. He also expanded his activities to drug and human trafficking. His regular sermons completely radicalized Taliban and their administration in Kabul. They imposed harsh laws prescribed by the Wahhabi Islam on the common Afghanis.

The Pakistani military and the ISI was fully complicit in helping Taliban administration to chart out and achieve its destructive goals. Pakistan willingly supplied manpower to Taliban by recruiting Pakistani and Afghani youths from its madrasas ensuring a steady supply of fighters to Taliban. Besides giving training to its foot soldiers, Pakistan had also supplied military hardware to the Mullah Omar government.

The al-Qaeda as a global terrorist organization demonstrated beyond doubt its immaculate planning and execution capabilities by the 9/11 attack. The operatives took flying lessons in the US, their planning meetings were held in Malaysia, and the plot leaders were from Hamburg, Germany. The funds were transferred from Dubai-based banks and the al-Qaeda leaders from Afghanistan oversaw all activities.

The 9/11 attack was a huge victory for the al-Qaeda and its protectors in Pakistan and Afghanistan. The well-coordinated strike hit multiple targets in the heart of the US. The attack was broadcast live around the world to an audience of hundreds of millions. The world was outraged. The North Atlantic Treaty Organization (NATO) for the first time invoked Article 5, allowing its members to respond collectively in self-defense. On 7 October, the US-led allied military forces launched an attack on Afghanistan. The US put pressure on Pakistan and the Arab countries to help in arresting the al-Qaeda militants, living under cover.

The US Congress quickly passed the USA PATRIOT Act (Uniting and Strengthening America by Providing Appropriate Tools Required to Intercept and Obstruct Terrorism). The Act has enormously expanded the search and surveillance powers of the FBI and other law enforcement agencies. Many insiders of al-Qaeda have confessed that bin Laden disastrously misjudged the possible US responses to the 9/11 attacks. He had imagined a few possibilities like a retreat from the Middle East along the lines of a US pullout from Somalia in 1993 or another series of cruise missile attacks on the Taliban camps. Neither of these two scenarios happened. The US campaign against the Taliban was relentless and using its full air power. Simultaneously, the Afghan Northern Alliance forces, which was fighting for the salvation of Afghanistan, also advanced from Panjshir valley to dislodge the Taliban forces from the country. Pakistan was sufficiently warned by President Bush not to mess up with the US campaign by providing Taliban with military hardware or ammunition.

The US Cover-Up

Is the Saudi connection to 9/11 one of the biggest cover-ups of the twenty-first century? Why did President Bush inexplicably censor 28 pages of the 800-page 9/11 Commission Report?³³ The pages were left blank, except for dotted lines where an estimated 7,200 words once stood. The Saudis deny any role in the attack and stick to the narrative that al-Qaeda acted alone with no state sponsors. Nonetheless, CIA found 'incontrovertible evidence' that extended to the Saudi royal family members, former diplomats and Saudi intelligence officers, who had helped the hijackers both financially and logistically. The intelligence file, cited in the report, directly implicates the Saudi embassy in Washington DC and the consulate in Los Angeles in the attacks, making 9/11 not just an act of terrorism, but an act of war.

A Saudi agent, Osama Basnan, set up an operating base in San Diego for the hijackers. They were provided rooms and cars on rent besides facilitating private meetings with the cleric Anwar al-Awlaki, who was the imam at a Saudi-funded mosque in the suburbs. The then Saudi Ambassador to the US, Prince Bandar and his wife sent checks totaling US$130,000 to Basnan while he was handling hijackers. Though the ambassador alleged that the money was for the sick wife of Basnan, the FBI investigations, however, confirmed that the money was used for hijackers. Other al-Qaeda funding has also been traced back to Ambassador Bandar and his embassy, so much so that by 2004, Riggs Bank of Washington DC even banned Saudis from being its clients.

Awlaki had taken over as the imam of Dar al-Hijrah mosque and the Islamic Center at Falls Church area in Virginia, in 2001. Imam Awlaki had met all the hijackers and arranged for their apartments and IDs through his handlers. He was a great admirer of bin Laden and had met him a couple of times. The imam was fully aware of the 9/11 attack and he had suspiciously fled the US by a Saudi flight well before the attacks. He was briefly detained at New York's John F.

---

³³Kean, Thomas (ed.), *The 9/11 Commission Report: Final Report of the National Commission on Terrorist Attacks Upon the United States: Executive Summary*, National Commission on Terrorist Attacks Upon the US, 2004, http://tinyurl.com/4tnwsjkp. Accessed on 5 September 2023.

Kennedy International Airport before being released into the custody of a Saudi embassy representatives.

Former Democratic senator Bob Graham had long suspected that many imams of California mosques, and preachers working under the Saudi Ministry of Islamic Affairs, were the strongest and most direct link between the hijackers and the Saudi operatives.[34] One of the key men was Fahad al-Thumairy, imam of King Fahad Mosque in Los Angeles who was known for his virulent anti-American views. Al-Thumairy was also an employee of the Saudi Ministry of Islamic Affairs, Dawah and Guidance. Another key person of the operation was Omar al-Bayoumi, al-Thumairy's handler, who used to move suspiciously among the Arab community in San Diego. They together were facilitating the hijackers' discreet stay and the flight training programs in the US.

The Manhattan-based law firm Kreindler & Kreindler, which represented the 9/11 victims' families for compensation, had brought forth many leads proving links between Saudi Arabia and the hijackers. Earlier, the law firm under Lee Kreindler, considered one of the founders of air disaster law in the US, had successfully fought civil suits on behalf of the victims of the 1998 Pan-Am Lockerbie bombing disaster, allegedly by Libyans. The firm had won a judgment against Libya securing a payment of US$3 billion as compensation to the victims' families. The relatives of 9/11 victims were aware of the success of the law firm. They were hoping that Lee Kreindler would eventually nail the culprits here too. Unfortunately, just over a year after the attack, Lee died of a stroke. The case was, however, handled by Jim Kreindler, successor to Lee.

Sometime in late 1998, a Somali al-Qaeda operative named Mohammad Sulaiman Barre established a branch of Dahabshiil, a Somali-based international funds-transfer company, in Karachi, Pakistan. Khalid Sheikh Mohammed, one of the 9/11 masterminds

---

[34] Golden, Tim, and Sebastian Rotella, 'The Saudi Connection: Inside the 9/11 Case that Divided the FBI', *The New York Times Magazine*, New York, 2020.

based in Karachi, was transferring money via Dubai to the US for training the hijackers through this firm. The law firm Kreindler holds that, in the wake of the US embassy bombings and the subsequent US pressure, the al-Qaeda operatives were using circuitous routes to transfer money and hence it had become harder to trace the money transfer trails.

The fate of the Kreindler case against Saudi Arabia is unclear. The Congress legislation, Justice Against Sponsors of Terrorism Act (JASTA), was passed to open doors for victims' families to hold responsible any member of the Saudi government, suspected in playing a role in the 9/11 attacks. President Obama vetoed the bill by arguing that it would remove the sovereign immunity and set a dangerous precedent. It was also argued that the US army personnel stationed around the world would become more vulnerable to lawsuits against them. Nevertheless, the Congress overrode the presidential veto and approved the legislation. It is known that Saudi is spending millions of dollars in engaging the lobbyist firms. President Trump during his campaign described Obama's veto as 'shameful'. Once in office, however, Trump seemingly reverted to the status quo. It seems unlikely that the Kreindler law firm will succeed in getting any compensation for the victims from the Saudi government.

The policy makers in America and Europe know well the connection between Wahhabi teachings and extremism that leads to terrorist acts like the 9/11 attack and the lone-wolf acts of terrorism in many parts of the world. In a way, Wahhabism is posing a serious threat to the US and the Western civilization as it is opposed to modernity, and the progressive ways of the liberal world.

After 9/11, the US however, had an opportunity to cap Wahhabism by replacing the monarchy in Saudi Arabia with a democratically-elected government as they envisioned for Iraq. The baffling question is, who convinced President Bush of a conspiracy theory that Iraq had possessed weapons of mass destruction and needed a punishment by direct intervention for a regime change. Either the advisers close to President Bush were heavily bribed by the

Saudi royal family to deflect attention from them or they were naive to believe that a regime-change in Saudi Arabia would antagonize 1.2 billion Muslims around the globe.

The whole world was aware that 15 out of the 19 attackers in the 9/11 incident were Saudi nationals, and the CIA and FBI had provided inputs to the Bush administration to establish their role in the heinous incident. These numbers included a member of the royal family and employees of the Ministry of Religious Affairs. Such persons were, however, dismissed by the Saudi royals as isolated rogues.

The bipartisan 9/11 Commission with Thomas Kean and Lee Hamilton as chairman and vice-chairman respectively, was set up to unravel the alleged conspiracy and role of different bodies including the foreign governments. The commission found no evidence directly or indirectly linking Iraq or Iran with the crime as they were not found in the loop of planning attacks. It is important to know that all the hijackers belonged to the Salafi brand of Islam. They were all radicalized and motivated by the Saudi-exported doctrine of Wahhabism. This intolerant ideology has also been the main discourse of all the American and European mosques, constructed by Saudi money and led by virulently anti-American imams.

It is absolutely naive to suspect Iran's role in the 9/11 attacks as Shias were regarded as heretics by the Wahhabis and it would be sacrilegious to consider them as partners of a Wahhabi conspiracy. In the case of Iraq, Saddam Hussein was secular, and not a devout Muslim. After his Kuwait invasion, the Saudi establishment however, began to feel increasingly uncomfortable with Saddam as he was behaving hegemonic in the region.

Saudi Arabia long remained a puzzle for the American agencies probing the 9/11 case. The most pertinent question was not who partnered the conspiracy, but what ideology inspired it. The focus should have been on the Wahhabi strain of Islam, which had long taken the centre stage in all mosques, Sunday schools and the Islamic study centres in the US. It had been transforming young Muslims into extremely bigoted and intolerant jihadists, ready to kill innocent people on the streets.

The Americans, European scholars and members of the civil society are fully aware that Wahhabism is the main source of Islamic extremism. Practically all terrorist organizations draw their inspiration from Wahhabism and funds from Saudi Arabia. Only a few exceptions like Hezbollah are linked to Shia Iran and that too, with its focus not to fight the West, but to support the Shia-backed regimes elsewhere, like Bashar al-Assad in Syria and Houthis in Yemen.

During the last 16 years, almost all the terror attacks including the 9/11, Boston Marathon bombing and San Bernardino shooting in the US were linked to Wahhabism. The role of Saudi-trained imams and the Salafi texts, used in mosques, were deliberately covered up at the highest levels of the US government. It is often 'soft-pedalled' to protect America's delicate alliance with the oil-rich Kingdom of Saudi Arabia.

The European Parliament in 2013 identified Wahhabism as the main source of global terrorism. The American administration and its successive presidents have to understand this fact. They should know that Wahhabism is an engineered perversion—an abomination which has spread like cancer into the Islamic world, and is now threatening to destroy its relationship with other religions. Wahhabism is not Islam, as Islam would never sanction murder, looting, atrocities and barbarism. Islam opposes despotism, injustice, greed and extremism. It is not in favour of anything which is not balanced and good, fair and merciful, kind and compassionate. The time has come for the world to realize that the abominable monster of jihadi terrorism is the legitimate baby of Wahhabism born in Saudi Arabia, which is fed and fueled by the riches of Arabian petrodollars. It is sad that the criminal misadventures of jihadis often become weapons in the hands of neo-imperialists to justify their military interventions.

Not only America and the European nations, but Asian countries too are under the grip of this disastrous perversion of faith. The 2019 Easter Sunday terror attacks in Sri Lanka, were masterminded by a radical Wahhabi mosque preacher named Zaharan Hashim. He staunchly supported ISIS ideology and subscribed to the extremist narrative of Salafi Islam. He used to put his sermons on online platforms attracting many educated youths to him. In 2014, he started a group called National Thowheed Jamath, which drew its ideology from the austere Wahhabi traditions that claimed to follow the faith as practised in the age of Prophet Mohammad. He believed that Sri Lankan Muslims should be ruled by Sharia laws and not the secular Sri Lankan laws.

Zaharan Hashim founded his own private mosque with foreign funds and targeted one of the richest business families for radicalization, as this was the signature practice used by the extremists, earlier in Boston, and later in Spain. Mohammad Yusuf Ibrahim was one of the richest business tycoons in spice export in Colombo. Members of Ibrahim's extended family say Ilham, Ibrahim's younger son was more devout than others in the family and that his young wife Fatima covered her entire face with a veil, unusual among Sri Lankan Muslims. The flamboyant elder son Insaaf Ibrahim, was trained to take over the business. The priest Zaharan Hashim was successful in brainwashing both the brothers to the extent of making them agree to be suicide bombers to kill non-believers.

A prominent teaching of Wahhabism is hate for other faiths and it works whether one is rich, poor, educated or uneducated. The police found out the role of the business family in the attack within hours and swarmed the Ibrahim mansion. At the gate of the mansion, the police was greeted by a woman, who then turned around and dashed up the stairs. It was Fatima, Ilham's wife. At the top of the stairs, in front of her three small kids, Fatima blew herself up, killing three police officers and all her small children including an eight-month-old baby. It shows that Ilham's entire family was radicalized by the priest, even though it was difficult to assess what role the women in the family played in the act. Fatima, however, was clearly complicit in the plan as she was prepared to kill herself once her husband committed the act.

Islam gives women their rightful place in society. Modern Muslim women aspire to become successful in their life as some of the bold and enterprising women in the early history of Islam, a great example being Khadija herself, the Prophet's wife, who was a successful businesswoman. But Wahhabism denies women every right and prefers them to be confined to their homes.

The global Muslim population, which has reached more than 1.6 billion and is spread all over the world, is under siege by Wahhabi–Salafi Islam. The challenge for the US and the European nations is to wake up and smell the coffee to put pressure on Saudi Arabia to stop exporting this dangerous ideology to the world.

The only alternative is to chart out a plan to spread the counter-narrative of a peaceful and tolerant strain of Islam like Sufism, and carve out a clear space for it among the Muslim communities across the world, including in the US.

The American and European sovereign nations have a right to reform the mosques, Sunday schools and the cultural centres attached to them by following the example of Morocco. In the aftermath of the 2007 Casablanca terror attack in Morocco, King Mohammed VI sought greater regulatory control over the religious realm of the country, purging Wahhabi-leaning imams from around 6,500 mosques, removing controversial lessons from the religious-education curricula, revamping the system of training imams and promoting the strain of Sufi Sunni Islam. The traditional Islam with its rich cultural and aesthetic heritage dates back to many centuries even before the birth of Wahhabism, which it apparently finds hard to digest. Today, global Muslims have two options before them: either the peaceful historical Islam that accommodates art, music, science, aesthetics and multiculturalism or the intolerant Wahhabi–Salafi Islam, a highly politicized version, full of hatred, dogmas, rigidities and bigotry.

2

SECTARIAN FAULT LINES AND THE FUTURE OF THE MIDDLE EAST

In the Middle East, Sunnis account for nearly 90 per cent of the population in Egypt, Jordan and Saudi Arabia. There is also a substantial majority of Sunnis in Qatar, UAE, Palestine, Turkey, Afghanistan and Pakistan, and a slight majority in Yemen, Syria and Kuwait. Shia Muslims are the majority in Iran, constituting around 95 per cent of the population; in Iraq, Azerbaijan and Bahrain they are above 70 per cent. They have a slight majority in Lebanon, while they are a minority in Yemen, Turkey, Kuwait, Syria, Saudi Arabia, Afghanistan and Pakistan. There are many sub-denominations of Shiism like Alawi in Syria, Alevi in Turkey, Zaydi–Houthis in Yemen, Ismaili Bohras in South Asia, etc.[35]

The divide between Sunnis and Shias is fundamentally about the political succession to Prophet Mohammad, as well as the qualifications of the successor and the scope of his responsibilities and duties. Nonetheless, the defining moment of the Sunni–Shia schism was the Battle of Karbala, which took place in Iraq in the year 680. The Battle of Karbala is highly significant as far as the Shia identity is concerned. Globally, Shias commemorate the event on the day of Ashura every year.

Sectarianism in the Middle East entered a new phase with the Islamic Revolution in January 1979. The leader Ayatollah Khomeini established a theocratic state by displacing the secular state under

---

[35]Robinson, H.M., et al., *Sectarianism in the Middle East: Implications for the United States,* RAND, Corporation, Santa Monica, California, 2018.

Mohammad Reza Pahlavi. The revolution also provoked the religious Wahhabi-Salafi leadership in the Kingdom of Saudi Arabia as they saw it as a regional threat and a challenge to its leadership. Inspired by the revolution in Iran, the Shias in Iraq, Lebanon, Syria, Bahrain and Yemen felt emboldened as they began to look towards Tehran for spiritual and political leadership.

Many Arab nations viewed Iran's emergence as a threat to Sunni dominance in the region. As a reaction, the Wahhabi-Salafi clerical leadership in Saudi Arabia seized the Grand Mosque (Masjid al-Haram) of Mecca in November 1979. They told the ruling royal family that enough was enough and that Saudi had to revert back to the puritanical fundamental principles of Islam as were practised during the early days, popularly known as Salafism. Though the leaders of the seizure were later caught and punished, Riyadh fully capitulated to their demands and agreed to strengthen the Wahhabi-Salafi clerical leadership, so as to help them spread their doctrine at home and abroad. In the back of their mind was the Shia Islamic Revolution, which needed to be countered squarely, and the only option was to overpower them by unleashing the extremist Salafi ideology in the region and beyond. A re-emergence of the two contrasting narratives inspired by two recent incidents was perhaps the main reason for the resurgence of sectarianism in the Middle East. Iran's regional power, however, began to grow after the US intervention in Afghanistan in 2001 and in Iraq in 2003. The core of the regional conflict in Yemen, Syria and Lebanon is also sectarianism, in which Iran and Saudi Arabia are in direct conflict.

Shiism as Official Religion

The crowning of Shah Ismail I (1501-1524), the founder of the Safavid dynasty, as king of Iran took place in 1501. A Turkish-speaking Shiite from Azerbaijan, he was a great warrior and a poet with a strong belief in Shia faith. He announced that Shia Islam would henceforth be the official religion of his state and brought all lands of Iran under a single ruler. The Safavid dynasty (1501–1722) had its origin in the Safavid order of Sufism. Like many outside Shiism, they venerated Imam Ali (601–661), the first of 12 Shia imams. Safavids with their genuine zeal for Shiism were determined to expand its area of influence. They were intense rivals of the Sunni Ottomans in the west and the Sunni Mughal Empire of the east. In particular, the Ottomans and Safavids competed for dominance in the heartland of the Middle East. That competition took sectarian overtones as Safavids became the Shia empire and the protector of Shiism. On the other hand the Ottomans, who ruled some of the Arab lands, had officially claimed the caliphate with Istanbul as its capital in 1517 to be the sole spokesman of Sunnism. However, there wasn't much of a real caliphate for both the Shias and Sunnis to fight over by the sixteenth century.

In fact, what the Ottomans had inherited was not the functional institution of the caliphate, but simply, the symbolic leadership of the Sunni world. The Ottomans and Safavids fought many wars. For a short time, Safavids also controlled Iraq and through state power, transformed the entire population under their command into Shias by coercion and persuasion. Under Safavids, Shia religious learning and culture flourished. They built their capital at Isfahan in 1660, in central Iran, and the grand architecture of the city, as seen today, is the legacy of the Safavid rule. In 1722, the Safavid Empire fell to Sunni armies from Afghanistan, which was then followed in power by the great Iranian king Nader Shah. Neither the Afghans nor Nader Shah were able to make Sunnism the official religion of Iran, and their triumph ended when Shias challenged the Sunni regional domination. Iranian Shiism endured with highly provocative consequences in the twentieth century.

Modern Iraq

The British Residency on al-Rashid Street in the heart of Baghdad was once occupied by the English diplomat, writer and archaeologist

Gertrude Bell. The Oxford-educated mountaineer and administrator first came to Baghdad in 1900. During the next ten years she explored the entire Middle East in her capacity as an archaeologist and a political officer. The British Empire thought of colonizing Iraq after the the First World War and Miss Bell charted the Iraqi course of history. She conceived the boundaries of Iraq and installed Emir Faisal of Mecca as its first ruler. She saw the new king, a puppet of the British Empire, as being well accepted by various tribes and sub-tribes. It was said that Miss Bell, however, developed a deep suspicion about the Shia community and grew impatient with their religious leaders. She believed that Shias were not loyal to the British Crown and always conspired against the British colonial power.

The state of modern Iraq was created as a kingdom under the British Mandate in 1921 and it was granted independence as a nation state in 1932. Nevertheless, Iraq did exist as a region or group of provinces for well over a millennium, under different rulers including the Abbasids, Mongols and the Ottomans. Fanar Haddad, scholar of Middle Eastern affairs, identified three types of identities held by the Iraqi Arabs: unified Iraqi nationalism, Sunni Iraqi nationalism and Shia Iraqi nationalism. All three types of nationalist identity exist simultaneously. The recent anti-Iran riots by the Shias across Iraq, however, arise from their unified Iraqi nationalism over sectarianism.

The Shia leadership of Najaf was mostly alien to Miss Bell and she had decided that the new state of Iraq would be entrusted to Sunnis. Under the British patronage, the Sunni Arabs took control of the new Iraqi army and parliament. The elements within the Sunni elites increasingly came to view the army as a tool to retain control of the state and to shape the Iraqi national identity. Prior to the British control in 1920, the Ottoman-trained Sunni Arab military and political officers were educated and trained in the Ottoman philosophy of a strong state. The Sunni minority ruled the following eight decades with the mindset of a majority.

When King Faisal's 23-year-old grandson Faisal II was overthrown and murdered in the 1958 coup, the Shias enjoyed power briefly, owing to the fact that the coup's leader Qasim's mother was a Shiite. Qasim was overthrown in another coup in 1963 and the eventual rise of Arab nationalism and Baathism completely marginalized the Shia community. The core of the Baathist party in the 1960s was composed of the Sunni Arab Iraqis who benefited hugely from the Saddam Hussein presidency. Whereas, the Shia Iraqis remained secondary citizens after the Iraqi revolution. They were sidelined and sometimes violently opposed by the Sunni regime. Unlike Sunnism, which envisioned a personal relationship between the worshipper and God, the Iraqi Shias were organized around Imams and Mujtahids.

Many power-friendly Shiites embraced Arab nationalism and rose to important positions in the Baath party. Baathism may have been secular and nationalistic on the surface, but, at heart, it professed a brutal Sunni hegemony. Traditionally, the tribal Sunni leadership had developed a strong streak of anti-Shiism under the influence of Wahhabism. The 35 years of Baath rule were hard for Shias, and the reign of Saddam Hussein was worse. He relentlessly mistreated them and even banned the public observance of Ashura and other Shia rituals. Millions of Shias were displaced from their land in the lower Tigris–Euphrates river basins, being forced to spend their lives in the slums of Saddam City in the northeast of Baghdad. Post the US invasion, the city was renamed after the murdered Shia leader Ayatollah Muhammad Sadiq al-Sadr. Every single Shia cleric family of Iraq suffered under the Saddam regime. Many relocated to Iran while some migrated to Europe. The Shias were looking to the US and waiting for an intervention.

During the buildup of the 2003 US invasion under George W. Bush, the Saudi monarchy had, however, warned the American administration in no uncertain terms, that if Saddam were to fall from power, the beneficiary would be Iran and Shias of Iraq, as they constitute the majority in the country. The House of Saud did not want Shias to rule an important Arab country in the heart of the Middle East. As per the 1744 treaty between Al Saud and the Salafi scholar Ibn Abd al-Wahhab, the supreme Sunni religious leaders of Saudi Arabia should always be direct descendants of Abd al-Wahhab, who decried that Shias and Sufis are heretics and hence should not be allowed to rule Muslim countries.

Bahrain is another Arab country, which has Sunni rulers, even though about 70 per cent of its native population is Shia. During the famous Arab Spring uprising, the House of Saud dispatched Saudi National Guards and brutally crushed the short-lived Shia uprising against the ruling family in Bahrain.

In March 2003, the Grand Ayatollah of Iraqi Shias, Sayyid Ali al-Husayni al-Sistani, told his community not to resist the US troops' march into Baghdad. When the US marines drove into the heart of the holy city of Karbala at midnight, they found it quiet and dark, save for the luminescent golden dome of the shrine of Imam Husayn—a scene that has dazzled many young American marines. The American administration was pleased by the fatwa of Ayatollah Sistani. In reality, the Sistani decree was less a favour to America than an opportunity for Shias in claiming Iraq. The Bush administration, however, was blissfully unaware of the implications of their act and the nuanced rivalry and hatred between Shia and Sunni sects. The fall of Saddam Hussein was the end of the Sunni rule in Iraq, which has totally changed the social matrix of Sunnis and Shias in the country. For the first time in the history of Islam, Shias would be the rulers of an Arab country. President Bush's vision was to make a regime change; to put down a tyrannical dictator and usher in an era of a democratic, secular and economically prosperous Iraqi state.

Shia Revival

The Shia revival in Iraq first manifested at a cultural and religious level. The holy cities and learning centres were opened. Hundreds and thousands of pilgrims visited Karbala and Najaf, creating a commercial stimulus and transnational links with the Middle

Eastern and South Asian countries. The revival rested mainly on three factors: a Shia-dominated government with a Shia prime minister in Baghdad, the rise of Iran as a regional power and the empowerment of Shias across Lebanon, Syria, Bahrain, Saudi Arabia, Kuwait, India and the UAE. All the three were interconnected, and each reinforced the other. President Obama's signing of the Iran nuclear deal, the European Union's granting of a new global respectability to the Rouhani regime in Iran and the recent success of the Iraqi forces in evicting the Islamic State fighters from Mosul and other parts of the country have given a new confidence to the Iraqi ground forces and the Shia militias in the region. The recent standoff between the four Sunni Arab countries—Saudi Arabia, Bahrain, UAE and Egypt with Qatar has further widened the Sunni–Shia fault lines in the Middle East. Qatar, a small country that shares gas fields with Iran, has signed agreements with Iran for imports of food and other essential items in view of a commercial embargo from their Sunni neighbours. The Saudi-led coalition is furious with Qatar for establishing a friendly relationship with a Shia Iran. The changed political equation has created a more level playing field for the Sunni–Shia balance of power in the region than in nearly 14 centuries.[36]

Sunni Insurgency and Islamic State in Iraq

The Sunni insurgency against the Shia-led central Iraqi government was joined by many forces in 2005. It also included the former Baathist army officers and the extreme Salafi jihadists. The insurgency was contextualized with ideology to complicate matters of power transfer for the US occupation forces when they leave Iraq. The insurgency group leader Abu Musab al-Zarqawi, rose from the ranks of al-Qaeda in Jordan. His message to both Sunnis and Shias was

---

[36]Nasr, Seyyed Vali Reza, *The Shia Revival: How Conflicts Within Islam will Shape the Future*, W.W. Norton & Company, London, 2006.

unequivocal, that the issues on the table were not about power-sharing with Shias, nor secularism, pluralism or democracy, but which sect would rule over Iraq.

The al-Qaeda leadership in Iraq issued a letter in the name of Zarqawi to all Sunnis calling Shias the lurking snakes, crafty and malicious scorpions and spying enemies with penetrating venom. They announced their battle to be at two levels: one with the Americans and the British and other with the Shias of Iraq. Zarqawi believed Shias to be more cunning than the American crusader masters. He knew that they would eventually stabilize their power base in Iraq and extend it across the region stretching from Iran, through Iraq, Syria, Lebanon and the Kingdom of Bahrain. The only option for the Iraqi Sunnis was to start a civil war and capture areas of Sunni majority and expel Shias from there. Zarqawi aimed to lead an insurgency that would usher in chaos and unpredictability in the nation with this aim. He was aware of the consequences of a civil war and its impact on the allied occupation forces in Iraq. In 2005, the Americans added more combat forces into the Iraqi war theatre and named it 'Surge' and mounted a strong attack against the insurgency groups along the Syria–Iraq border. Zarqawi strongly retaliated with three days of mayhem, during which suicide bombings and other brutalities killed many and maimed hundreds of Shias and their religious leaders. The attack was followed by postings on the al-Qaeda websites, which called for a full-scale war on heretic Shias all over Iraq. These were the initial days when the Internet was increasingly being used to spread jihadi messages and technology-driven global terrorism emerged for the first time.

The 'flattening of the world'[37] paved the way for an unprecedented growth of al-Qaeda. Globalization had been its friend, in that it helped to solidify revival of the Muslim identity in many ways. It enabled the Muslims in one country to better understand and

---

[37]Friedman, Thomas L., *The World Is Flat: The Globalized World in the Twenty-First Century*, Penguin Books, 2007.

sympathize with their brothers and sisters in another country and also to express solidarity with them. This was possible through the Internet and different social media platforms. The flattening process also intensified the feelings of discrimination and injustice done by the West to them in the name of regime changes in different countries. The unresolved Palestinian issue and the violence unleashed by Israel on the occupied West Bank had always remained etched in the minds of generations of Muslims.

The flattening of the world also led to more urbanization and large scale migration of educated unemployed Arab youths to the West. The fast Internet and electronic mails helped young Muslims form a strong and effective network amongst them. The new communication technology has been a boon to underground extremist organizations like al-Qaeda and its affiliates. They started transferring money through hawala networks (hand to hand financing system) and recruited through websites by promoting hatred towards other faiths.

What the world witnessed in Iraq after the American invasion was a clear surge in the supply chain of suicide bombers. Hundreds of suicide bombers were recruited from the Wahhabi Islam hotspots like Chechnya, Afghanistan, Somalia and Pakistan. They were in a rage not because of the long Israeli occupation of the West Bank or the American occupation of Iraq. Instead, the compelling message of jihad spread through the Wahhabi mosques, Sunday schools and various extremist e-platforms clearly had something to do with it. Islamic texts were used selectively to lure the youth for committing suicide for the 'greater cause of Islam'. The flattened world also helped them create a 'virtual caliphate' using all its communicational possibilities. The horrific video of the beheading of the Wall Street Journal reporter Daniel Pearl by Islamist militants in Pakistan, was shared on the Internet all over the world. Ironically, the same beheading videos were also used for recruitments. The new world makes it much easier for the terrorists to globalize their violent acts. With the Internet at their disposal, they need not go to any media organization to spread their messages. Instead, they can do it on their own by directly uploading them on any e-platforms like Facebook or YouTube.

Terrorist groups use the Internet to raise funds as well. Al-Qaeda always depended heavily on donations and smartly weaved a global fundraising network comprising foundations, charities, non-governmental organizations and other financial institutions, which use websites and Internet-based chatrooms for their interactions and money transactions. Recruiters also use more interactive Internet technology to identify and rope in potential members to their group from a young population. The terrorist outfits like Hamas, al-Qaeda and many Pakistan-based groups do not operate strictly on a hierarchical chain of command, but allow groups to work as affiliates, as done by Boko Haram in Nigeria and al-Shabaab in Somalia. Dozens of sites support terrorism and there are many loosely networked extremist groups in the Philippines, Indonesia, India, France, Britain, Pakistan, Chechnya, Somalia and Nigeria. They exchange ideas and practical information among them about how to build bombs, establish terror cells and carry out attacks. Majority of the al-Qaeda operatives involved in the 9/11 attacks had used the Internet for all their planning and coordination activities.

In 2004, Zarqawi and his group—The Society for Unity of God and Jihad (Jamaat al-Tawhid wal-Jihad), pledged allegiance to Osama bin Laden, who in turn appointed Zarqawi as his deputy. After the bin Laden endorsement, Zarqawi's operations in Iraq continued to gain strength. His military capabilities became more sophisticated as he tapped in new sources of financial support and started conversation with former Sunni Iraqi army commanders to improve his arsenal. He organized the guerrilla groups in towns across the Euphrates river valley. He also developed a network in Jordan and Syria and took responsibility for major operations in Amman in November 2005. His group carefully created an anti-Shia narrative among the Sunni circles of Iraq and the Shia revival was seen as a monumental calamity in the fortune of Islam.

The larger Arab world and Sunni Muslims in general were suspicious of the US actions in the Middle East, considering that they perceived it as a grand conspiracy to weaken Sunni Islam. This served as a new call to expand the scope of confrontation with the US as sectarian feelings constituted an important aspect of the Arab world's reaction beyond the development in Iraq. A message had gone across the global Sunni and Arab communities, that the US had snatched Iraq from the hands of 'true Islam' and delivered it to 'heretic' Shias. The US invasion of Iraq in 2003 triggered the weakening of the traditional Sunni Arab bastions, and the regimes in Cairo, Amman and Riyadh, were forced to provide a larger space for Shia Iran.

President Obama believed that it was imperative for the US to engage with Iran to keep them from achieving the nuclear threshold. The deal would push back the threshold level by 15 years and cut off their pathways effectively. Once they are better integrated with the global communities, Tehran would behave in a more responsible way. Israel has consistently raised the pitch against the nuclearization of Iran, seemingly to widen the fault lines between Sunnis and Shias in the Middle East.

Hostility to Shiite Iran

Sectarianism in the Middle East has been growing out of proportion. It is like a giant prism: people view their neighbours through it and governments use it to size up their rivals in the region. The conflict in Syria, Yemen and Iraq is proxy sectarian wars between Saudi Arabia and Iran—Sunni- and Shia-dominated nations, respectively, of the region. Within each country, the orthodox clerics speak harsh language about each other's beliefs. Saudi Arabia's hard push of the Wahhabi–Salafi creed of Islam, has influenced the spread of sectarian rhetoric across the world. This, in turn, influences the Iranian perception of Sunnis and breeds in them a strong intolerance towards Sunnis.

The ruling family of Saudi Arabia believes that Iran is behind the military success of Houthis in Yemen, Hezbollah in Lebanon and Bashar al-Assad in Syria. The Islamic State, one of the most intolerant jihadi groups, also strongly hates Shias and followers of the Sufi Sunni Islam, owing to their Wahhabi influence. After the collapse of ISIS and its caliphate in Syria and Iraq, many sleeper cells with similar ideology have emerged in Syria, Yemen, Afghanistan, Libya and pockets of northern Iraq.

Significance of Iran to US Strategic Interests

Seyyed Hossein Nasr, Iranian–American professor from Georgetown University, Washington DC, routinely briefed high-ranking officials of the American administration about the geostrategic importance of Iran and the nuances of its relationship with the Sunni Arab world. In reality, William Burns, former US deputy secretary of state, developed the contours of the interim nuclear agreement secretly in 2013 with his Iranian counterparts, paving way for the later negotiations. It is the continuation of the same effort which later culminated in the signing of the historic nuclear deal with Iran in 2015.

The deal, obviously, has invited several criticisms including from prominent personalities like John Boehner, the speaker of the US congress, who rejected it saying that it was 'unacceptable'. Nevertheless, President Obama stood his ground and made it clear in his remarks that the deal was not based on trust but on verification. He also maintained that it was the best option for the US and its allies and the world to integrate Iran with the rest of the world.

In March 2004, a series of bomb blasts in Baghdad and Karbala killed as many as 143 Shias who were commemorating Ashura.[38] It was one of the deadliest attacks in Iraq after President Bush declared an end to major combat operations in the country on 1 May 2003. A Wahhabi cleric in Saudi Arabia who followed the Hanbali school of Islamic jurisprudence, variously described as

---

[22]Arraf, Jane, and Brent Sadler, 'Deadly Attacks Rock Baghdad, Karbala', *CNN*, 2 March 2004, http://tinyurl.com/h8jknups. Accessed on 5 September 2023.

Wahhabi, used his website to justify this act of utmost cruelty by condemning the observance of the Shia holy day as 'the biggest display of idolatry' and saying in reference to the Shia sect, 'they are not our brothers'. He accused Shias of forming an 'axis of evil, linking Washington, Tel Aviv and Najaf,' the holy city of Shias and a conspiracy to disenfranchise Sunnis. Saudi Arabia believes that the US, its closest ally, is complicit in making a Shia revival possible. At the same time, the US and Western democracies know the role of Saudi establishment in globally spreading Salafism, which is a violent brand of Islam. Its consequences include the emergence of al-Qaeda, the Islamic State and other jihadi groups.

The Saudi-led Sunni camp is scared of the Shia Crescent expanding from Beirut to Tehran. Paul Bremer, who led the US administration in Iraq, following the 2003 invasion of the country, said that the attacks were intended to provoke sectarian violence among Sunnis and Shias. The strike came after weeks of the coalition getting a copy of a letter written by Zarqawi to the al-Qaeda leadership in Pakistan or Afghanistan about keeping alive the insurgency against Shiites and taking credit for other attacks in the region.

The Saudi-led Wahhabi Salafists are not only attacking Shias, but are also taking over the mainstream Hanafi, Sunni and Sufi Islam elsewhere in the world. In one country after the other, Saudi Arabia is spending millions of petrodollars for this purpose. A result of this is the spread of sectarian strife in the Islamic world. The Shias are targeted with unprecedented ferocity from Saudi Arabia to Pakistan and from Tunisia to Indonesia. Such sectarian violence is not confined to the villages of Syria or Pakistan, but it is poisoning the relationship between different sects in every Islamic community.

One of the key reasons of dispute between Qatar and Saudi Arabia, is the former's relationship with Shia Iran. Although the majority of Qataris and its ruling Al Thani family follow Wahhabism, the compelling geopolitical matrix forces Qatar to keep a friendly relationship with Iran. Qatar's Shia community comprises around

45 main clans divided between three major groups. The first group comprises people originally from Bahrain, the second from the al-Hasa region of Saudi Arabia and the third is a non-Arab group from Iran. Shias have enjoyed freedom of worship in Qatar for decades. They have their own mosques, halls for religious ceremonies (*hussainias*) and even Shia religious courts. Shias and Sunnis have lived in harmony in Qatar for ages. Being a small island nation, protruding like a thumb into the Persian Gulf, Qatar shares its gas field with Iran. The country has, over a period of time, carved a place for itself as one of the important leaders of the Sunni Arab world.

After 9/11, the Bush administration decided to annually host an event, the US-Islamic World Forum, in Doha, mainly to engage the Sunni Arab countries in the realms of politics, media, academia and civil society issues. The focus was not academic dialogue, but developing an actionable agenda for the governments and the civil society. The annual meeting was always held in Doha, Qatar, except the one in April 2011, which was held in Washington DC. The Brookings Institution was given the responsibility to organize the annual event. In an effort to institutionalize pan-Arabism, Iranian academics or government functionaries were never invited to these events in Doha. The royal family of Saudi Arabia was irked by the US administration for holding such an important annual event outside Riyadh, Saudi Arabia.

The first meeting of the forum[39] was held in January 2004, in which over 150 leaders and experts from the US and 37 Muslim countries participated. The emir of Qatar, Sheikh Hamad bin Khalifa Al Thani, delivered the keynote address. Since then, the event has been organized annually by Qatar's Ministry of Foreign Affairs in cooperation with the US Center for Middle East Policy. By hosting such an important annual event in Doha, the Qatari Emir emerged as a key leader of the Sunni Arab world. The emergence of Qatar

---

[23]The Brookings Institution, *Annual Report 2004*, Washington DC, 2004, https://tinyurl.com/4ywmhwpm. Accessed on 15 September 2023.

as a leading voice of moderation in the Middle East is not palatable with the young and ambitious Crown Prince MBS of Saudi Arabia.

An increasingly warmer relationship between Doha, Ankara and Tehran has brought Tel Aviv closer to Cairo and Riyadh. The sectarian narrative of the Middle East, however, is counterbalanced by a warmer relationship between Turkey, Iran and Qatar. Riyadh views Iran as an existential threat, yet Qatar, like Turkey, is strengthening its multilayered relationship with Iran. There are no Shias in Libya, but it faces a powerful insurgency from jihadist Sunni groups that fight the Sunni-dominated Government of National Unity inspired by the Islamic State ideology. The fact is that the Middle East never was, and can never be, strictly divided along the ethno-sectarian lines. The heavily mixed population in the cities and provinces and the intermarriages between sects, complicate the arguments for division. In the late 1990s and the early 2000s, Saudi Arabia started moderating both the elements of sectarianism. The government began a rapprochement with Iran, and a reformist camp within the ruling clique, led by the then Crown Prince Abdullah, sought to reduce the influence of Wahhabi extremism in Saudi Arabia in the aftermath of the 9/11 attacks. The militant Wahhabism has undergone several facelifts from time to time, but underneath, the ideology remains the same—whether it is Taliban, the various clones of al-Qaeda, the dreaded Islamic State or the al-Nusra Front, which is the Syrian version of al-Qaeda. Backed by the Saudi petrodollar, the al-Nusra Front is still causing havoc in the lives of millions of innocent Syrians. These extremists, flush with Saudi dollars, have been targeting Christians, Jews, Yazidis, Shiite and other sects of Muslims just because of the fact that they are different from them. In fact, it is their fellow Sunnis themselves, who have been most beleaguered by this exported doctrine of hate.

In the meanwhile, pressure is mounting on Crown Prince MBS to effect some serious moderation to Wahhabism. Riyadh has spent billions of US dollars exporting the ultra-conservative interpretation of Islam through thousands of mosques, madrasas, Islamic centres and Sunday schools in Western countries. From Asia to Africa, from Europe to America, this theological perversion has brought shame to the global Muslim community. Many former jihadists are of the view that Saudi Arabia has changed Islam with their money. Wahhabi Salafism has been devastating in its impact. Virtually every terrorist or jihadist group abusing the name of Islam, be it al-Qaeda and its offshoots in Syria or the Boko Haram in Nigeria, has been inspired by this death cult. In 2013, Iran's president, Hassan Rouhani, proposed an initiative called World against Violence and Extremism (WAVE). The United Nations should build on that framework to foster greater dialogue between different religions and their sects to counter this medieval fanaticism.

The conflict in the Middle Eastern countries, in reality, is much more nuanced than a simple sectarian war. Saudi Arabia's rhetoric, which is deeply entrenched in Wahhabism, is very distinct from the Islamic State's use of anti-Shiism to settle political and economic scores with Bashar al-Assad in Syria and the Shia prime minister in Iraq. There are different kinds of sectarianism at play in the Muslim countries. Some Sunni groups and states have integrated sectarian themes into the very fabric of their political, cultural and educational systems. In other words, sectarianism has been institutionalized in such places. The most prominent example is, of course, Saudi Arabia and its centuries-old antagonism towards Shiites. Muhammad ibn Abd al-Wahhab, the father of Wahhabism, made anti-Shiism a core component of his doctrine. The formal interpretation of Saudi Arabia's Islam is ideologically sectarian and condemning of all other schools of Islamic thought. The state and many citizen groups put millions of US dollars every year into evangelism (*dawah*), which includes establishment of mosques, schools and financial support to media organizations that promote their interpretation of Islam. Continued and conscious exercise of sectarian policies and discourses is likely to be a feature of the Middle Eastern politics for years to come as different groups are determined to encourage and push their sectarian agenda in the region. Apparently, such perpetrators of conflict are put in motion to target groups. Now, Syria and Iraq are the two sectarian crucibles, not because Shias, Sunnis or any other groups can only manage to settle their differences violently, but because some outside forces have been actively encouraging them to do so. In short, there are various drivers of the Sunni–Shia conflict in the Middle East.

The humiliations faced by Sunnis and the spread of a virulent Wahhabism led to al-Qaeda receiving significant support in Iraq, which led to a spate of bombings against Shia targets and shrines, after the 2003 invasion. A large number of Shias were killed in suicide and car bombings. However, Shias responded in the following years by killing Sunnis on a large scale. Sectarian killings by both sides intensified until they were brought under control by the US operation named 'Surge' in 2007, when President Bush sent an extra troop of 20,000 soldiers to stabilize the situation. The US had encouraged the Sunni tribal leadership to turn against the al-Qaeda in Iraq. Nonetheless, they remained hostile to Nouri al-Maliki's Shia majority government, and this helped to create conditions for the rise of a strident Wahhabi narrative against Shias, which eventually led to the rise of the ISI or the Islamic State in Iraq. Saudi Arabia supplied the maximum jihadist fighters from the region to the ranks of the Islamic State to indirectly punish Iran. In Syria and Iraq, on the other hand, Iran funded and supported its proxies like Hezbollah, to counter the Sunni groups led by Saudi Arabia.

Any of the prominent Sunni or Shia extremist groups, like the al-Qaeda, ISIS or Hezbollah have not defined their movements in sectarian terms, and they often use anti-imperialist, anti-Zionist and anti-American narratives to justify their jihadi acts. After developing a political wing in Lebanon, Hezbollah is now sharing the government in Beirut. They fought along with Iranian militias in Syria and joined hands with Houthis in Yemen against the Saudi-backed Sunni forces. Remnants of the former Baathist regime and jihadists from around the world congregated in Syria and Iraq and formed the Islamic State there. They employed the Sunni Wahhabi rhetoric to mount resistance to the rise of the Shia power in the region.

Abu Musab al-Zarqawi, who founded the al-Qaeda franchise in Iraq and organized the Islamic State, evoked ancient anti-Shia fatwas or religious rulings, to spark a civil war in the hope that the Shia majority would eventually capitulate to the Sunni jihadi forces. During the sectarian war in Iraq, around quarter of a million people have been killed and displaced internally.

That a sectarian rhetoric dehumanizes the other is the centuries-old narrative. The Wahhabi Sunni hardliners use all kinds of harsh and derogatory words like *'rafida'* (rejecters of the faith), 'crypto-Persians' and 'heretics' to describe Shia Muslims. Shias describe Sunni opponents as *'takfirs'* (who declare fellow Muslims as apostates). Recently, this cycle of demonization has been amplified significantly throughout the Islamic world.

The political leadership of the Islamic Republic of Iran has smartly refrained from painting the situation in the Middle East as a Sunni–Shia conflict. Javad Zarif, the articulate and soft-spoken Foreign Minister of Iran, always maintained that Iran was on the right side of the conflict in Yemen, Syria and Iraq. He also warned that the extremists and takfiris would be a threat to both Sunnis and Shias. The Islamic republic has warned the Western democracies of the dangers of supporting the Salafi extremists at the cost of disturbing the power balance in the Middle East. Sunni and Shia Muslims have co-existed in harmony for many more years in the history of Islam than they have fought each other. In many countries it has become common for members of the two sects to even intermarry and pray at the same mosques. They share faith in the Quran and the Prophet's saying, and perform similar prayers, although they differ in rituals and in the interpretation of the Islamic laws.

Both the sects also have subdivisions. The Sunni sect comprises four traditional schools of jurisprudence: Hanafi, Shafi, Maliki and Hanbali, the last spawning the Wahhabi and Salafi movements in Saudi Arabia. Sunni, a broad umbrella term for the non-Shia Islam, is together on the importance of the Quran and Sunnah, but, allows differences in legal opinion. The Shia sect has following subdivisions:

Ithna Ashari (those who follow 12 imams), Ismaili (those who follow 7 imams), Zaydi (Yemeni sect of Shias) and Alawite (Syrian sect of Shias).

The Shia groups, supported by Iran, have recently won decisive political and sectarian battles in Syria, Yemen, Lebanon and Iraq. The regime of President Bashar al-Assad, who has been ruling since 1970, relies mainly on the support of Alawites, a heterodox Shia sect, that makes up about 13 per cent of the Syrian population. Alawites dominate the military and security services of the country and form the backbone of the forces, fighting in support of the Assad Regime in the Syrian civil war.

The bewildered Arab neighbors of Iraq, including Saudi Arabia and Jordan could not fully comprehend why the US administration allowed the Shiite to come into power in a major Arab country. On the flip side, the US intent was to effect a regime change in Iraq without knowing its implications or the nuances of the historical sectarian fault lines of Islam. King Abdullah II of Jordan had warned in an interview with *The Washington Post* that Iran's growing influence in Iraq could be resonated throughout the Middle East and could lead to a 'crescent' of dominant Shia movements stretching from Tehran to Baghdad, and from Lebanon to Damascus and Sanaa.[40] Later Abdullah backtracked and modified his statement, saying that what he meant was not Shiite as a religion, but as one sect of the community politically backed by the Republic of Iran. Egypt's strongman Hosni Mubarak had put this in perspective and declared that most Shiites living in the Arab countries 'are loyal to Iran, and not to the countries they are living in'.[41] Unfortunately, these alarms have a slightly hysterical edge to them.

---

[40] Wright, Robin, and Peter Baker, 'Iraq, Jordan See Threat To Election From Iran', *The Washington Post*, 8 December 2004, https://tinyurl.com/ct4ur8bf. Accessed on 24 September 2023.

[41] 'Mubarak's Shia Remarks Stir Anger', *Al Jazeera*, 10 April 2006, https://tinyurl.com/fdadnnbn. Accessed on 24 September 2023.

The 2020 protest of the Iraqi Shias against the Iranian influence in their country by vandalizing the Iranian Consulate in Najaf is proof for the fact that Shias in the Arab countries are loyal to their respective countries and not to Iran. Upfront, Shia Arabs, like Sunni Arabs, are loyal to their countries, but only that they seek freedom to practice their faith as it is allowed by Qatar, Lebanon and Oman.

The genie of sectarianism is any way out of the bottle. But, evidence points to the fact that ethno-nationalism is beginning to moderate and dilute the sectarian passions, as is seen in Iraq. Among the ordinary Shiites in Iraq, there is less sympathy towards Iran, including to its system of governance. In the July 2006 war of Lebanon with Israel, Iran fully supported the extremist outfit Hezbollah out of its Shiite solidarity. Now, it is evident that there is total convergence between Iran and Hezbollah in countering the US–Israel plan to reshape the Middle East. Iran also supports the Palestinian wing of Muslim Brotherhood called Hamas, a patently Wahhabi–Salafi movement. The solidarity with the Palestinian cause is well appreciated in the Arab capitals, but accepting Iran as a regional power is definitely going to get less traction.

At this point of time, it is not easy to predict how the sectarian struggle would turn out in the Middle East, and where and when the next big battle would be fought between Sunnis and Shias. What is clear is that the future of the Middle East is in jeopardy as long as the lengthening shadows of sectarian conflict hang over it. This is a conflict that will not go away any time soon and is likely to shape the future of 1.6 billion Muslims across the world.

3

RISE OF THE SHIA CRESCENT IN THE MIDDLE EAST

The term 'Shia Crescent' was first used by King Abdullah of Jordan, at the time when Iran was reportedly interfering in Iraq in the run-up to the 2005 parliamentary elections. What he was referring to was a notionally crescent-shaped region in the Middle East, where the majority population follows Shia Islam or where there is a strong minority in the population. The king was indirectly suggesting the emergence of a Shia power across the nations in the region. As a consequence, all Sunni Iraqis boycotted the elections, leading to a Shia-dominated government coming into power. A general perception was that the Shia-dominated Iraq would be under the influence of Shia Iran. The common religious practices followed by the Shiite communities provide potential for cooperation between countries with significant Shia populations, including the Alawite-dominated Syria, Iraq and Bahrain. If such cooperation is extended to Hezbollah in Lebanon and the powerful Shia Houthis of Zayidi sect in Yemen, that completes the Shia Crescent King Abdullah was referring to, in the Middle East.

Addressing the International Islamic Unity Conference in Tehran on 27 December 2015, Hassan Rouhani, the Iranian president, called all Muslim countries to unite and strive for improving the public image of Islam, elaborating that there was 'neither a Shiite nor a Sunni crescent. We have an Islamic moon.'[42] In January 2016, Crown

---

[42]'Rouhani: It's Up to Muslims to Fix Islam's Image', *VOANews*, 27 December 2015, https://tinyurl.com/yh39sbcr. Accessed on 24 September 2023.

Prince of Saudi Arabia, MBS, said that the Arab world was confronted 'by a Shia full moon', rather than just a Shia Crescent, as a result of the expanded activities of its proxies in Yemen, Lebanon, Iraq and Syria.[43] Nevertheless, Iranian leaders always underscored their commitment to pan-Islamic unity. They downplay the Shia character of the Islamic Republic of Iran while speaking on foreign policy issues, and continue to express its pan-Islamic nature, as opposed to it being Shia-centric. However, Iran's strategic approach in the Middle East has been focussed on supporting the Shia armed groups in the region since 2003. Working through non-state actors, Iran has greatly expanded its regional influence and stabilized its allegedly furtive idea of a Shia Crescent, passing through different countries like Iraq, Syria, Lebanon and Yemen.

King Abdullah had argued that the centre of Shia power indeed was Iran. Nevertheless, Iran's influence has been growing steadily with Arab Shiite communities since the US invasion of Iraq in 2003. Iran pursues an aggressive foreign policy across the Middle East, whether it is fighting a war through its proxies in Syria, or trying to control the politics of Iraq, Syria and Lebanon. With signing of the nuclear deal between Iran and the P5+1 nations (the five UN Security Council members and Germany), the international economic sanctions on Iran had ended briefly, but it was re-imposed back in 2017 by the Trump administration with more severity. The Kingdom of Saudi Arabia rightly feared increased Iranian power in the region, particularly in countries where sectarianism was raging. The animosity is very real on both sides. But, it is often overwhelmed by Arab nationalism, as was seen during the anti-Iranian demonstrations in Iraq in the early 2020.

One of the milestones in the regional groupings came in 1979 when Egypt signed a peace treaty with Israel.[44] Feeling isolated,

---

[43]'Young Prince in a Hurry', *The Economist*, 9 January 2016, https://tinyurl.com/5m7z6rnn. Accessed on 24 September 2023.
[44]Israel Ministry of Foreign Affairs, *Treaty of Peace between Israel and Egypt: Foreign Affairs Press Release*, March 26 1979.

Hafez al-Assad of Syria thought that Syria needed new friends. Iran took initiative and played an important role in sustaining a strategic presence of Syria in Lebanon by delivering military and economic assistance to it through Hezbollah. The relationship has always been uncomfortable because of the ideological differences between the two countries. Syria was led by Hafez al-Assad, an Alawite, a sect of Shia Islam, but secular in disposition and closer to Sufi Sunni Islam. Iran, on the other hand, is a Shia-majority nation, and has been an Islamic Republic ruled by clergy since 1979. Syria never steadfastly supported Iran on any policy issues and the relationship was tradable. At one point, Bashar al-Assad even negotiated with Israel for Golan Heights and promised to improve relations with the US, and in exchange, was willing to trash his relationship with Iran.

Arab Spring in Syria

The uprising in Syria, led by the educated middle class transformed into a full-fledged civil war against the government led by President Bashar al-Assad and the majority followers of Sunni Islam. From the outset, Iran came to Assad's aid by ensuring access to the Lebanese fighters and keeping Saudi Arabia from extending its influence in the Levant. Nevertheless, most of Syria's military and political elites, including Bashar Assad himself, worried that an over-reliance on Iran, would limit their flexibility when it comes to post-war reconstruction, economic development and the future diplomatic relations with the West.

The Trump administration seemed to be willing to cede Syria to Russia. But Washington should have understood that, in reality, it was not acceding to Russia, but to Iran. Russia was only interested in keeping the air bases in Syria and occupying the space vacated by the US. Under no circumstances did Israel want Iran's hegemony in Syria. However, Tehran had political ambitions with respect to Syria for years and had invested huge resources in making Syria a pro-Shiite country. The process began during the period of Hafez al-Assad, when a network of educational and cultural institutions were created across Syria. The objective was to promote Shiism in all regions of Syria. The Syrian regime let the Iranian preachers work freely in Damascus, the Alawite-inhabited coastal towns and beyond. In both urban and rural parts of Syria, Sunnis who adopted Shia faith received special privileges and preferential treatment in the disbursement of aid funds. Raqqa, before it was captured and declared capital of the IS, was one of the cities in the Euphrates river valley with huge Iranian investments. Iran charities had built many public buildings, mosques and hussainias there. The Wahhabi–Salafi warriors of Islamic State destroyed and plundered all the buildings and symbols of Shia Muslims in Raqqa. As of 2009, there were over 500 hussainias in Syria and Shias had renovated all their holy places in Damascus.

Savage battles were fought between the forces loyal to Bashar al-Assad and the Sunni insurgency groups, spearheaded by the Islamic State and Saudi Arabia. The government forces were being supported by hundreds of recruits, from Lebanon identifying themselves as Abu al-Fadl Abbas Brigade, named after the half-brother of Imam Hussain. Hezbollah fighters were also operating in the Lebanon border of Syrian villages, on the way to Homs, a city in Western Syria, creating a territorial continuity for Alawite control under the Iranian influence. The continuity is extremely critical for Iran, since it links Lebanon and Damascus to the Alawite coast. Iran aims to have a network of militias affiliated to them in place in Syria, regardless of what happens to Assad. The war in Syria is moving at a slow pace, but the forces loyal to the Assad regime, with American help, have shrunk the space of ISIS fighters and their territorial hold. Hezbollah is not a Lebanese national movement, but a creation of Iran and subject to its exclusive authority. Hezbollah chief Hassan Nasrallah is a close ally of Tehran and its religious leadership and the outfit is funded by Iranian petrodollars.

Tehran is making efforts to recruit fighters from Iraq, UAE and Pakistan to fight in Syria. For Iran, the Syrian war is important, as it is against a radical Sunni uprising, which views Shias as infidels, deserving to be annihilated. The Iranian establishment views it as war within Islam. If the extremist camp of the Wahhabi–Salafi Sunnis and the al-Qaeda are not defeated in Syria, they will assert themselves in Iraq and threaten to take over the Persian Gulf, posing a real danger to the regional influence of Iran. The current stand-off between Qatar and the Sunni Arab nations has provided a great opening for Iran to align itself with Qatar, an important Sunni Arab monarchy in the region.

An 'arc of power' or a 'Shia Crescent' is a metaphor used for the regional domination of Iran's Shiite regime. The Iranian sphere of power now stretches across Iraq, where Iran has joined the Shia regime in fighting ISIS, and to Syria where Tehran has worked to keep a fellow Alawite President in power throughout the continuing civil war. It stretches to Lebanon, where the Iranian backed Shia Hezbollah is a real force vying to gain political legitimacy. And, it has spread to Yemen, where Houthi rebels have recently taken control of the government under constant Saudi air attacks. It is the 2003 US invasion of Iraq and the Arab Spring that paved the way for Iran to get an opening in Iraq, Yemen, Bahrain and Syria and redraw the map of the Middle East. An important date for the Iranian influence in Iraq was the 2005 general elections, which brought a Shia-led coalition to power. The coalition government drafted the first constitution of Iraq. In 2014, the Islamic State, after capturing Mosul and other Sunni-dominated areas, threatened Baghdad. President Obama offered help saying that the US would provide air support to the Iraqi Shiite regime. At that critical moment, Iran came forward to help Iraq. It sent advisers and weapons that enabled Iraq to prevent the fall of Baghdad. In the offensive at Tikrit, the former stronghold of Saddam Hussein, as many as 20,000 Shia militiamen were mobilized to fight along with Iraqi soldiers, who were trained by the US.

The 1991 uprisings in Iraq were a series of popular rebellions in northern and southern Iraq during a ceasefire in the Gulf war. Both Shiite groups and Kurds were up in arms against President Saddam Hussein. The Iraqi population was fatigued by the prolonged Iran–Iraq conflict and the Gulf War that took place within a single decade totally devastating the economy and progress of the country.

President George H.W. Bush had been urging Iraqi Shias and other rebel groups to fight against Saddam Hussein and depose him. After the liberation of Kuwait, the US abandoned Iraq and the Saddam regime through strong tactics totally crushed the Shia and Kurdish uprisings. The US government watched in mute silence when Saddam brutally slaughtered and gassed thousands of Shias and Kurds across Iraq. As a consequence, all prominent Shia clergy and businessmen fled to Iran while ordinary Iranians developed a strong sympathy with Iraq. For decades, Syria was a good friend of Iran. But at the onset of Syrian uprising, President Bashar Assad brutally killed his own people who were asking for elections and change in leadership.

Saudi Arabia stepped up pressure on President Obama to intervene in Syria and the Republican members of the Arms Services Committee were advising the President and the White House to declare the Sunni inhabited cities of Syria as a no-fly zone. The chairman of the Joint Chiefs of Staff, Martin Dempsey, was not enthusiastic about putting American boots in Syria and creating a no-fly zone. In 2012, General Petraeus and Secretary Hillary Clinton wanted to arm the Syrian rebels, but President Obama rejected the proposal. In hindsight, the decision appears to be right, as all the weapons would have ended up with ISIS fighters, as all rebel groups subsequently coalesced together when the conflict took sectarian overtones. Nonetheless, President Obama talked about redlines with the Bashar Assad regime. Once, Obama famously said that if the Syrian regime used chemical weapons, then the US would directly intervene and make a regime change.[45] In 2013, the Assad regime used

---

[45]'Remarks by the President in Address to the Nation on Syria', *The White*

gas on several occasions to kill hundreds of women and children, and the global communities were outraged by the images. Surprisingly, the White House advisers used their Russian channel and at the behest of President Putin negotiated a deal with the US, based on which all chemical weapons would be handed over to Russia and all factories would be closed.

President Assad agreed as the entire operation was conducted by Russians. Apparently, only a part of the chemical weapons were shifted out of Syria and the rest were left with the regime which they selectively used against the Sunni insurgency. The inability of the US to confront Assad in a meaningful way opened doors for al-Qaeda and ISIS to occupy space in Syria and establish the emirate with a caliph. The big ticket entry of these terror groups pushed Syria further closer to Iran and Hezbollah bolstering the fight against the Sunni groups. Syria is no more an ally of Iran, it is more of a proxy.

Arab Spring in Yemen

The Arab Spring broke out in Yemen in 2011, led by the nation's educated middle class and youths, against the oppressive and corrupt regime of dictator Ali Abdullah Saleh. He brutally killed the protesters on the streets and launched a war against the restive Houthis, Zayidi Shiites, who make up more than half of the country's population. Iran gave all support to the Houthis. President Saleh stepped down by making a deal with his Vice President to get immunity for prosecution. Later, to take revenge against his successor, Saleh conspired with Houthi rebels and captured the capital Sanaa in September 2014. They forced the successor of Saleh to flee the country and he later took refuge in the neighbouring Saudi Arabia. Soon, Iran and its ally militia installed the Houthis in command.

House President Barack Obama, 10 September 2013, Press Release, https://tinyurl.com/2kw54n74. Accessed on 15 September 2023.

As the events unraveled, the US kept out of the quagmire and in the process, Iran fully arrived as one of the major regional players.

Ali Abdullah Saleh was constantly playing with fire after stepping down as President of Yemen during the Arab Spring. First, he allied with Houthis—the old enemies of his regime as he had fought them for almost a decade. He then allied with Saudi Arabia only to cheat them later. His death in 2017 was expected. The Houthis killed Saleh and launched Iranian-supplied ballistic missiles on Riyadh Airport, in Saudi Arabia. It was indicative of their growing power, which in turn reflected the Iranian power and its regional domination. Houthis were seeking to punish the people in the capital Sanaa and punish members of the General People's Congress—Saleh's political party. After Saleh's death, it was clear that Houthis were the only major power in Yemen. They increasingly proved their military capabilities and Saleh's remaining forces were eventually neutralized by the Houthis. The Houthis cover a large swathe of Yemen's territory thanks to the support provided by Iran and Hezbollah. A large area under the Houthis' control, however, suffers from electricity outages, which has contributed to the region suffering from one of the world's worst Cholera outbreaks. To check the enemies conspiring against them, the Houthi administration also shut Internet access to their territories.

The Saudi Crown Prince MBS, in desperation, opened dialogue with the Islah group, the counterpart of Muslim Brotherhood in Yemen, with its leadership in Riyadh. The Houthis fired the next ballistic missile, this time targeting the venue of the meeting near Riyadh. Saudi Arabia retaliated by attacking parts of the capital city of Sanaa, killing many innocent women and children and destroying several heritage buildings.

Yemen is strategic to Iran because of the Bab el-Mandeb strait and the long borders it shares with Saudi, as Saudi Arabia is Iran's regional and sectarian enemy. Therefore, Iran has strategic interests in Yemen, as it does in Syria, Iraq and Lebanon. Iran is seeking to drag Saudi Arabia deeper into the messy Yemeni conflict in order for Iran to take full control of the Syrian and Iraqi situations. The

Iranian support and interventions of Houthis constitute a threat to Saudi national security. Yemen could be used as a pretext to put pressure on Saudi Arabia regarding other regional issues and it makes the Iranian interest in the region primarily political. Saudi Arabia has two options in the Yemeni civil war. It could continue the war, but, with the humanitarian situation deteriorating further, it may not be sustainable for long. The Sunni alliance forces have not been able to resolve the conflict for years, as they have no Saudi boots on ground. The other option is, to negotiate with Houthis directly, for a durable, long-term settlement.

Turning Point for Iran

The geopolitical calculus in the Middle East, however, changed after the 2003 US invasion of Iraq. In the years that followed, Iraq imploded with sectarian violence, undermining the American position in the region. The Iranian interest in Iraq soon doubled because of Karbala, a region, which during the middle ages, was part of the greater Persia. Iran now enjoys influence in a large area, stretching from the Mediterranean to the confines of Central Asia. It has a strong support base in the radicalized Hezbollah in Lebanon and among the Houthi tribesmen in Yemen. Iran has also developed a nuclear technology that practically constitutes a threshold to bomb-making.

The political leadership in Tehran has shown maturity and vision to join the US and the five European nations to negotiate a peaceful agreement to suspend the nuclear weaponization programme. The deal allows the nuclear programme in its basic level and lifts all economic sanctions imposed by the US and its European allies. Perhaps, the biggest effect of the agreement will be that the accord creates a better context for the US–Iranian cooperation in the Middle East where their interests overlap the most. Both the US and Iran want to dismantle and destroy ISIS; they both want to weaken al-Qaeda in the Middle East and Afghanistan. In Syria, Iran is engaged with Russia in dismantling and pushing out the Islamic State fighters from all enclaves along the Euphrates river valley. The US wants to remove Bashar al-Assad from power, but Iran and Russia argue that his deposition will bring back Sunni jihadists back to Syria, a scenario not acceptable to the US. The big challenge for the US administration is to forge a strategic relationship with major Sunni nations, who are responsible for spreading the Wahhabi ideology and transforming members of the global Muslim communities—Arabs and non-Arabs, into militant jihadis. The young and educated Muslim youths are radicalized by social media encrypted sites, hosted by the Islamic State volunteers, who inspire them to commit violence of varying degrees including by transforming into lethal suicide bombers.

The International Atomic Energy Agency (IAEA) Director General Yukiya Amano has often clarified that the Vienna based agency is technical rather than a political one, underscoring the need for its work to be based on facts alone. In September 2017, the IAEA reported that Iran under the JCPOA was in total compliance with the 2015 agreement made between Iran and the P5+1 countries together with the European Union.[46] This marks the eighth time, the agency in its regular reports, mandated by the JCPOA, has confirmed that the nuclear deal was working—and the reports underscored that not once the agency found Iran to be out of compliance.

In a bizarre move, President Donald Trump decided to ignore the evidence and declare Iran out of compliance in defiance of all the experts. On 8 May 2018, Trump announced the US withdrawal from JCPOA. In November 2018, the US sanctions came back into effect, forcing Iran to dramatically alter its policies, including its support of militia groups in the region and its development of ballistic missiles. All security experts in Washington DC and in European countries were of the opinion that the Trump administration's approach to Iran was dangerous.

---

[46]International Atomic Energy Agency, *IAEA Annual Report 2017*, Vienna, Austria, 2017.

The American foreign policy cannot be built on alternative facts. Amazingly, Nikki Haley, then US Ambassador to the UN, tried to manufacture a case against staying in the deal, by citing violations that did not happen, implying that there were hundreds of suspicious sites left uninspected, which was not true, and against the views of European allies. The IAEA knows the in and out of the Iran nuclear program and it knows better than any other entity, so it makes sense that its report, which stated Iran was in compliance with its commitments, were accepted across the board, except perhaps, by the unhinged President Trump. In the aftermath of the Baghdad airport strike, on 5 January 2020, which killed the Iranian General Qassem Soleimani, Iran however, declared that it would no longer be restricted by the deal, but would still continue to coordinate with the IAEA, leaving open the possibility of resuming the compliance.

Iran's Military Capabilities

One of Iran's critical assets has been its military development over the past decade. Iran-made military equipment is now an important factor in the regional arms markets in Iraq, Syria and Lebanon, as Iran trades with the governments as well as the militia groups. In June 2017, Iran for the first time, fired medium range missiles on Islamic State targets in Syria. It successfully produced and tested long-range ballistic missiles, main battle tanks and unmanned aerial drones, in addition to domestically built submarines and attack boats. Iran's strategy is to increase its power, centred on the promotion of cross-border Shia solidarity to boost its economy in the post-sanction times.

President Putin's direct military intervention in Syria in 2015 brought Iran and Russia on the same strategic page as a powerful counterforce to the Saudi–US bloc. Perhaps the single best organized and most aggressive alliance currently active in the Middle East is the bloc of states gathered around the Islamic Republic of Iran. It is marching steadily ahead, motivated by clear strategic goals, powerful ideological backing and long experience of supporting resistance forces in the Middle East. The Russian entry and withdrawal of the US has strengthened Iran and its allies and made them powerful in the regional context. Iran is currently actively supporting proxies in many conflict zones in the region. In addition, there are many Iranian charities active among Shia populations in Kuwait, Saudi Arabia and Bahrain.

Iran's strategic goal is to emerge as a dominant power in the Middle East and, eventually, in the entire Islamic world. It seeks rollback of the US's influence in the region. President Donald Trump's anti-Iranian rhetoric on not re-certifying the nuclear deal came despite the fact that the IAEA had put on record that Iran's compliance to the pact was perfect. As a matter of fact, the European allies and other stakeholders of the accord have made it clear that, in case the US decided to walk away from the deal, they can see it through alone without the support of the allies.

Iran is actively working to establish a contiguous line of pro-Iranian entities from the Iran–Iraq border to the Mediterranean sea, extending to the Arabic speaking side of the Persian Gulf, reducing the influence of Saudi Arabia in this area. The advance brings Iran close to securing an overland route that would run from Tehran, via Baghdad, to the Mediterranean. This would make it easier for Iran to supply Hezbollah with arms and fighters from Iraq, Afghanistan and Pakistan. Such a land bridge is anathema to Saudi Arabia and Israel. President Trump was on record as saying that the US had no interest in a regime change in Syria and it was only interested in defeating ISIS. On 9 September however, the American forces pushed Kurdish and Arab fighters north of Deir ez-Zor. The American commanders on the ground say that they want these allies known as the Syrian Democratic Forces (SDF) to push south along the Euphrates river valley, to capture towns such as Bukamal along the Iraqi border, before the regime and its allies get there. As a part of the understanding to make sure that the major powers do not run straight into each other, America called Russia to hold back Syrian forces from crossing the Euphrates.

It is in Russia's strategic interest to push Syrian forces across the river, attack Raqqa and move towards the Iraqi border. In the meanwhile, battle-hardened and well-supplied Shia militias in Iraq are headed for crossing the border too. They intend to capture the Iraqi border, crossing back to control the highway, west to Jordan and Syria. The US, under the influence of Israel, is pushing Russia to remove the Assad forces and their allies from Golan Heights as a bargain to extend a ceasefire with the rebel forces and end the war in the South. The Assad regime wants to control the border crossing with Jordan and close to al-Tanf, a US special forces base that sits on the Baghdad–Damascus highway.

The Western diplomats are delusional about Bashar al-Assad's eventual departure. He is a dictator, who has butchered hundreds and thousands of his compatriots and allowed many more to be killed by warring groups, and in the process turned many historical cities with thriving culture into heaps of rubble. Syrians with skill, who would have rebuilt the country, have fled or migrated to Europe and the neighbouring countries. Those who are left, live in poverty in a dysfunctional state. The fear the Trump administration and the Israeli prime minister Netanyahu share is of the growing influence of Iran in Damascus which is likely to be further expanded as it props up the sticky state and helps it to rebuild.

Israeli intelligence claims that Iran will soon be establishing air and naval bases in Syria besides securing mining rights in the country. Iranian firms have already won fat contracts in oil, gas and agricultural sectors. It has, on 12 September 2017, signed a contract to import Iranian power plants for the ruined city of Aleppo. A deal has also been made recently by an Iranian firm to operate Syria's third largest mobile-phone network. Israel, in the meanwhile, is making extra efforts at the highest level, even talking with President Putin, to forestall the Iranian influence and restrict its power in the region. The strategic interest of Russia is to keep Bashar al-Assad in power and that could only be possible by the support of Hezbollah and Iran. Israel is surely sceptical of the presence of Hezbollah fighters close to its border. It bled Israel in 2006 and the border war with Lebanon had ended in a draw. The Syrian civil war has helped Hezbollah evolve from a militia into a professional army capable of fighting brigade-scale battles. It looks like Iran will hold a strong sway from Mesopotamia to the Mediterranean in the years to come.

Iran has trained and deployed thousands of Shia Afghans as shock troops in Syria's sectarian war. The members of the Afghan unit, the Fatemiyoun Division wear a shoulder patch, recounting words of praise from Iran's supreme leader, as a badge of honour. Afghanistan may well become the next sectarian battleground between Iran, the declared guardian of Shiites, and Saudi Arabia, the long sponsor of conservative Sunni doctrine. Many Shia fighters were given Iranian passports, when they were sent to Syria to fight for the pro-Assad regime along with Lebanon's Hezbollah. They have returned to their villages in Bamiyan Province, where Taliban leadership massacred more than 300 Shiites in 2001.

In Iraq, a Shia Muslim militia named Harakat Hezbollah al-Nujaba, under the leadership of the cleric, Akram al-Kaabi, recaptured from the Islamic State, the town of Qayrawan, which is strategic in land route connectivity with Damascus. The Nujaba group, which has more than 10,000 fighters, is now one of the most important militia in Iraq. Though entirely made up of Iraqi Arab Shias, it is loyal to Tehran and is helping it in creating a safe supply route to Damascus. The route will run through a string of small towns including Qayrawan. To open it up, the Iranian-backed militias are pushing into southeast Syria, near the Iraqi border, where some of the US forces are based.

The Nujaba militia is only an example of the way Iran is seeking to expand its influence in Iraq and across the region. Akram al-Kaabi has repeatedly said that Nujaba is aligned with Iran. He elaborated that the group follows '*Velayat-e Faqih*', meaning 'the guardianship of the jurist', which is the ideological cornerstone of Iran's theocratic system of governance. If Iran can open this route, they will have access to Hezbollah in Lebanon, all the way through Iraq and Syria. Iran, which backs the Assad-regime in Syria, has stated that it wants to see its influence extend through Iraq, to its allies in Damascus, and beyond to Hezbollah, in Lebanon.

The current route that Iran is pushing to open through Iraq was not its first choice. Soon after Iran became involved in Syria in 2011, the Iranians attempted to open a logistic supply line through the Kurdish region in northern Iraq. The Kurdish leadership resented the move. Nevertheless, the new route bypasses the Kurdish region. If Iran succeeds in making this route serviceable, Sunnis will be displaced. The Kurdistan region will be under threat and so the Christian community will also come under threat. The cleric leader Akram al-Kaabi, has had a chequered career as a fighter. The Nujaba, during the Syrian conflict, gelled well with the allies as a fierce fighting force under the dynamic leadership of al-Kaabi. They flourished and expanded the group: more arms, more people, more money. The money came from Iran.

Iranian Nationalism

The young Iranians, in the uniforms of the Islamic Revolutionary Guard Corps (IRGC), who have given their lives in Syria, Yemen and Iraq, are the new heroes of the Islamic Republic. Their images are on the billboards in all squares of the major cities and towns. After years of cynicism, sneering and desperation, Iran's middle classes have been overwhelmed by a wave of nationalistic fervour.

The change in attitude, which was in the making for several years, can be attributed to two related factors: the amplification of anti-Iranian rhetoric by the Trump regime and the growing competition from Saudi Arabia, Iran's sectarian rival for regional leadership. The middle class Iranians were horrified when the US president denounced the nuclear treaty of Iran and described it as 'the worst deal ever negotiated' and promised to tear it up notwithstanding the fact that the deal was signed along with the US and all of its major European allies. The European Union has clarified that they would not walk away with the US as long as they find the deal good and Iran is following the IAEA norms. The people of Iran watched in horror when President Trump joined Saudi King Salman and others in the 'war dance' during his visit to Saudi Arabia in May 2017. To please their American guests, the kingdom even agreed to purchase more than a billion worth of military hardware from the military-industrial complex of the US.

For the first time after the 1979 Islamic Revolution, the Iranians are finding something to be proud of and worth celebrating as the Iranian-led militias are playing a central role in defeating the Islamic State in Syria and Iraq, and getting an upper hand in Yemen against the Saudi-led coalition forces, increasing the country's influence in the region. Today, two of the most popular heroes in Iran—a country with thriving film and music industries—are not actors or singers, but two major figures from the political and administrative realm of Iran: General Qassem Suleimani, recently assassinated leader of Iran's regional military campaign and Mohammad Javad Zarif, the voice of reason and a balanced Iran.

The wave of the new nationalism was set in motion with the election of the moderate leader Hassan Rouhani as President of the country in 2013. This was the first ray of hope for the urban middle class of Iran since the brutal crackdown on protests on the street following the 2009 presidential elections, which were widely perceived as manipulated. The state's theocratic ideology has long dictated an artificial version of nationalism, where everything related to Shia Islam was glorified and the pre-Islamic history of Iran was trashed.

However, in October 2017, the government allowed one of the top former palaces of Shah of Iran to be used for a grand multimedia performance, where actors reenacted parts of the epic poem Shahnameh, or the Book of Kings, which describes Iran's long pre-Islamic history. Images of Persepolis, the ancient Palace of Darius the Great, were projected on the palace building. More than 5,000 families in their fine suits and ladies in designer outfits attended the cultural event.

Qatar and the New Middle East Equation

The expulsion of Qatar from the GCC countries has given Iran an opportunity to strike a diplomatically important alliance with Qatar alongside Russia and Turkey. Tehran lacks the ground, and air forces, for projecting might beyond its borders. It seeks to overcome this limitation by developing a ballistic missile program and turning the asymmetric regional conflicts to its advantage. The Iranians are partially successful in tactfully isolating Saudi Arabia from other Sunni Arab countries like Qatar and Turkey. This has brought, for the first time after the Islamic Revolution, countries like the Arab Sunni Qatar, Turkey and Shia Iran on the same side of the Middle East equation. With a military base established in Qatar, Turkey has plans to eventually station more troops in Qatari soil.

The Saudi royal family used President Donald Trump's 'America First' agenda to commit more than a billion US dollar investments in the US by ordering military hardware for the kingdom. This gave Trump talking points about creating jobs in America. It appeared that Saudi funds will also be available towards a new women's initiative launched by Ivanka Trump, the President's daughter. Historically, Saudi royal family always used petrodollars to ensure family security and deflect the attention of the US and European democracies from the issue of Islamic terrorism, which in fact, is the product of Wahhabi Salafism, vigorously pushed by Saudi Arabia since 1979.

Saudi Arabia, in May 2017, hosted a summit of Heads of State from the Islamic World, with the exception of Iran and its allies, at Riyadh. In his welcome remarks, the Saudi King Salman said that the regime in Tehran 'represents the tip of spear of terrorism'.[47]

---

[47] 'Saudi King Says Iran at Forefront of Global Terrorism', *Reuters*, 21 May 2017, https://tinyurl.com/5n9by8zd. Accessed on 23 May 2023.

President Trump, in his remarks, used undiplomatic language, saying 'all nations of conscience must work together to isolate Iran.'[48] He ignored the conflict in Yemen, where the US jets were used to bomb innocent people and where millions of people were starving because of food shortages. Turkish journalist Mustafa Akyol, in his New York Times column wrote, 'This whole meeting looked like a "Sunni international," in which the main non-Sunni power in Muslim world, Iran, was bashed by both the American President and his Sunni hosts.'[49] It is not rocket science to understand that all the radical Islamic terrorists were inspired by Wahhabism that advocates a strict conservative morality and intolerance, which is the state religion of Saudi Arabia.

Javad Zarif, Iran's foreign minister, in an article written on the website of the London-based *Al Araby Al-Jadeed* news network, wrote that the state-sanctioned orthodox brand of Islam—Wahhabism—was behind the growth of extremism among the Sunni Muslims and President Trump should confront the Saudi royal family to stop fomenting radicalism. Unfortunately, he said nothing during his trip to the Wahhabi kingdom. Instead, he appeared at the opening ceremony of the Saudi-run Global Center for Combating Extremist Ideology. The obvious question was how a nation which sponsors terrorism by spreading hatred and bigotry through its state ideology could combat extremism.

The Shia-majority Iraq and the Sunni-led Saudi Arabia were estranged from each other for decades after the Iraqi invasion of Kuwait in 1990. The delusional president, Donald Trump and his national security team at the White House, in their overdrive to isolate Iran, pushed Saudi Arabia to bridge its differences with Iraq

---

[48]'In Riyadh speech, Trump calls for isolation of Iran', *Gulf News*, 21 May 2017, https://tinyurl.com/39w42963. Accessed on 22 May 2023.

[49]Akyol, Mustafa, and Wajahat Ali, '"This Wasn't a Speech About Islam"', *The New York Times*, 21 May 2017, https://tinyurl.com/29auu8fy. Accessed on 23 September 2023.

and move closer to it. Nevertheless, the relationship remains still plagued by suspicion. Saudi Arabia recently opened its embassy in Baghdad and started service of the Saudi Airlines flight after a gap of a quarter of a century. But, the emergence of Saudi's arch-rival Iran as a key player in Iraq came as a surprise to Riyadh and Washington. Unfortunately, the present US administration has framed much of its Middle East security policy and agenda around isolating Iran, which they see as a malign influence that poses an existential threat to Israel and other American allies in the region.

The maverick Crown Prince MBS felt emboldened by their recent outreach to the Shiite factions in Iraq, through their leaders like Muqtada al-Sadr and Qasim al-Araji, the Iraqi interior minister close to Iran. They were invited to Saudi Arabia in July 2017, hoping to cultivate al-Sadr and other Shiite leaders, who can be a counterweight to the Iranian influence in Iraq.

Iraq is the only Arab country in the Middle East, where Shia Arabs make up the majority of the population. Iran has sought influence by stoking sectarianism and gaining allegiance of the Shias in the country. Saudi Arabia's strategy is to win them back by reviving the country's Arab nationalism and setting Iraqis against the Persian Iran. Arab nationalism was largely smothered when Iraq's former ruling Baath party was banned after the US invasion. Apparently, many Iranian-backed factions in Iraq are trying to sully the country's rapprochement with Saudi Arabia. Their leadership has cited the case of more than 3,000 Saudis joining ISIS, to prove their point. Shia clerics also oppose the opening of Saudi Consulate in the holy city of Najaf. But, overall, Saudi's charm offensive is gaining traction in Iraq. Many, including the Muqtada al-Sadr group, view the prospect of any deep Irani engagement as a colonization drive by the Persian Empire. But MBS's Iraqi outreach initiatives are continuing as an overall strategy for the region, which is to isolate Iran.

Saudis could not find an al-Sadr who can offer an alternative to Hezbollah, in Lebanon. Since the Lebanese civil war in 1990,

Hezbollah has been firmly entrenched in the Shia-dominated region of southern Lebanon and southern Beirut. With Iranian support, Hezbollah has opened schools and hospitals, besides providing business loans and fielding candidates in the last Parliament elections. They are also important stakeholders in the present national unity government of Saad Hariri. Its military capabilities and fighting skills are robust, as was seen in Syria and Yemen. It has deployed thousands of ballistic missiles along the Israeli border. The mass outfit also owns an underground fiber-optic communication network in addition to several underground bunkers and supply tunnels. During the last three decades, Hezbollah's singular focus was to keep Israel at a safe distance.

Hezbollah in Lebanon

Hezbollah is a force to reckon with. Its fighters are engaged in real time fighting in Yemen and Syria. It has also raised a battalion of Shia fighters from Afghanistan and Pakistan. They figure in all the conflicts that matter to Iran. More significantly, Hezbollah helped recruit, train and arm new militant groups in Iraq, Syria and Yemen advancing the agenda of Iran. It was founded in the 1980s with Iran's financial support to vacate the Israeli occupation of southern Lebanon. Over the decades, Hezbollah has evolved into a virtual arm of Iran's Revolutionary Guard Corps, providing connective tissues for the growing network of powerful militias. Iran and Hezbollah complement each other. Both are Shiite powers in a part of the world which is predominantly Sunni. For Iran, a Persian country bordered by Arab-speaking nations, Hezbollah is not only just a military power, but also an Arab-speaking force of fighters and operatives who can easily gel with the Arab masses. It is a great military and strategic asset to Iran which has profoundly influenced the course of conflicts across the Middle East.

The Iran-led Shia militias are collaborating across the borders. Hezbollah fighters are the elite commandos, who train Afghans, Pakistanis and Iraqis and fight together with Sunnis under the overall leadership of Iran. The Arabic word '*hezbollah*', which is the name of Lebanon's Shia political party with deep ideological ties to Iran, means 'party of God'. Most of them endorse Velayat-e Faqih, the concept that Iran's supreme leader is both the leader of the highest political power in the country and the paramount religious authority. They have enough reasons to fight Sunni jihadists like al-Qaeda and the Islamic State besides the US and Israel. Tehran's rising influence has made both Iran and its allies a target of military and diplomatic actions from Saudi Arabia, Israel and the US, who consider Hezbollah a terrorist organization. In reality, Hezbollah has become active in so many places and against so many enemies, that detractors have described it as 'the Blackwater of Iran', after the infamous mercenary firm.

In Syria, Hezbollah has made its greatest foreign investment and paid the highest price in terms of manpower. Its leaders have portrayed the war as a conspiracy by Israel, the US and Saudi Arabia to use Sunni extremists of the Islamic State and the al-Qaeda clones to destroy Syria, and weaken the pro-Iranian axis in the region. In their view, it is their pious duty to directly intervene and provide 'resistance' against the alliance of evil.

Middle East Policy of Iran

The guiding principle of Tehran's Middle East policy is Shia empowerment. Therefore, the Iranian regime has patronized Shia parties and militias in a fashion that resembles Moscow's strategy towards Third World's communist movements during the Cold War. Tehran used different proxy armies to push back Saudi influence and enhance its influence in the region. The jury, however, is still out on whether the sectarianization of the Iranian foreign policy will be a costly mistake or not. On one side, the policy has worked well and enhanced the regional power of Iran.

The Sunni Arab countries, which are falling out of the Saudi camp because of the American pressure to cooperate with Israel, have come closer to Iran. Recently, nations like Qatar and Turkey have formed a group, which is mentored by Russia. Strategic and close relations with Russia and China contribute to Iran's power as it provides a counterweight to the US efforts to isolate Tehran. Russian and Chinese opposition to strong action against Iran has consistently blocked sanction resolutions against it at the UN Security Council. Russia sells weapons and nuclear material to Iran. Similarly, China buys oil from Iran and supplies consumer goods to it.

Iran has structures for a modern, prosperous state—lots of oil and gas (the world's fourth and second biggest respectively), a young population under the age of 35, developed infrastructure and good communication facilities. As of 2012, the republic has more than one mobile phone per head, and more than 50 million Internet users, a rate much higher than Saudi Arabia and Egypt. It has huge digital talents and exports about US$50 million worth software annually. Iranian women spend more on make-up, per head, than any other nation; the young are very fashion-conscious and the young women often wear short skirts and fashionable clothes under their black robes. Iranians love to eat, consume and shop, and continue to patronize international brands.

The regional confrontation between Iran and Saudi Arabia, two nations geographically separated by the Persian Gulf, is deeply rooted in sectarian, political and economic competitions. They follow two rival sects of Islam with a long history of violence and they are fighting proxy battles, often violently, in different countries. The domestic struggle of Saudi Arabia may stem from a series of foreign policy failures. Riyadh's military intervention in Yemen, launched with much fanfare in 2015, to counter the Iran-aligned Houthis rebels, has become a political quagmire. The crown prince and de facto ruler MBS is pushing the can down the road turning it into a major humanitarian disaster

Saudi's rift with Qatar and Jordan has pushed smaller Arab countries closer to Iran. Turkey emerged as a major player in the Middle East with its close links to Qatar and Iran. They also brought

Russia into the equation to counter the US's influence. In Syria, the Sunni jihadists groups, supported by Saudi Arabia, failed to topple the government of Bashar al-Assad. Putin's aggressive policies gave full naval, air and military support to the Syrian leader Bashar Assad. On the grounds Shia militia and the Iranian proxy boots prevailed in the conflict and uprooted the Islamic State fighters.

Riyadh tried in vain to stir trouble in Lebanon by forcing Saad Hariri to resign, during a private visit to Riyadh. They were planning to topple the coalition government, in which Hezbollah is an important stakeholder. Under the power-sharing agreement with Sunni Muslims and Christians, Shia members of the parliament, belonging to Hezbollah, occupy the speaker's chair in the Lebanese parliament.

Saudi Arabia and its allies view Iran's foreign policy as sectarian and expansionist. They argue that Iran has been exploiting the political unrest to support its militant Shia clients and undermine the Sunni dominated status quo in the region. They see Iran's endgame as a transnational, pro-Iranian Shia polity, stretching from Iran to Lebanon and from Iraq to Syria—something akin to a resurrected Persian empire. Undoubtedly, the Islamic Republic's foreign policies are aimed at advancing its strategic interests. Sectarianism plays an important role in them. It is also a fact that, for most of its history, Iran has been following a largely non-sectarian path. Even now, it is aligned with the Sunni Qatar and Turkey.

The sectarian elements in the Iranian foreign policy have, however, increased after the US invasion of Iraq and the Arab Spring in 2011. The rise of Sunni jihadism fuelled by Salafism and the subsequent rise of militant anti-Shia narrative spread by the Islamic State fighters, had ignited the conflicts in Iraq, Syria, Bahrain and Yemen. Fearful of each other's intentions, the behavior of Iran and Saudi Arabia moved sharply towards sectarian directions. Since its allies felt threatened in Iraq, Syria, and Yemen, Iran doubled down on its pro-Shia strategy as a way of protecting its regional interests and investments. The IRGC is Iran's premier military organization and the leading agency in its strategic activities including the proxy wars in the Middle East.

Iran has two levels of foreign policy, both of which are overseen by its Supreme Leader. They are subject to his authority, but differ in content and form. The first level is the state-to-state policy, which is largely managed by the elected government in Tehran. The second level is Iran's relation with the non-state actors, which is overseen by the IRGC and mostly managed outside the Iranian parliament. Iran remains the most vocal opponent of anti-Americanism and anti-Zionism. Iran's most ardent allies are non-state actors, mostly Shia Islamist groups. Iran is famously closer to India than to its Muslim neighbour Pakistan. Recently with Indian collaboration, Iran has developed the Chabahar Port, to give easy access to India and facilitate trade with Afghanistan and Central Asia.

In terms of the military budget, Tehran spends US$6.3 billion on its defence each year, while the budget of Riyadh is US$56 billion. The gap is enormous and appears more impressive than it really is, until you take into account the fact that Saudi Arabia gets all its weapons from the US at steep prices. Of course, it also comes with a lot of kickbacks to the royal family princes. Iran, which prides itself in manufacturing most of its weapons domestically, has found impressive success in rocket technology. In terms of solid hardware, Saudi Arabia beats Iran in the number of fighter jets and attack aircraft. Most of Iran's jets are outdated American models from the Shah era. Nonetheless, modern aircraft are being acquired from Russia and China and are in use in the Iranian Air Force. The naval strength of Iran is very impressive with lots of vessels and submarines acquired from Russia and some manufactured domestically too. A direct conflict, involving two of the major producers of crude oil, is unlikely. If, God forbid, it ever happens, it will send oil prices skyrocketing since a major share of the oil trade relies on the route through the Persian Gulf.

According to a 2015 BBC report, President Hassan Rouhani has given US$19.8 million to the IRGC as its annual cyber security budget. The IRGC forces are projecting their power across the Middle East, sending military advisers, volunteers and training professionals to the Iraq, Yemen and Syria governments as well as different militia groups. Analysts say that Tehran has successfully produced and tested long-range ballistic missiles, main battle tanks and unarmed aerial vehicles, in addition to domestically built submarines and attack boats. In November and December of 2017, the Houthi rebels in Yemen fired long-range ballistic missiles targeting Riyadh and they were built in Iran.

The rise of various Sunni jihadi groups like Islamic State and al-Qaeda shaped Iran's role in the Middle East more broadly as the defender of Shia Muslims. Russia's direct military intervention in Syria in 2015 put Iran and Russia on the same strategic side as a powerful counterforce to the US–Saudi bloc. Iran has gained economically and politically by siding with Qatar in the ongoing Saudi–Qatari diplomatic rift. It increased its food supplies and signed gas agreements for explorations in the shared gas fields with Qatar. Iran sewed a formidable political, economic and military bloc with Russia, Turkey and Qatar against Saudi Arabia.

President Bashar al-Assad made a dubious claim about Iran saying that it does not have any ambitions in Syria. 'We would never allow any country to influence our sovereignty. We would not accept it, and the Iranians don't want either,' he said.[50] Nevertheless, the facts are different. Iran is fully involved in Syria, and the country has fallen under Tehran's absolute control. The Iranian advisers with Hezbollah fighters are managing the post-IS regime of Syria. Bashar al-Assad has no choice but to rely on Iran proxies for funds and paramilitary fighters.

Syria serves Iran in three ways. First, it prevents the collapse of Iran's purported 'Shia Crescent' by keeping the Assad regime

---

[50] 'Syria's President Speaks', *Foreign Affairs*, No. March/April 2015, 25 January 2015, www.foreignaffairs.com/interviews/syrias-president-speaks. Accessed on 28 September 2023.

intact. Second, it maintains Iran's direct route to Lebanon. Third, it facilitates the movement of Iran's armaments to Hezbollah through Syria. During the civil war in Syria, they were singularly responsible for preventing Syria from falling into the hands of the hostile Islamic State jihadis. Iran has not entirely outsourced its involvement in Syria to its proxies. On the contrary, General Amir Ali Hajizadeh, commander of the IRGC Aerospace Force (Islamic Revolutionary Guard Corps Aerospace Force), said in a recent interview to the German magazine *Der Spiegel* that Iran builds and operates missile plants in Syria. Many senior commanders of Hezbollah were killed during Syrian operations in the Golan Heights. The involvement of top-ranking IRGC and Hezbollah commanders speaks volumes on what Iran has given to the Syrian war. Israel is upset by the Hezbollah commanders' involvement in the Golan Heights as they feared that the southern Lebanon and Golan Heights war theatre would merge together and pose a formidable threat to the security of Israel.

The Persia–Arab divide is a real one, and in terms of Islam, the Iranians' Shia version stands in contrast to the faith of the majority Sunni Arabs. The dominant view among the Arabs during the 50s and 60s was based on the nationalist narrative of President Nasser of Egypt and Hafez al-Assad of Syria. Symbolically, the Arab nationalists even reject the term 'Persian Gulf', preferring to call that body of water which connects the world's richest oil reserves, the 'Arab Gulf'. Nonetheless, after 1979, Saudi Arabia with the control of its enormous wealth, weakened and replaced Arab nationalism with the Salafi brand of jihadi Islam. It is ultra-conservative, rigid and represents a very extreme and uncompromising view of Islam, which is completely averse to Shiism.

The Iranian leadership, however, always talks about the pan-Islamic unity or *Wahdat*. Much of the drive behind Iran's pan-Islamic outlook is first and foremost political, and it is undertaken with a view of enhancing Iran's geopolitical position. It also occurs in the context of the regime's ambition to become the leader of the Islamic world.

It is a goal hindered by the Persian and Shia characteristics of the Islamic Republic. Iran's antipathy for Wahhabism and Salafi jihadism is unsurprising. Both teach that Shiism is a deviant sect and its followers are beyond the fold of Islam. Saudi Arabia's top cleric, Grand Mufti Abdulaziz Al al-Sheikh, told a Saudi journalist in September 2016: 'You must understand, Iranians are not Muslims. They are the sons of Zoroastrians. Their hostility to Muslims is ancient, especially with Sunnis.'[51]

---

[51] Payton, Matt, '"Iranians are not Muslims," says Saudi Arabia's Grand Mufti', *The Independent*, 7 September 2016.

4

SAUDI ARABIA AND IRAN: A TALE OF TWO RIVAL STATES

The identity conflicts between Arabs and Persians are more than a thousand years old as they are ethnically two different races. The struggle between Saudi Arabia and Iran is a persistent feature of Middle Eastern geopolitics. It has been exacerbated on various occasions since the 1979 Iranian Islamic Revolution. Various events that followed, including the war started between Iran and Iraq in 1980, the Iraqi invasion of Kuwait in 1990, the US-led invasion of Iraq in 2003 as well as the Arab Spring of 2011, led to periodic flare-ups of tension between them, which never cooled down completely. Their rivalry always had an underpinning of sectarian and regional dimensions. Both the countries hold a firm regional standing: Iran has a large, young and educated population with significant oil reserves and a long history of nationhood, while Saudi Arabia holds vast oil reserves and is the custodian of two of Islam's holiest sites—Mecca and Medina.

In 1925, the Shah of Iran annexed Khuzestan, an Arab enclave at the border of Iraq, to Persia, and this alarmed Saudi King Abdul Aziz. Then Saudi Arabia signed a bilateral treaty with Britain in 1927 to establish buffer governments in the Gulf and recognized three nations for it: Bahrain, Kuwait and Oman. Saudi Arabia also signed a treaty with Britain to sabotage the Iranian claims to Bahrain. Iran complained to the League of the Nations and requested to return it back to Iran. Saudi Arabia and Iran continued to maintain diplomatic relations, but they got strained when Iran signed the Baghdad Pact. After Britain's departure from the Middle East by 1971, both Iran and Saudi Arabia continued to have good relations until the Islamic Revolution in 1979.

US and the Twin Pillar Policy

President Richard Nixon encouraged Iran and Saudi Arabia, two leading nations of the region, to be policemen of the Gulf and protect the region from the influence of communism and the Baathist regime of Iraq. As the 'twin pillars' of the US in the Middle East in 1971, Iran and Saudi would operate together as the local guardians of the US interests in the region. This came to be known as the Twin Pillar Policy. Both the countries made special efforts not to trigger identity politics as there were strong differences between them in terms of faith and nationality. Iran enthusiastically assumed the role of a regional policeman under Mohammad Reza Pahlavi, while Saudi Arabia also played an important role as the US's ally in the Arab world. Cooperation between Iran and Saudi Arabia under the Twin Pillar Policy extended to different joint operations in defeating the communist regimes in North Yemen, Zaire, Somalia and Oman. However, following the assassination of King Faisal of Saudi Arabia in 1975, the kingdom began to assert a new approach towards oil, its major resource.

The Shah of Iran declared publicly that oil was undervalued for years and the OPEC (Organization of the Petroleum Exporting Countries) needed to urgently affect a price hike. Saudi Arabia, as de facto leader of OPEC, however, refused to toe the Shah line on price hike and stood to gain brownie points from the industrialized Western countries. Iran was heavily dependent on its oil revenues for keeping pace with the needs of a large educated population and funding the high military spending. The domestic sentiments grew against Shah's economic policies and a strong undercurrent eventually toppled the Pahlavi dynasty.

The revolution was inspired and led by Ayatollah Khomeini from France. Later, on his arrival in Tehran, Khomeini was given a rousing reception by the people of his country. Khomeini claimed broad Islamic support for the revolution and was quick to criticize the 'decadence' of the Wahhabi Saudi monarchy. His claim that a Shiite theocracy would be the authoritative voice of Islam in Iran, clashed with the Saudi Kingdom's assumed religious legitimacy as the guardian of two holy mosques in Mecca and Medina. Iran further upset Saudi Arabia by showing solidarity with the fellow Shias in the oil-rich eastern regions of Saudi Arabia. And then, at the behest of Saudi Arabia's King Khalid, Iraqi dictator Saddam Hussein attacked Iran. The Saudis had given billions of US dollars to the Saddam Hussein campaign. In retaliation, Iran struck Saudi tankers, and the kingdom responded by shooting down two Iranian jets. By the end of war, an estimated 750,000 Iranians and 500,000 Iraqis lost their lives. After the Iran war, Saddam Hussein invaded Kuwait in 1990 and this, anyway, brought Iran and Saudi Arabia together, not as friends, but as two countries working together for regional cooperation.

It was after the US–British invasion of Iraq in 2003, however, that the entire regional dynamics went for a total shake-up. With Saddam Hussein, Saudis had been able to present as an effective counterweight to Iran's regional ambitions. After the invasion, however, the new Shia-dominated government in Iraq was supported by Iran, upsetting the Kingdom of Saudi Arabia. Saudi had never imagined a major Shia Arab country in their neighbourhood. It rightly feared Iran's increasing interference in the region, for the first time, challenging its supremacy in the neighbourhood.

Saudi Arabia was actively involved in Syria to overthrow President Bashar al-Assad. It was mainly aimed at destroying the Syrian–Iranian alliance. The American invasion of Iraq in 2003, the Lebanon War in 2006 and the Iran–Iraq–Syria pipeline programme, all led to strengthening the ties between Iran and Syria. These developments, in turn, worsened the ties between Syria and Saudi Arabia. The Assad regime of Syria received support from Iran and the local Shia Alawite population. Saudi Arabia is also afraid of its Shia population in the eastern province of the kingdom rising against the government, especially after the Arab Spring. Just over 74 per cent of the Syrian population practices Sunni Islam and hence Saudi Arabia hopes to get an upper hand in case the Assad regime falls. Therefore, Saudi Arabia sends a large number of young jihadis to wage war against the Alawite political regime.

Traditionally, majority of the Syrain Sunnis followed Sufi traditions and rejected the bigoted Wahhabi–Salafi ideology, advocated by Saudi Arabia. Jihadi groups like Free Syrian Army (FSA) and Jabhat al-Nusra were allied to the al-Qaeda and were actively supported by it financially and logistically. After the entry of ISIS, the Syrian civil war morphed into a complete sectarian war, instead of a political struggle for democracy.

Saudi–Iranian Competition

The history of the Saudi–Iranian competition is deep and dates back to the seventh century. Saudi Arabia was established in 1927 as the Kingdom of Nejd and Hejaz, and a Saudi–Iranian friendship treaty was signed in 1929. Iran is primarily a Shia-majority nation, while the ultra-conservative Wahhabi–Salafi sect, which detests Shia Muslims, dominates in Saudi Arabia. The reign of Mohammad Reza Pahlavi, who ruled Iran between 1941 and 1979, was secular. He maintained an excellent relationship with Israel and Saudi Arabia. Gregory Aftandilian, an expert on Middle East politics, observed in *The Arab Weekly* that Iran and Saudi Arabia were on the same side of the global Cold War. However, the latter was worried that the Shah was trying to recreate the Persian Empire with American assistance.[52]

For all the military training and arms sales to the Saudi Arabia in the 1970s, it was apparent to any observer that the US had

---

[52]Aftandilian, Gregory, 'Saudi Fear Re-enactment of "Twin Pillar" Strategy', *The Arab Weekly*, 22 May 2015, https://tinyurl.com/28cpkraj. Accessed on 6 September 2023.

considered Iran as an equal and competent partner. The seizing of three islands by Iran off the coast of the United Arab Emirates in 1971 was unexpected and it upset the Arab countries. Iran had been playing the role of the 'policeman' in the Persian Gulf, more than the Saudis. In the mid-1970s, Iranian troops with British special forces were sent to southwestern Oman to crush a Marxist-led insurgency. The US also engaged in strategic alliances to counter the emergence of the socialist Baath party in Iraq and Syria.

The Shia Islamic Revolution of 1979, however, totally changed the sectarian equations, and Saudi Arabia began to see Iran as a regional threat thereafter. The relation between Iran and the US also deteriorated after the revolution. After Ayatollah Khomeini's emergence to power, the sectarian rivalry increased as Iran nullified friendship with Israel, declared war on Saddam Hussein's Baathist regime and branded the Saudi kingdom as an illegitimate monarchy.

The relationship between Iran and Saudi Arabia has been at the centre of many major political shifts that occurred in the Middle East after the US invasion of Iraq in 2003. The battle for regional dominance played out in various ways and in multiple forms in the region. The clash has been ideological, sectarian as well as of the military. Syria's Alawite Shia President Bashar al-Assad, who was backed by Iran, gradually gained the upper hand against the Saudi-backed Sunni rebels in the country while in Yemen, a Saudi-led coalition backed by Iran, has been attacking Shia Houthi fighters.

Both the countries are engaged in proxy wars in the entire Middle East and their relationship is defined by long-standing theological fault lines. Each has aspirations of Islamic leadership, and each pursues different versions of Islam. And here comes the next level of complexity: the political game now extends from 'Saudi versus Iran' to 'US versus Iran'. The unequivocal support from President Trump and his family for Riyadh, as a counter to Tehran, extends to unquestioning support for the kingdom's impetuous Crown Prince MBS, who conceitedly secured his power base in the monarchy. The Crown Prince has been targeting internal enemies through a deadly purge of senior princes in the administration, military and religious leadership. But there are wheels within wheels: even as the US backs Saudi Arabia, it continues to support Lebanon, including providing it military aid.

The US and Israel along with Riyadh branded Iran as a destabilizing factor in the Middle East and designed a policy to isolate it in the region. The ruthless ambition of the Crown Prince MBS is on full display at home with his crackdown on the big businessmen and senior members of the royal family. It is also known across the Middle East that his over-enthusiasm is driven by the urgency to check the Iranian influence in the region. Whether he likes it or not, Iran is all set to become the dominant power in the region from Iraq to Lebanon. The Irani policy-makers know well that Tehran may not be in full control in Baghdad, Damascus and Beirut, but thanks to its proxies and allies, it can decisively shape their battlefields and politics. Once a cautious and passive regional power, Saudi Arabia in recent years has found a new meaning and purpose in its foreign and security policies. Rather than carefully pushing Iran back and garnering broad support for this effort from the rest of the world, Saudi's approach, however, has been often haphazard, unsettling and counterproductive.

Saudi-Led Campaign in Yemen

The Saudi-led campaign called 'Operation Decisive Storm'[53] began in March 2015 with the aim of forcing Houthi rebels to withdraw from the Yemeni capital Sanaa and install Yemen's internationally recognized government in its place. Saudi Arabia deployed 150,000 soldiers, 100 fighter jets and navy units. Despite the 20 months of aerial bombardment and an estimated cost of US$5 billion by Saudi alone, the war is still to see an end. The Houthis control northwest Yemen and their alliance with the ousted President Saleh had further deepened their control in the region. The Houthis enjoyed broader

---

[53]'Anti-terror Islamic alliance to meet in Riyadh', *Al Arabiya News*, 26 March 2015.

support from various tribes and sects of the country. There were many reasons for their success as an armed rebel movement, but first and foremost was their intimate knowledge of the rugged mountains and canyons in which they operate.

The Houthis and the tribesmen, who make up the majority of their loosely formed force, have long understood Yemen's mountains, which are an effective force multiplier. Mountains favour defensive warfare. Those who invaded Yemen in the past—the Ottomans twice, and the Egyptians later—quickly discovered that mountainous northwest Yemen, just like Afghanistan, is a graveyard for invaders. Second, the Houthi leadership has forged personal and organizational relationships with the tribal clans, most of whom are Zaydi Shias.

As a Zaydi Shia organization, Houthis' rise to power set off alarm bells in Saudi Arabia, which views them as proxies of Iran. To fight Houthis on the ground, Saudi Arabia had pitched militias and ISIS fighters escaped from Syria. The forces, comprising southern separatists, soldiers loyal to the government and militant Salafist tribesmen, were used as proxies of the Saudi-led coalition.

Houthis, who hail from Yemen's northern coffee-growing Saada province, get their name from their late leader, Hussein Badreddin Houthi, and now led by his brother Abdul Malik Houthi, a charismatic figure, often compared to Hassan Nasrallah of Hezbollah. The Houthis have been fighting the Yemeni central government since 2004, when the movement was founded to strengthen the rights of the Zaydi sect, which represents between 30 to 40 per cent of Yemeni population. The Houthi movement came into being basically to fight the discrimination against the tribes of northern region by the former Saleh administration. Yemen never had sectarian issues in the past and there was no animosity between Shia and Sunni sects. During a Houthi uprising following the Arab Spring, Saudi Arabia launched an aerial attack on the protesters, after which Iran entered the scene and eventually, contours of conflict changed in favour of the Houthi fighters.

Riyadh feared that Houthis, under the guidance of Hezbollah and Iran, would morph into a deadly fighting force on its southern border. After three years of Saudi air bombardments and over 10,000 casualties, the Houthi forces are capable of firing ballistic missiles reaching up to Riyadh airport from Yemen. Saudi Arabia now says that it is Hezbollah who is providing expertise and technology to Houthis to launch ballistic missiles. Over the time, Iran has transferred Iranian-built Ababil series UAVs (drones), fitted with high explosive warheads to them. They are capable of engaging with high-value targets, such as radars and Patriot missile batteries. Anti-ship and man-portable missiles have also been suspected to be transferred to Yemen. Reliable sources have confirmed that Tehran has provided specialist manpower of Afghan and Shiite Arabs to train and lead Houthis besides acting as logistical advisers to them.

Yemen has a long border with Saudi Arabia and none with Iran. Saudi Arabia's intervention in Yemen, at the initiative of Crown Prince MBS, on behalf of the Yemeni government forces against the Iranian-backed Houthi rebels, has been costly and inconclusive even after years of Saudi bombing that killed more than 3,000 civilians.

It could lead to the very outcome that Riyadh wanted to prevent at any cost—the transformation of Houthi rebels into something akin to Lebanon's Hezbollah, except that it is right next door sharing a long border with Saudi Arabia. Many analysts observed that there was a strong possibility of the Houthis, with the help of Hezbollah and Iran militias, capturing the entire Yemen and completely governing the country.

Houthi rebels strategically fired an Iran-made ballistic missile on the Riyadh airport to give a warning to the Saudi royal dispensation. Fortunately, the missiles were intercepted without causing any damage. The Crown Prince was counseled many times not to resort to counterattacks and escalate the conflict with the poor Arab fellow nation. Recently, the United Arab Emirates has withdrawn from the coalition with Saudi Arabia in the Yemen conflict. The Americans are trying to enforce a ceasefire and bring back the warring parties to the negotiating table.

The Saudi-led blockade of Qatar has been a total disaster and a failed policy initiative of Crown Prince MBS. The effort to tame Qatar's assertive regional foreign policies has not worked, and the issue has gone on the back-burner of international diplomacy. As a result of the economic embargo and the closing of skies for Qatar Airways, the country found new friends in Turkey and Iran. They signed treaties to broaden and foster long-term economic, political and military relationships. Turkey established an army base in Qatar and Iran promised military support in case of any misadventure by the maverick Crown Prince.

The Saudi Goof-Up in Lebanon

What Crown Prince MBS attempted to do with Lebanon's prime minister was even more bizarre. The PM, Saad Hariri was invited to spend his weekend in a resort of the Crown Prince, outside Riyadh. The prime minister of a sovereign nation was taken into the protective custody of another country disregarding all the international protocol. And he was forced to announce his resignation as the prime minister of Lebanon, blaming Hezbollah and Iran for hatching a conspiracy to assassinate him. This incident involving Hariri, once a favourite ally of Riyadh, bewildered many in Lebanon and outside the country. Hariri is a Sunni follower, which is significant, given the role of Saudi Arabia in Lebanon.

From 1975 to 1990, Lebanon witnessed a deadly civil war between its diverse religious sects. In the end, a power sharing formula was worked out after a series of discussions, talks and coalition deals, like the 1989's Taif Accord. Under this, the prime minister of Lebanon must be a Sunni (backed by Riyadh); its president, a Maronite Christian; and the speaker of parliament, a Shia. In this precarious coexistence, it was perhaps Hariri's willingness to astutely share power with Hezbollah (a Shia political party) that saw him prevail for long.

Hezbollah is an important political party and represents the Shia minority of Lebanon. Any Sunni prime minister of the country has no choice but to strike a deal with Shias and Christians, if he or she wants to run the government. After forcing Saad Hariri to resign in November 2017, Riyadh claimed that Lebanon had begun a war against it, blaming Hezbollah for the missile attack on Riyadh from Yemen. Saudi ordered its citizens to leave Lebanon immediately and raised the spectre of military hostilities. Significantly, both Saudi Arabia and Israel strongly detest Hezbollah for their own reasons and have joined hands to punish their common enemy. This move, which is likely to backfire, is like playing into the hands of Iran and Hezbollah, who duplicitously pose as rule-abiding.

The African tale of the old king and his young prince is quite relevant to Crown Prince MBS. The story goes like this: a king sends his young prince to learn the rhythms of the jungle. On his first outing, against the din of buzzing insects and singing birds, the young prince could make out only the roars of lions and the trumpets of elephants. The prince returns again and again and begins to pick up less obvious sounds, until he can hear the rustle of a snake and the beat of a butterfly's wings. The king tells him to keep going back until he can sense the danger in the stillness and the hope in the sunrise.

To be fit to rule, the prince must be able to hear that which does not make a sound. If Crown Prince MBS's goal is to counter Iran, Riyadh is picking the wrong battlefields; Lebanon and Yemen are peripheral countries, where wars are costly and complex, outcomes are ambiguous and returns low. In the Middle East, the balance of power is determined in Syria and Iraq. But in these countries, the costs are high and the risk even higher. And in both these countries, Iran is well ahead of the curve. It has the network's expertise, experience and strategic patience required to fight and win proxy wars at low cost, with plenty of disingenuous deniability. Seeking to beat Iran at this game, without proper preparedness, is dangerous and costly. It is not easy to roll back Iran in the Middle East. Iran has another strength: It has demonstrated that it will be there for its friends and allies in good and bad times. Saudi Arabia does not have the same consistency.

Impact of Arab Spring

The Arab Spring of 2011 is a very important milestone in the history of Saudi–Iran rivalry. It has profoundly transformed the political landscape of the Middle East and elevated sectarian fault lines to an unprecedented level. The Wahhabi–Salafi narrative of the Sunni Arab countries against Shias was intensified, aggravating the polarization further. The religious minorities in Saudi Arabia, Bahrain and Yemen started protesting against the ruling elites. Therefore, one of the key consequences was the revival of the contest between Saudi Arabia and Iran in the fields of proxy conflicts as was happening in Lebanon, Yemen, Bahrain and Syria. Attempts by Saudi Arabia and Iran to expand their regional influences, by interfering in the internal ethno-sectarian affairs of the Middle Eastern countries, worsened the instability of the region. Iran and Saudi got sucked into the region's bloody civil wars through the Iran-backed Hezbollah and Shia militias in Syria and Iraq, and with Saudi National Guards in Bahrain and Yemen respectively, to strengthen their client regimes.

Tensions between the tacit Sunni Arab countries, led by Saudi Arabia and the Islamic Republic of Iran, basically boiled down to two things. One is the battle to be the dominant power in the Middle East, while the other is the fight for dominance between the ideologies represented by the two rival countries. A vast majority of Muslims in the world are Sunnis, amounting to about 80 per cent. They are spread all over the globe and it is the dominant faith of North Africa and the Middle East. Only Iran, Iraq, Azerbaijan and Bahrain have a Shia majority, although there is a significant Shia population in Yemen, Lebanon, Kuwait, Syria and Qatar.

The events of the Arab Spring, however, proved to be a game changer for the Islamic Republic of Iran. The overthrow of a few Arab dictators and the chaos caused by the emergence of social media, paved the way for a more assertive foreign policy in the Middle East. The wave of democratization also reached, among others, countries with a sizable Shia population. Iran has constantly supported the demand for political reforms in Bahrain, the island-country with a Shia majority and a Sunni ruling monarchy. The oil-rich eastern region (Hasa region) of Saudi Arabia also has a large number of Shias. The Iranian regime has been harshly criticizing Saudi Arabia for the mistreatment of its Shia community in the region. The execution of the Saudi Shia cleric Nimr al-Nimr and many others had created a diplomatic crisis between Riyadh and Tehran in early 2016. The leader of the Lebanese Shia party Hezbollah had decried Saudi Arabia's act of beheading the leading Shia cleric as 'tyrannical, criminal and terroristic'.

The Islamic Republic of Iran not only mobilized Shia communities from the Middle East but also from the South Asian nations like Pakistan and Afghanistan for its political ends. The fragmentation of Iraq is a geopolitical victory for Tehran as the Saddam regime was a champion of Arab nationalism. The collapse of the Baathist state secured the Islamic Republic an opportunity to interfere in the local affairs of Iraq. The Iranian regime attempted successfully to fill the vacuum after the departure of the US troops from Iraq in 2011. The Shia-dominated Iraqi government in Baghdad has increasingly relied on Iranian aid to deal with the threats posed by ISIS and other Sunni extremist groups.

Amazingly, Saudi policy towards Iraq has become increasingly conciliatory, and the maverick Prince is even seen courting some Shia leaders like Muqtada al-Sadr, a known critic of Irani policies in Iraq, as part of this policy. Engaged in multiple fronts across the region, to project its influence and defend various interests, Iran is a more confident country now than it was two decades ago. Despite low oil prices and stringent economic sanction by the US-led European nations, Iran continues to survive as a strong self-confident nation, and is slowly transforming into a regional power exerting influence in several countries.

In 2001, Iran and Saudi Arabia signed a security pact dealing with terrorism and drug trafficking. In subsequent years, there were two major developments that had a cascading effect on the overall Saudi–Iran relations. The first was the US war on terror, following the 9/11 attacks in 2003, and the other, the Arab Spring in 2011. While the former removed Iraq as a major power in the Middle East, the latter destabilized Syria and Egypt—two important Arab nations. These events also redefined the rivalry between Saudi Arabia and Iran, with each country supporting different extremist groups and crafting new policy outlooks for them.

The Saudi policy has totally transformed since 1979, after the siege of the Grand Mosque of Mecca and the Iranian Islamic Revolution in the same year. It was in the subsequent years that the Arabian Kingdom spent billions of petrodollars to spread the Wahhabi–Salafi strain of Islam through its different cultural and political arms across the globe to far-reaching consequences. Of late, however, Saudi's rulers seem to have begun to realize the damage it has caused to the country's economic and religious standing on the global stage. Under the leadership of King Salman and his assertive and ambitious crown prince, a plan of economic, social and religious reform has been announced to help reduce the kingdom's dependence on oil revenue and to, at least peripherally, purge the Wahhabi–Salafi strain of intolerant jihadi Islam. For the first time since 1979, the kingdom is now potentially fighting a war within Islam. He has even famously said that he was not reforming, but restoring Islam.

Crown Prince MBS has expanded Saudi military involvement in foreign wars. The most important and critical of them is the military campaign in the neighboring Yemen, to fight the Houthi rebels, without putting Saudi boots on the ground. Saudi Arabia over the years has funded Pakistan and Egypt. Both the countries have, however, refused Saudi requests to provide ground troops to fight on behalf of Saudi Arabia in foreign lands. Upset about it, the Saudi royals have downgraded their relationship with Pakistan. They allege that Houthis are militarily supported by Iran's Republican Guards and Hezbollah fighters from Lebanon.

Under the Obama administration, the US policy towards Iran was reset. In July 2015, JCPOA between Iran and six major Western powers was signed. This had a major ripple effect on the entire Middle East. The US and the European countries want to see Iran join the 'community of nations', but the Sunni Arab countries, led by Saudi Arabia, remain fearful of Iran's emergence as a regional power. The nuclear deal also increased tension between the Sunni Saudi Arabia and Shia Iran. Israel saw an opportunity in it and for the first time voiced the concern of Arab nations about the nuclearization of Iran.

The Saudi–Iran rivalry is likely to intensify with time and the main area of contention will be Iran's continued support to its proxy groups in the Middle Eastern countries including Yemen and Bahrain. Iran is indirectly fighting in Yemen and Syria. Although Saudi's support to its proxies is not as strong as Iran's, its presence nonetheless intensifies the tension between the two countries. Saudi Arabia does not have a strong support in Iraq; it has avoided providing any open support to ISIS. Nonetheless, it is in the public domain that ISIS is receiving financial support from Saudi contacts in Syria. The Saudi royal family suspects that with support from the Islamic Brotherhood, ISIS may also come back to confront them. However, the Salafi jihadist militants in Syria are fully backed by Saudi Arabia and they are also formally allied with the al-Qaeda and its affiliates.

On the economic front, Saudi Arabia and Iran will continue to compete in the international oil market, once the economic sanction is lifted. Saudis are using oil as a weapon, refusing to reduce production and thereby preventing Iran from selling its oil at higher prices. More economic competition is on the cards as Iran is slowly emerging as a player on the international trading market. The harsh economic blockade on Qatar by the Arab countries, led by Saudi Arabia, has also caused fissures in the GCC, which is contrary to Saudi's desire to present a unified Arab front against Iran. In the next 10 or 15 years, new areas of friction and competition might evolve, especially after the JCPOA term expires in 2030.

Some of the Gulf analysts were of the view that Crown Prince MBS made an effort at restructuring the geopolitics and geo-economics of the region. The moves, however, were sudden and destabilizing, enhancing the chance of fresh regional flare-ups and proxy wars. They feared that this could have led to creating more refugees and more shattered cities like Mosul, Sanaa and Aleppo, besides quadrupling the cost of reconstruction. Many diplomats feared that it was not just Saudi Arabia whose actions seemed unpredictable; the US, led by President Donald Trump, was not predictable either. The US administration had issued a statement that it stood with its Gulf allies and their complaints to the United Nations 'against the Iranian regime's aggression and blatant violations of international law.'[54]

Iran and Cross-Border Alliances

Iran's strategy for increasing its power has been centred on the promotion of cross-border Shia solidarity and development of a resistance or sanction economy. During the Iran–Iraq War (1980–1988), the Sunni-dominated Saddam regime, aided by the US and the Sunni Arab countries, seriously damaged Iran. Since then, Iranians have cultivated strong political, economic and sectarian ties with the Iraqi Shias, hoping to eliminate any future Iraqi threats to Iranian security. Iran's main objective was to reduce the influence of Sunni extremist groups in Iraq and keep Baghdad safe from any future Sunni dominance in public administration. The rise of various Sunni extremist groups, including the Islamic State, shaped Iran's role in the Middle East more broadly as the defender of Shia

---

[54]'White House Statement on Iranian-Supported Missile Attacks Against Saudi Arabia', *US Embassy in Yemen*, 8 November 2017, Press Release, https://tinyurl.com/3cyxaxfj. Accessed on 22 August 2023.

Muslims. President Vladimir Putin's direct intervention in favour of Bashar al-Assad in Syria with a strong air support brought Iran and Russia on the same strategic side as a powerful counterforce to the US–Saudi bloc.

Resistance economy[55] is Iran's clever strategy to survive in a hostile global economic environment. Designed to counter the corrosive effects of the US-led economic sanction, it seeks to reduce economic vulnerabilities to global and regional economic shocks through domestic capacity building, developing a knowledge-based economy and improving industrial production. The other big objective is to decrease dependence on oil and gas, Iran's principal sources of revenue. Iran wants the US to, at least, reduce its footprints in the Middle East, if not totally pack up and leave the region.

The Arab Spring has created a new set of openings in which Iran could seek to expand its influence while Saudi Arabia could only struggle to maintain the status quo. When a Saudi-friendly regime was threatened by any force, Iranians supported the opposition, while the Saudis tried to prop them up. When the Iranian ally Syria was on the brink of collapse, Saudi Arabia tried to push it over the edge while Iran, with the support of Russia and Hezbollah, pulled it back and restored the regime. In Bahrain, the Shia-majority staged pro-democracy protests against the Sunni monarchy; Saudi Arabia, fearing Iranian influence, sent in the army and brutally crushed the protests.

In Yemen, Iran stepped up its financial and military aid for the Shia Zaydi sect of Houthi rebels; after the rebels seized the capital Sanaa in the early 2015 and moved to take the rest of it, Saudi Arabia along with UAE, launched an air bombing campaign to stop them. Nevertheless, the Houthi rebels dug their heels in and managed to hold the capital city. Subsequently, the Saudi Arabian navy blocked the Yemeni seaports and stopped all humanitarian help. When the world media showed pictures of starving Yemen

---

[55]Takeyh, Ray, 'Iran's "Resistance Economy" Debate', *Council on Foreign Relations*, 7 April 2016, https://tinyurl.com/2jmump4t. Accessed on 6 September 2023.

infants and children, the Saudis, under intense UN and Western pressure, lifted the blockade and allowed the humanitarian help to reach the hospitals.

The total US retreat from the Middle East made it possible for Iran, Saudi Arabia and other regional powers to play an increasing role in the civil conflicts of countries like Lebanon, Iraq and Syria.

Arab Betrayal of Palestinians

Donald Trump often boasts that he is a smart dealmaker. He was resolved to take on challenges, when he took presidency of the US in January 2017, fanciful at the idea of succeeding where other presidents failed. He assigned the responsibility of Palestinian–Israel negotiations to his son-in-law Jared Kushner, a devout Jew and a senior adviser in the White House, without security clearance. He had no background knowledge of the complex Palestine–Israel issue and the White House efforts were greeted with suspicion in Arab capitals.

President Trump and his team looked at the convergence of factors that make the moment ripe, including willingness of the Saudi and Israeli camps to isolate Iran, which all of them consider the larger threat. With that in mind, the Egyptian president was given the job to broker reconciliation between Mahmoud Abbas who presides over the West Palestinian Bank, and Hamas, the organization which controls Gaza. A deal was envisioned to cement the Palestinian Authority as the representative of the Palestinian people. Trump's sudden announcement of shifting the US embassy to Jerusalem from Tel Aviv, embarrassed all the Arab nations except Saudi Arabia. President Trump did a job that no earlier US presidents had done, and as a consequence, all the groups favouring Palestine came on a single platform. Palestinians are protesting Trump's provocative decision to recognize Jerusalem as the sole capital of Israel. Half of Jerusalem, especially the eastern part of it, had been envisioned as the future capital of a Palestinian state, if two states ever became a reality.

Meanwhile, Crown Prince MBS and the UAE leadership are trying to strangle Jordan's economy until it agrees to their terms, submits to their leadership in the region and agrees to Trump's so-called 'ultimate deal' on the complex Palestine issue. This is another ill-conceived move by the Crown Prince to bring Jordan and Palestine leadership in line with the Saudi wishes, to have a close working relationship with Israel and the US. It is ultimately aimed at pushing through a purported peace plan that Jared Kushner, a Jew raised with orthodox traditions, had been drafting under the guidance of Israel.

As part of pressure tactic to submit Jordan to its demands, including by threatening to strangle its economy, the Saudi authorities detained the Arab Bank Chairman Sabih al-Masri, while he was on a private visit to Riyadh. Sabih al-Masri's multi-billion dollar investments are considered to be the cornerstone of Jordan economy. Headquartered in Amman, Arab Bank is Jordan's largest lender and a major economic engine throughout the Middle East and North Africa. According to Arab analysts, Saudi Arabia and the UAE have put pressure on Jordan to accept the recent US recognition of Jerusalem as the capital of Israel and a heavily stripped down version of the Palestinian state. Jordan had strongly sided with Palestinians and totally rejected the US move to shift the US embassy to Jerusalem.

Another very contentious, sensitive and challenging issue, faced by the Crown Prince in Saudi Arabia, is the moderation of the Wahhabi–Salafi version of Islam, giving space to the moderate or Sufi Sunni Islam, which is devotional and tolerant. The unwritten alliance between the House of Saud and the eighteenth century reformist scholar Muhammad ibn Abd al-Wahhab is fortified and remains unquestioned to this day. However, Crown Prince MBS's quest to moderate Islam indicates a desire to shift these tectonic plates of history and introduce reforms, which have been thought to be impossible for decades. In his efforts to restructure Saudi Arabia's religious establishment, Crown Prince MBS has reigned in the *mutaween* (religious police) by stripping them of their power to arrest individuals. Women will be allowed to drive, enter sports stadiums, watch movies and travel without male escorts. Decisions have been taken to open music concerts and movie theatres. Many hardcore Wahhabi and Salafi clerics have been arrested for expressing dissent following the decision. A council of scholars from around the world has been set up by the king to combat the extremist teachings globally. Liberalizing the Saudi society is also integral to Crown Prince MBS's plan of modernizing the kingdom.

The Saudi foreign policy, under the Crown Prince, is misguided if they take much solace from Trump's support for Saudi's regional policies in the Middle East. Irrespective of what the US does, increasing the rhetoric against Iran and compelling smaller fellow Sunni Arab nations like Qatar and Jordan to accept their leadership, will only weaken Saudi's position in the Arab political order. It is ridiculous how Saudi Arabia is undermining its own political position by escalating conflict with Iran and working to bring Qatar forcefully into compliance.

Saudi Arabia has been thinking that its security relationship with the US was giving the kingdom many military advantages over Iran, but in reality, much of its political strength in the region comes from the Kingdom's strong position and traditional goodwill within the Arab world. But the Arab order has become fragile due to the unhinged policies of the US president and Crown Prince MBS in the Middle East. Trump's recent announcement, to recognize Jerusalem as the new capital of Israel, was received with violent demonstrations in all the Arab and Muslim capitals.

The heads of states of the Organization of Islamic Countries (OIC) met in an emergency session at Istanbul in Turkey, following President Trump's announcement. The meeting was boycotted by Saudi Arabia along with its allies like UAE, Bahrain and Egypt, but attended by all other Arab Muslim nations, including Iran.

The weakening of Saudi's own position, caused by the Arab Spring, civil wars and, lately, the unpredictable responses of the Trump administration, posed a serious challenge to Riyadh and a real opportunity for Tehran. Notching up hostility towards Iran is likely to prolong the war in Yemen and Saudi Arabia cozying with Israel and accepting the Palestine peace plan, proposed by President Trump and Jared Kushner, would also further compromise the Saudi position in the Middle East.

Syrian Quagmire and Sinking Saudi Prospects

What is incubating in Syria right now, within the Sunni opposition to President Bashar al-Assad, is a metaphor for how divisions between Arab countries pose a greater threat to Saudi Arabia, than the challenge from Iran. In contrast to the disciplined, tightly consolidated Iran-led Shia coalition, supporting the Syrian government, the Sunni opposition is highly fragmented. There are different opposition groups ranging from jihadists affiliated to al-Qaeda and Salafists groups like Jaish al-Islam. Given the way of propping up the Syrian government by Iran, Russia and different Shia militias, it is unlikely that these Sunni groups will pose an existential threat to Bashar al-Assad any time soon. Moreover, some of the Sunni jihadists groups from Syria, like Hayat Tahrir al-Sham, may even turn their attention to the Arab world, posing security and political challenges to Saudi Arabia. The battle-hardened Sunni groups in Syria could also spill over to the other parts of the region, further eroding the Saudi position on Iran. Saudi Arabia has potentially amplified this risk of blowback from Syria by dangerously using divisions within the Sunni Arab community as a flashpoint in its relations with Qatar.

Saudi Arabia considers the Muslim Brotherhood a terrorist organization and a real threat to the House of Saud, while Qatar kept its doors open to this nearly century-old Islamist political organization, with deep roots in several Arab countries. By pushing the Muslim Brotherhood out of the Sunni equation, Saudi Arabia along with Egypt and UAE are creating an opening for more extremist organizations like the Islamic State and the sundry clones of al-Qaeda with deep roots in Syria.

Thousands of foreign ISIS fighters and their family members escaped from Syria after the US-backed Syrian Democratic Forces (SDF) intensified military campaigns in eastern Syria. Many fighters fled unfettered to the south and west through the Syrian army lines; some even went into hiding near Damascus and the northwest region. Some others bribed their safe passage to Turkey by using US dollars, with a hope of eventually returning to Europe. The US military advisers are concerned that a Turkish offensive against the Kurdish-dominated SDF in Afrin, northern Syria, is worsening the problem.

Turkey is using Sunni rebels to fight Kurds. Saudi Arabia and Jordan use Sunni rebels to fight the pro-Assad regime forces. The SDF is working with the US forces to defeat, degrade and dismantle ISIS. They had greatly succeeded in defeating it from the upper Euphrates river valley, including the de facto capital Raqqa. More than 40,000 foreign fighters from 120 countries, once part of ISIS with active participation in the fight, are now spread across the region. Thousands died in the battlefield of Syria and Iraq. Surviving jihadis, however, are slipping away to Yemen, Libya or the Philippines, while some others are hiding in Turkey and on the Syria–Iraqi border. To believe that these foreign fighters would quietly leave Syria and return to their old jobs as shopkeepers in Paris, Brussels and Copenhagen, is ludicrous.

The countries involved in the Syrian war are not owning, but renting a war. The pro-Assad group or pro-Iranian Shiite mercenaries are from Iraq, Lebanon, Pakistan and Afghanistan. Russia, which entered the Middle East for the first time as a superpower, make no mistake, is the kingmaker in Syria. The ground fighters are outsourced to the private Russian company, Wagner, to fight and take casualties. The pro-Kurdish fighters, supported by the Americans, are fighting ISIS remnants in northern Syria. Various pro-Saudi and Jordanian Sunni rebel groups make up the anti-Syrian-regime force. The complex Syrian civil war can be described as a 3D battlefield with multiple actors and shifting alliances. Unfortunately, in Syria, no one owns the war and, hence, no one is fixing it.

Jared Kushner, chief architect of the US's deal on Palestine, has pushed Saudi Arabia very close to Israel as a potential partner. This partnership has, however, totally upset Palestine, Jordan and many other Arab nations. Undoubtedly, the real threat to the Sunni Arab countries in the Gulf, and beyond, is the Salafi radical Islamic groups, more than anything else. The vacuum created by the withdrawal of the US from the Middle East is being filled by the Russians, Turkey, Iran and Qatar. Unfortunately, the Saudi's ruling royalty understands it as a good time to be friends with Israel. The recent domestic upheaval in Saudi Arabia, which saw the arrest of many powerful princes, high profile business tycoons and hardline clergymen by Crown Prince MBS has been seen as attempts to crush dissent and consolidate his power base under the false pretext of cracking down on corruption. The fast pace of political and religious changes are compelling Saudi Arabia to align with Israel. Iran is not worried about this 'unholy alliance', on the contrary, Iran has emerged as a soft power in the region attempting to better its image with the larger Arab constituency.

The final status of Jerusalem has been one of the most vexatious questions of the Israeli–Palestinian conflict. President Trump's declaration of Jerusalem as Israel's capital was seen as deciding an issue that was supposed to be left to negotiations. Trump's move would have further destabilized an already volatile region. According to the Turkish president, the US president was plunging the region and the world into fire with no end in sight. Turkey also said that it would cut its diplomatic ties with Israel in case the US shifted its embassy premises in Jerusalem. Crown Prince MBS was also embarrassed by Trump's untimely declaration. Arguably, it will be difficult to rekindle peace efforts in the region as all Arab and non-Arab Muslim countries have strongly condemned the move by the US.

The Palestinians make up 37 per cent of Jerusalem's 850,000 population. Many live in overcrowded homes and neighbourhoods, unable to get permits to build or extend their buildings. The international community considers East Jerusalem as an occupied territory. But, that half of the city also contains sites holy to all the three major monotheistic religions. It includes the Western Wall, the most sacred site in the world for Jews, and the Haram al-Sharif (the noble sanctuary), a sacred site for Muslims. The Palestinian leadership and the world at large agree to make East Jerusalem as the capital of Palestine in the two-nation agreement. The Israelis disagree, and time and again, Netanyahu, the present Israeli prime minister, has said that Israel would not even consider making concessions over Jerusalem.

Saudi Arabia is trying to liberalize its economy and the civil society while fighting extremism and various terror groups, all of whom follow the ultra-conservative Salafi strain of Islam and unabashedly spread it across on the strength of Saudi Arabia's deep pockets. Meanwhile, Iran continues to back the proxy groups Saudi Arabia is trying to liberalize its economy and the civil society, while fighting extremism and various terror groups, all of whom follow the ultra-conservative Salafi strain of Islam and who unabashedly spread it across on the strength of Saudi Arabia's deep pockets. Meanwhile, Iran continues to back the proxy groups supported by Saudi Arabia and the US, fighting the Salafists in various regions of the Middle East.

The Jerusalem decision by the US in a complex way strengthens Iran's leverage in the region. A series of avoidable decisions, like the forced resignation of Saad Hariri, prime minister of Lebanon, declaration of Jerusalem as Israel's capital and the arrest of Palestinian billionaire Sabih al-Masri to pressurize Jordan, backfired and benefited Iran. Turkey, on 13 December 2017, hosted an OIC summit in Istanbul, to denounce Trump's decision. Iran's president, along with the heads of nations from Kuwait, Jordan, Qatar, and many other Muslim nations, attended, while Saudi and its group of countries sent low-level delegation. The foreign minister of Iran, Javad Zarif, after the meeting, tweeted: 'Inspired by a very high level participation at an extraordinary OIC summit. Despite a handful of telling exceptions.'[56]

---

[56]'High Level Participation at OIC Summit on Quds Inspiring: Iran's FM', *Tasnim News Agency*, 13 December 2017, https://tinyurl.com/4enp4utp. Accessed on 30 August 2023.

For decades now, Riyadh has been keeping a low profile and engaging in spreading the Wahhabi strain of Salafi Islam across the world by constructing mosques and Islamic centres using its high oil wealth. These centres and mosques were loaded with Salafi jihadi literature meant to hijack and transform the worldview of Islam along Wahhabi lines. After all this, the Saudi military and intelligence machine is now pursuing a brutal war in Yemen with indiscriminate bombing of its cities and, in the process, causing untold mayhem and misery to millions of its people, including women and children. Its economic and air blockade against the tiny emirate of Qatar led to pushing it into the arms of Iran and Turkey. After many such failed foreign policy misadventures, the kingdom under a naive Crown Prince is now licking its wounds. The sloppy handling of the regional issues has embarrassed all its friends, who had cautioned the crown prince from any future misadventures in the region. The common denominator is the Saudi's competition with Iran for the coveted position of the regional hegemon.

The Yemen war was the Crown Prince's signature policy initiative. Failing in Yemen is fundamentally a black mark on his credibility. Apparently, he was the one to double down on the sea blockade, air attacks and trying to enlist the Houthis against the Kingdom. The Saudis on social media are sensitive to the charge that they are using starvation and disease as weapons to defeat the Yemenis. The White House and the US state department are, for the first time, ignoring the worst humanitarian crisis in the region and looking the other way to the blockade. Top US commanders familiar with the crisis say that Iran has accomplished more in Yemen in the last five years, than it did in building up Hezbollah in Lebanon in 20 years. When war began in Yemen, Iran had only limited connections with the Houthis, and now it is a robust relationship. Iran is smartly navigating the conflict and financially punishing Saudi Arabia by making it spend billions of US dollars per month as compared to Iran's expenditure in the country, which is pittance. Iran is helping Houthis in missile capabilities. They have fired more than a hundred missiles on Saudi cities and bases, including at Riyadh airport. Russia always vetoes any resolution which the US brings in to condemn Iran for providing missile technology and expertise to Yemeni rebels.

Iran's influence has gone up from almost zero in the 1990s to an exceptional level in the entire Middle East today. The Shia Houthi rebels, who had staged a coup in Yemen in 2014, later deepened their control over the country slowly. That was mainly a local development, but Riyadh reacted to it through aerial bombings, without putting its boots on the ground. Houthis are backed by Hezbollah fighters from Lebanon, which is backed by Iran and is now bleeding Saudi Arabia. Assad's Alawite regime with support from Hezbollah, Iran and Russia had won the Syrian civil war, where the jihadist Sunni groups, supported by Saudi Arabia were defeated comprehensively. The Saudi influence in Iraq evaporated after most of the Sunni majority provinces joined ISIS caliphate in 2014, which was later recaptured by the Shia government of Iraq and Shia militias supported by Iran.

Saudi Arabia's struggle against Iran has everything to do with the Sunni-Shia binary and nothing with economics. Both are oil-rich states, both are members of the OPEC and also members of the same cartel. Iran is an avowedly Shiite state while Saudi Arabia is ruled by a hard-line Sunni Wahhabi government, and the conflict is primarily over religion.

The biggest danger in the Middle East is that Crown Prince MBS and Jared Kushner appear to have a skewed and unrealistic understanding of the world around them. Antics like that of the forced resignation of the Lebanon prime minister are not going to frighten the Iranians or Hezbollah. Iran has decided to avoid any confrontation with the US. In Iraq, it will support the re-election of Abadi as prime minister, which the US also wants. Iran knows well that it has come on the winning side in Iraq and Syria and it underplays its success in the region. The Islamic republic has also realized that the crown prince was using strident anti-Iranian rhetoric only to secure and stabilize his power base in the kingdom and does not want any confrontation with it. Nobody gains much from another war in the Middle East, but wars are usually started by those who miscalculate their own strengths. Both Saudi Arabia with Crown Prince MBS and the US under President Trump have acted like 'wild cards' in the regional pack.

The Middle East today is a dangerously pressurized regional system, with few safety valves for conflict resolution. Qatar with Iran and Turkey could be seen as a new robust safety valve to counter Saudi Arabia's hegemony. Qatar, by building bridges with Muslim Brotherhood and Shia Iran, has created new pathways for dialogue and conflict resolution, both inside and outside the Arab world. If Qatar continues to be isolated by Saudi Arabia and kept out of GCC long enough, Doha will become more dependent on Turkey and Iran and would be a net loss to Riyadh. If Saudi Arabia continues to deviate from its traditional path at the behest of President Trump's unreliable partnership, it is likely to weaken its own regional position and strengthen Iran. Like it or not, the Middle East has moved from being a Saudi-centric region to an Iranian-, Turkish-, Russian- and Qatar-centric region.

The US cannot effectively confront Tehran and its proxies until it understands and appreciates Iran's role in state-building in the Middle East that is decimated by conflicts. During the last five years, there has been an exponential increase in Iran's influence in the region. The Iraqi Shia militias, battle-hardened by fighting the US forces, began fighting in Syria alongside the Assad forces in 2012. Hezbollah captured the strategic Syrian town of Qusair from the opposition fighters in 2013. Shiite militias were pivotal in capturing Aleppo in December 2016, which arguably secured the survival of the Assad regime. Over the last two years, relentless bombing of Homs and Ghouta areas led to a humanitarian crisis, with the surviving population being forced to migrate along with rebels.

The Iranian proxies do not just turn up for battle, fight the battle and return home. Hezbollah's 'state within state' model in Lebanon was once the exception, but now it is a model being replicated by other militia groups with devastating impact. Iran has trained all these groups to exploit the disorder and fill the vacuum by providing services and security to often desperate communities in a conflict zone.

One of the important branches of the IRGC, Quds Force, under the leadership of the late General Qassim Suleimani was responsible for all the Iranian operations outside the Irani border. He is considered Iran's one of the most respected, cunning and autonomous figures, directly reporting to the Supreme Leader Ayatollah Khomeini. He was arming and guiding Iran's proxies in Yemen, Iraq, Syria and Lebanon and helping them to co-opt or take over the local humanitarian organization and charities as a measure for acquiring legitimacy and popularity. Iran is ensuring that aid is distributed through these proxies. His accomplishment shaped the creation of a Shiite axis of influence in all the major Arab countries of the Middle East.

The proxy war calculus may be changing after the assassination of General Suleimani by a US drone attack on 2 January 2020, along with Abu Mahdi al-Muhandis, commander of Al-Hashd al-Shaabi. Iran retaliated by firing dozens of ballistic missiles at the Ain al-Asad Airbase and Anbar in Iraq and the military facility in Erbil.

In the meanwhile, the anti-Iran sentiment is gaining traction in Iraq and recently, many observers have noticed that the Iraqi middle class is upset by the Iranian interference in the local governance and they squarely blame Iran for its economic hardships. Iraqis also resent cultural influence of the Iranian religious figures, which is especially pervasive in cities with a majority Shia population. The burning of the Iranian consulate in the holy city of Najaf is significant because it is the home of Shia religious authorities, headed by the Grand Ayatollah Ali al-Sistani. The consulate destruction is a sign that many Shia Iraqis have abandoned their sense of religious solidarity with Iran as a Shia state. The unrest is restricted mainly to the Shia heartlands and not seen in Sunni or Kurdish areas. The Iraqi Shias are reverting back to their Arab nationalism and Saudi Arabia is also trying to moderate its Wahhabi–Salafi brand of rigid Islam. These developments are important for the US to reset their Middle East policies post-COVID-19.

Beijing Accord

The Americans have been important players in the Middle East since 1938 when oil companies discovered the first oil well. The emergence of Saudi Arabia's Crown Prince MBS led to a cooling off in their relationship with the US President Biden in office. Biden's 'pragmatic realism' was to lead to a steady downsizing of US's military role in the Middle East.[57] China, the second largest economy and a rising regional Asian power, steadily increased its footprints in the Middle Eastern capitals.

Under the leadership of Crown Prince MBS, Saudi Arabia's foreign policy pivoted to China, which led Chinese mediation for normalizing relations between Iran and Saudi Arabia. The immediate consequence of the Beijing Accord is ending the proxy war in Yemen, where Houthi rebels, aligned with Iran, battled Saudi forces for eight years. The United Nations estimated that more than 377,000 people may have died from violence, starvation and disease during the war.

The Saudi–Iran deal brokered by China has elevated its global status and evidently dashed Israel's hopes to build anti-Iranian coalition with Saudi Arabia.[58] On the flipside China, unlike the US, comes with a cleaner record and has warm ties with both—it is a leading buyer of Saudi oil and the largest trading partner of Iran. This has allowed China to use its economic leverage to bring both countries together.

---

[57] Ahmed, Talmiz, 'Will West Asia Become Ground-Zero for Ending Euro-Atlantic Dominance', *India Narrative*, 10 June 2023, https://tinyurl.com/2aatyn6s. Accessed on 28 September 2023.

[58] Baker, Peter, 'Chinese-Brokered Deal Upends Mideast Diplomacy and Challenge US', *The New York Times*, 11 March, 2023, https://tinyurl.com/vnmveesc. Accessed on 28 September 2023.

5

RADICALIZATION OF MUSLIM YOUTH IN EUROPE AND AMERICA

Social and political reform movements in many Muslim countries encouraged their governments to permit students' travel to European countries for higher education from the early nineteenth century. Muslim students were constantly present in the metropolises of Europe, especially the UK after the end of the Second World War and the decolonization of many Asian and African countries. The partition of Indian subcontinent in 1947 on the basis of religious identity displaced millions of Muslims and Hindus from their homeland. The initial migrants to the UK were those uprooted from both the communities. At that time, England was rebuilding after the devastation of the war with Nazi Germany. While England needed a large labour force, the poverty in these people's home countries was forcing them into migration. They were barely educated and only very few even knew the English language properly. Similarly, there was a large scale migration of Turks to a Germany that was divided into West and East, as large cities like Frankfurt had been flattened by the intense bombing of the Allied forces. To rebuild the cities and highways, it needed a large number of skilled workforces. French colonies of North and Central Africa saw a steady migration of labour and semi-skilled work force to the major cities of France. The pattern of migration was similar in Belgium, Italy and Netherlands.

The liberal democracies of northern Europe, like Denmark, Sweden and Norway, with their economic opportunities, allowed a large number of Muslims as legal migrants. Language played a critical role in how migrants moved across the European nations. The

English-knowing migrants from the former British colonies in Asia and Africa moved to the UK, while French-speaking migrants from North and Central Africa, moved to France and Belgium. Migrants, who spoke Dutch, from Suriname and Indonesia, moved to Holland and Belgium. The South Asians and French-speaking migrants from the north, preferred to stay with their own communities in the new lands, reproducing their social structures and culture, based on their ethnicity and the place of origin.

Muslim Migration to Spain

The Muslim migration to Spain began as early as 710, when the first Arabs and the North African Berbers conquered the Iberian Peninsula, before the arrival of Abd al-Rahman I in Spain in 755. Abd al-Rahman was a member of the Umayyad ruling family of Syria who founded the Umayyad dynasty in Spain. They focussed on southern Spain (Andalusia) and built a civilization.[59] Here they treated Christians and Jews with utmost tolerance, as a result of which many embraced Islam. They patronized arts, music, culture, and made an important contribution to the progress of science and medicine, establishing one of largest and most progressive cities in Medieval Europe—Cordoba. By the tenth century, Cordoba could boast of a population of 500,000. According to the chronicles of the day, the city had 700 mosques, some 60,000 palaces and 70 libraries—one reportedly housing 500,000 manuscripts and employing staff of researchers, bookbinders and library supervisors. Europe's first street lights were installed in the city of Cordoba for five miles connecting Madinat al-Zahra, the residence of the caliph. It was constructed by using ivory, onyx, marble and stucco, and it took about 40 years to build. Unfortunately, it was destroyed in the eleventh century. Its restoration began in the early years of this century and is still underway.

---

[59]Speers, Peter C., 'Islam in Spain', *IslamiCity*, 10 October 2020, https://tinyurl.com/4yht25hp. Accessed on 7 September 2023.

By the eleventh and twelfth centuries, Christian re-conquest began. The Arabs did not surrender easily. Their internal bickering further accentuated the slow retreat to the south. Nonetheless, the work of the Alhambra palace began in 1238 by Muhammad ibn al-Ahmar, who sought safety when King Ferdinand of Aragon laid siege on Granada. After compromising, he returned to Granada and wrote on the wall of the Alhambra: 'There is no victor but God.' The Christian kings had surrounded Granada by re-taking Toledo, Cordoba and Seville. Only Granada survived.

In 1482, internal quarrels in the Muslim kingdom spilt hostile factions and the unity among the surrounding Christian sovereigns forced Granada to fall after ten years. In 1492, the victor King Ferdinand and Queen Isabella hoisted the banner of the Christian Spanish Empire over Alhambra, and sent Christopher Columbus to America. Muslim cultures that fell under Spanish expansions gradually got marginalized in the development of Christian Spain.

The recent wave of immigration, following the civil war in the Middle East, has brought many Muslims to Spain; the Islamic Spanish population has almost doubled from about a million in 2007 to more than two million in 2017. The Spanish Left is now supporting the conversion of the church back into a place for holding interfaith meetings. At one level, it has also become fashionable for the Leftists to romanticize the Islamic past of Spain in the wake of the new developments. Whereas, there is also a great resentment among the majority of Christians in Spain that the Islamists would soon bring Allah back to the Cathedral of Cordoba, and the tsunami of Islamic supremacy would submerge the country's decaying Christianity. There are thousands of churches left in the lurch after being deserted by the believers in different parts of the country.

Muslims in Britain

During the reign of Queen Victoria, the first mosque of England was built at Woking, Surrey, about 30 miles from London. Gottlieb

Wilhelm Leitner was an orientalist, born of Jewish parents in Hungary. After working as an interpreter for the British army during the Crimean War, Dr Leitner travelled to England at the age of 17 to study at King's College. His passion for Islamic and Hindu culture meant that, aged just 21, he became professor of Arabic with Mohammedan law at King's. He, an expert on Kashmir, had lived several years in India and became principal of Government College, Lahore. It was in 1883 that he acquired the site, an extensive area in Woking, for the Royal Dramatic College, and started the Oriental Institute there. He also built a mosque there in 1889 with financial support from the Begum of Bhopal and named it after the Mughal emperor Shah Jahan. It became the first mosque in Europe outside Moorish Spain, as well as the first mosque to be built in Britain. The Woking mosque was popular among Mohammedans as it was there they gathered to offer Eid prayers and also to meet Munshi Abdul Karim, who was a close confidant, secretary and teacher of Urdu to the reigning Queen Victoria of the British Empire.[60] The *Birmingham Daily Post* in an article in May 1891 wrote that Munshi Abdul Karim, who was a *hafiz* (one who has memorized the entire the Quran) had also been invited to lead the Eid prayers at the mosque in those days.

After a gap of 84 years, the second mosque in Britain was constructed in 1973 at Regent Park in the heart of London city.[61] It was in 1940 when the British government was persuaded to donate a site in London for the Muslim community to build a mosque. It was, in fact, Churchill's war cabinet, which authorized the acquisition of a site for building the mosque in London on 24 October 1940. A prime location of 2.3 acres was presented by the British Government

---

[60]Basu, Shrabani, *Victoria and Abdul: The True Story of the Queen's Closet Confident*, Bloomsbury, London, 2010.

[61]'History of the London Central Mosque & The Islamic Cultural Centre', *London Central Mosque Trust & The Islamic Cultural Centre*, https://tinyurl.com/mr47c3nn. Accessed on 28 September 2023.

as an unconditional gift to the Muslim community so that they could conduct their affairs according to their faith. Al-Azhar University in Cairo, Egypt, had delegated an imam to the newly built mosque in central London and it continued to do so for many decades. The funding originally was provided by King Faisal of Saudi Arabia. Later, the practice of imams coming from the Al-Azhar University was discontinued and slowly the Sufi Sunni imams were replaced by the Hanbali, Wahhabi–Salafi imams. The Board of Trustees of the Regent Mosque Centre comprised the Muslim Ambassadors and High Commissioners accredited in London. Nonetheless, during the recent years, the Centre receives its entire financial and academic support from the Muslim World League of Saudi Arabia.

Along with the overall increase of immigrants in Europe, Muslim population has grown manifold during the 1970s and 1980s. They brought their families and got permanent citizenship there. The Saudi Arabian religious leadership saw an opportunity to construct more mosques and Islamic centres and aggressively pushed the Saudi version of Wahhabi–Salafi Islam, with liberal grants to the Muslim community leadership. It is estimated that Saudi establishment has spent about US$2–3 billion on the construction of mosques, Islamic centres and the ideological education of preachers in Saudi universities. Presently there are 2,700 Sunni mosques across Britain, out of which, 425 are built after demolishing Christian churches or on the ruins of English Christianity.

All the major British cities have a good percentage of Muslim population—Manchester has 15.8 per cent, Birmingham has 21.8 per cent and Bradford has 24.7 per cent. During the last four decades, through the concerted efforts of the English-speaking Arab preachers, flushed by Saudi dollars, they have been espousing the virtues of Wahhabism and the ways of the Salafi brand of Islam. The weekly sermons (*khutba*) before the Friday prayers and the kind of teachings given through the study centres, have totally transformed them. These propaganda factories also produce Wahhabi–Salafi ideologues to populate the universities and colleges of Britain.

The famous British University Union Hall is converted into a mosque every Friday and the *muezzin*'s call for prayers (*azan*) reverberates through the high-domed Victorian Halls. The khutba is usually delivered by young students (who will have attended the summer schools in a Saudi university) where they talk about the atrocities committed by the West on the Muslim nations globally. Compelling and passionate arguments are also made to motivate youths to sign as volunteers for jihad. Fiery speeches would take place calling for jihad in Chechnya, Kashmir and Afghanistan. The Islamic University of Medinah reserves about 85 per cent seats for foreign students besides conducting summer schools for visiting students from Europe and North America.

It was those Muslim youths, educated from the elite British schools and universities, who would later transform themselves into suicide bombers and ISIS volunteers wreaking havoc in the Middle Eastern countries. It is this Wahhabi Salafism, which is being presented as the true form of Islam in most parts of the world. The al-Qaeda, ISIS, Boko Haram, al Shabaab, Afghan Taliban, Tehrik-e-Taliban of Pakistan and all other terrorist groups subscribe to this hostile and intolerant reading of Islam. Along with the mosques, about 100 Sharia courts also operate in Britain. They are very secretive and settle financial and family disputes as per the Islamic Sharia law. They deliver judgments which can be given full legal status if approved in the national law courts. Mostly, they are unfair to women and backed by intimidations. The courts mainly operate in cities like London, Manchester, Bradford, Birmingham and Nuneaton, and are run by the Muslim Arbitration Tribunal (MAT), a body whose rulings are enforced through the state courts under the 1996 Arbitration Act.

The bottom line is that the radicalization of the British Muslims[62] among its second and third generations is total, and the elephant in

---

[62] Al-Alawi, Irfan, 'Radicalization of Young British Muslims', *Gatestone Institute: International Policy Council*, 13 February 2012, https://tinyurl.com/4phrct2c. Accessed on 28 September 2023.

the room, without doubt, is Wahhabism and Salafism, romanticized and articulated smartly by the Saudi preachers over the years. They have grown up with a twisted version of Islam that has given them a negative view of other faiths and an intolerant sectarian understanding of their own.

The ISIS executioner known to the world as 'Jihadi John' has been identified as Mohammed Emwazi, born in Kuwait, but raised in London. Emwazi is one of the thousands of British nationals who have travelled to Syria and Iraq to train and fight for ISIS. The 27-year-old Emwazi, belonged to a well-to-do family in West London. He graduated from the University of Westminster with a degree in computer programming. The world came to know about him in 2014, through the YouTube video of the execution of the American photojournalist James Foley, in which Emwazi speaks to the camera in a British accent. He continued to make videos threatening the US and documenting the murders of other hostages, including many Westerners. The issue is not how many of them travelled to Syria or Iraq to join ISIS and returned back to Britain; the overarching concern is of the ideology that has conquered the young generation of British Muslims.

British Muslims are a tapestry of various strands of the global Muslim community with a current population of 1.6 to 1.8 million, of which around two-third are of South Asian backgrounds. Over 50 per cent are born in the UK and about the same per cent is under the age of 30. Salafi teachings are widespread in all the Sunni mosques across Britain, but only some openly identify themselves as a Salafi. The most important among the Salafi mosques are the Green Lane mosque and the Salafi Institute in Birmingham, Masjid ibn-Taymiyyah in Brixton, London and the Islamic Centre in Luton.

The main organization responsible for spreading Salafism in Great Britain is the Society for the Revival of the Prophetic Way or Jamiyyah Ihyaa' Minhaaj al Sunnah (JIMAS)[63], under the leadership

---

[63] Hamid, Sadek, 'Salafism in the UK: The Reasons for its Success', *Fondazione Oasis*, 27 March 2019, https://tinyurl.com/239wftt4. Accessed on 7 Spetember 2023.

of Manwar Ali, alias Abu Muntasir. Considered to be the father of Salafi dawah (preaching) in the country, he is largely responsible for the spread of Salafism among Muslim youth through his speeches at the Islamic study circles at mosques, community centres and universities across the UK. The young Abu Muntasir during his teenage years had gone through all the common tensions experienced by the second generation British Muslim youths seeking to reconcile their religious upbringing at home with the influence of a liberal non-Muslim British society. Having decided to dedicate himself to a committed religious identity, he sought to learn Islam through English-language books. He saw a huge contradiction between the liberal Islam and Islam taught in the mosques through the texts prepared by Saudi Wahhabi ideology. He later visited Saudi Arabia to study in the Islamic University of Medinah, which is the hot hub of Salafi ideology.

Salafism as a religious paradigm has evolved over a period and it needs to be understood contextually in relation to its theological claims and historical developments. It is a religious stream within the Hanbali Sunni Islam, which is based on the pure, undiluted teachings of the Quran, the Sunnah and the practices of the Salaf, the early generations of Muslims. As the religious paradigm became established in Britain by the mid-90s through a network of mosques, publication, media and a large body of literature available on the Internet, the Salafi trend attracted mainly the second generation of South Asian Muslim youths, with a large number of Black and White converts. Its followers were, on an average, between the age of 18 and 30, geographically located close to the Salafi mosques.

Under the leadership of Abu Muntasir, Salafism transformed into a religious cult by reviving the 'pure' Islamic practices and forms of a protest religion. JIMAS members became conspicuous for wearing military jackets, trousers and boots. They started prefixing their names with 'Abu', meaning 'father of', or 'Umm', meaning 'mother of'. Salafi Muslims were characterized by an exclusivist and intolerant attitude, giving out the impression that they belonged to the 'saved sect'. Uncompromising and harsh critiques of other sectarian trends also helped to polarize Salafis against other Muslims. This produced tensions, fallouts between friends, family members and Islamic organizations. Factions based on Muslim ethnicities and the factions within the JIMAS eventually caused the organization to split, which is how it remains to this day.

The members of JIMAS got split in three identifiable factions: 'purists,' 'politicos' and 'jihadists'. Among them, the purists were loyal to the principles of Salafism and the Saudi state, and resisted any attempt to challenge the rulers. They were close to Wahhabism and believed in peacefully preaching the need for reforming the beliefs and rituals of other sects. While politicos agreed with the Salafi purists on most things, they argued that the Salafi leadership should also take into consideration the changing socio-political realities of the world. The jihadis, on the other hand, are impatient with the status quo. Many of them have participated in the war in Afghanistan and Chechnya and have wanted to take direct action to effect a change. All the three share Salafi positions in matters of theology and differ in their analysis and approach of solving the problems in the Muslim world. Britain experienced as many as five terrorist attacks in 2017 at different locations. This indicated clearly that the jihadi faction had become dominant among the youths.

Influential modern Sufi scholars such as Muhammad Hisham Kabbani have attempted to respond to Salafi polemics against Sufism, by taking doctrinal objections head-on and using the same primary textual sources to defend their interpretations of theology and ritual practices. Kabbani's seven-volume *Encyclopedia of Islamic Doctrine* was among the major publications produced to offer a scholarly rebuttal to the Salafis' anti-Sufi literature.

The attraction of Salafism among the young Muslims in Britain may be mainly because of five reasons. First, globalization of the well-funded Saudi Salafi discourse through the mosques and the massive online and offline availability of Salafi literature, besides the influx of graduates and preachers from the Islamic University of Saudi Arabia.

Second, the British-born Muslims' search for religious identity and their urge to restore their religious confidence. Third, the appeal of Salafism both as a result of external influences and competition with other Islamic sects and the intra-Salafi debates arising out of fragmentation. Fourth, the counter-response of traditional Islamic perspectives, which persuaded Salafis to be more reflective and accommodating. Fifth, attempts to moderate its ways following the 9/11 and other terrorist attacks.

Despite the evolution of Salafism and its appeal for the British youth, there is also a visible traction for 'traditional Islam' promulgated by charismatic American scholars like Hamza Yusuf. He argues strongly by invoking his deep knowledge of Islam and the relevance of music, literature and science. Moderate Salafis praise his logic in private but publicly dismiss him as Sufi. Hamza Yusuf's message was echoed by other prominent English scholars like Abdal Hakim Murad, a Cambridge professor of Islamic Studies, and the American Islamic scholar Shaykh Nuh Keller, who is based in Jordan. Many prominent scholars in the UK also describe themselves as 'hybrids' (Wahhabi–Sufi). By all account, the influence of Salafism on the British Muslim communities has been far and deep for various reasons including the easy availability of its literature and the presence of its preachers in mosques across the country.

France and Islam

Napoleon Bonaparte occupied Egypt between 1798 and 1801. The occupation was short-lived, but helped in developing a systematic inventory of the country's historic monuments. The French army colonized Algeria between 1830 and 1857; this was France's first African colony, as well as the largest one nearest to France. Tunisia was made a French protectorate in 1881, while the French West Africa was colonized between 1880 and 1912, the year in which Morocco was also made a protectorate. During the First World War, France was an ally of Russia and Britain in the conflict with the Ottoman

Empire and Germany. In 1920, the League of Nations gave France a mandate to rule Syria and Lebanon. However, Lebanon got its independence in 1941, and Syria in 1946. Tunisia and Morocco were freed in 1956, while Mali and Senegal got freedom in 1960, and Algeria in 1962. Early in the nineteenth century, a few of Napoleon's Muslim soldiers settled in the Rhone valley in France; towards the end of that century, there were about 800 Muslims living in Paris, most of them students. The influx of Algerian workers began in 1900, which was followed by Moroccans a few years later.[64]

In 1914, on the eve of the First World War, there were about 30,000 North Africans in France and the war led to a massive increase in their number; 132,000, mostly Algerians, who were recruited to work on French farms and factories, while a further 175,000 served in the army. Some 25,000 died in action during the war. After the war, the majority of the survivors returned home and as a result, only 100,000 were left in France in 1919. The economic depression of the 1930s led many to return to their home country. After the Second World War, immigration of skilled and unskilled workforce was encouraged in order to meet the needs of reconstruction and industrial expansion. Before 1962, the majority of them were Algerian workers, but after the Algerian independence, the French government encouraged immigration from other former colonies of France.

There is no religion-based census in France, but those who were born outside, are estimated to be around 1,700,000. Muslims are concentrated around the industrial towns. The highest number lives in Paris and its suburbs. Unlike in Britain, where Muslims developed their own ghettos in the inner cities, in France, they settled in the suburbs of small towns. Between the two wars, the French Muslims were relatively lax in their religious observations. The employers

---

[64]Chtatou, Mohamed, 'An Overview of French Colonialism In The Maghreb – Analysis', *Eurasia Review*, 5 March 2019, https://tinyurl.com/3wafvjk3. Accessed on 7 September 2023.

usually provided them with temporary wooden structures for Friday prayers. Construction of the famous Paris Mosque began in 1922 and was completed in 1926. It was ostensibly built in recognition of services rendered by the Muslims who lost their lives in defending France.

Once, France used to be a great Muslim colonial power; the ruling class, as a result, wanted to build a grand mosque in Paris to celebrate their rule over the Muslim countries in West and North Africa. France separates state and religion. However, the state made a substantial contribution towards the building costs of the mosque. The problem was circumvented by routing the funds through a charitable organization in Algiers. It was done on an understanding that the funds would be used for a 'Muslim Institute' that would comprise Turkish baths, a shopping area, a library, as well as a mosque. The Sultan of Morocco inaugurated the mosque, and the Persian carpet to be used in it was presented by Mohammad Reza Pahlavi of Iran.

The Muslim population of France is 5,760,000, which is 8.8 per cent of the total population of the country. Presently, France has about 2,200 mosques and the French Muslim council leadership wants them to double it in the next five years. The Muslim World League of Saudi Arabia has pumped millions of euros into the construction of mosques and as salaries of imams during the 1980s and 90s. The transnational Islamic movements like Tablighi Jamaat, Salafists and the Muslim Brotherhood operated aggressively in some of the poorest neighbourhoods of France after 1979. Nonetheless, during the second phase, i.e. 1990–2000, the state tried to control French Islam through a representative council.

In the French Sunni Islam, there is no clerical hierarchy like the Catholic Church, which can act as an interlocutor with the state. For the Ministry of the Interior, it was difficult to build Islam in France after long acceding managerial powers, including that of the Grand Mosque of Paris, to Algeria. In the 2000s, France struggled to contain the growing influence of Muslim Brotherhood, which operated freely through the Union of Islamic Organisations of France.

The transformation of French Muslim communities over the last 60 years has been amazing. Now, their identity is based exclusively on Islam and they reject all values of the French society as anti-Islamic. Salafism is the dominant discourse in the majority of the mosques, particularly in the suburban communities. Mostly, youths from traditional families are attracted to its fold. The purists and the jihadi factions of Salafism are mainly localized in the inner city mosques and in the suburbs of large cities. Living separately and having practically no social or cultural interaction with the mainstream French societies, the second and third generations of French Muslims have become convinced that they no longer belong to the national mainstream community.

To understand and analyse French Islam one has to regard it as a market. According to the classical economic theory, supply and demand finds a balance in the market. This applies to religion as well, when it is regarded as a product. The Muslims' search for the real Islam constitutes a market. By selling goods to the potential consumers of this product, firms try to improve their market share and hope to make a profit. By claiming to supply products that represent the true Islam, these firms compete with one another and try to undermine their competitors' market share. For this purpose, they develop sales strategies, expand their communication abilities, launch advertising campaigns and claim that they alone are capable of fulfilling their consumers' needs.

The competition is ardent in the French Islamic market due to a high number of Muslim organizations. The volatility in the market is directly linked to the volatility in the global Islamic market. Thus, in economic terms, re-Islamization is an interactive process, since each stage in re-Islamization in the global or the national field can only be successful if there is a balance in the supply of product and the demand for it.

One of the reasons why Salafism has become the main form of re-Islamization among the young French Muslims, as well as the young French Muslim converts, is that it is directly imported from the 'holy land' of Saudi Arabia, where Islam is supposed to be practised in its pure form, which in reality, is only a myth.

The Muslim World League of Saudi Arabia trained many French-speaking Moroccan imams in Saudi Islamic universities with the Wahhabi and Salafi ideology. These imams did their job exceedingly well. They also radicalized the second and third generations of French Muslim youths. The Paris bombing, Brussels airport bombing and the attacks on visitors and holidaymakers in other cities, speak volumes about the level to which these Muslim youths have been radicalized.

The deep penetration of Salafi ideology in France can be gauged by the story of Emilie Konig, daughter of a policeman from a small town of Brittany, where she converted to Islam as a teenager. Once she started using the Salafi dress code, covering herself from head to toe in black *abaya* and veil, she began to be scorned at by the general public in France, and eventually, she left for Syria where she joined the Islamic State as a propagandist and a recruiter. She surrendered after the fall of Raqqa and is presently kept in a prison jointly administered by the US and the Syrian Kurdish Forces.

In 2012, a French journalist made a documentary titled *Emilie Konig vs Ummu Tawwab*. It was shot before she had left for Syria. She used to be entirely veiled except for a slit for her eyes. In her interview she recalls her journey and the virtues of Wahhabism and Salafism. Once in Syria, she worked in the recruitment division of ISIS and posted many propaganda videos on social media. In one of those videos, she was seen target-practicing and making a full-throated appeal to support the Islamic State and join the force as volunteers to strengthen its caliphate.

The French law enforcement department has estimated that about 690 French jihadis are still in Syria of which 43 per cent are women. They have been picked up after the fall of Raqqa, to be returned to their home countries including France, Britain, Russia, Kazakhstan and Indonesia.

The reforms proposed by the French President Macron have to be implemented in a transparent and realistic manner and they cannot be done without fully engaging the French Muslim community.⁶⁵ The French-speaking Morocco has initiated reforms by purging the Wahhabi–Salafi brand of Islam and restoring the Hanafi Sufi Sunni traditions that preach tolerance and respect for other faiths. During the colonial times, the Moroccan and Islamic culture used to coexist with the French culture. The French even encouraged elements of these cultures, mentoring Sufi traditions, such as trance music and the celebration of saints.

The good news is that since 2004, Morocco has been developing a training strategy for imams to establish its moderate ideology in French mosques via the Ministry of Religious Endowments and Islamic Affairs. Morocco has also made a commitment to the French Ministry of the Interior to provide them with training courses. The Moroccan government efforts may be scaled up to counter the Salafi and Wahhabi narrative of Islam among the French Muslims so as to restore the tolerant traditions of Islam.⁶⁶

Islam in US and Canada

When the first West African slaves were shipped to the New World, beginning in 1501, Islam was already well established in West Africa. For 350 years, Muslim men, women and children arrived as slaves and introduced the new monotheistic religion to post-Columbian America. Islam did not quite survive among the slaves in America, except in some rudimentary forms, which is linked to the origin of African Islam. After the official end of slavery, African Americans were only permitted to practice Christianity and it would remain a

---

⁶⁵Aloune, Rim-Sarah, 'Islam, made in France? Debating the reform of Muslim organizations and foreign funding for religion', *Brookings*, 1 May 2019, https://tinyurl.com/yasnsf8c. Accessed on 7 September 2023.
⁶⁶Fakir, Intissar, 'The Moroccan Monarchy's Political Agenda for Reviving Sufi Orders - Islamic Institutions in Arab States: Mapping the Dynamics of Control, Co-Option, and Contention,' *Carnegie Endowment for International Peace*, 7 June 2021, https://tinyurl.com/3xbany6f. Accessed on 27 September 2023.

singular religious choice for them.

Islam came to the US as a viable and sustainable religious alternative only when it was adopted by the African American communities, through the religious movement called Nation of Islam (NOI), which offered a multiple identity reformulation to African–American Islam. Nonetheless, a major shift came through the immigrant communities in the early twentieth century, when the Ahmadiyya movement got traction in the northeastern cities of the US. It too was mainly addressed to African Americans. Although they did not become Ahmadis, they used this introduction to Islam as an opening to study and practice the orthodox Sunni Islam and eventually set up their own communities in the 1950s and 70s.

A change in the US immigration laws in the 1960s, however, opened the doors for a large number of immigrants who would come with a greater emphasis on sustaining their religious, cultural and ethnic identity including Islam. More Arabic-speaking immigrants followed and a large number of South Asian immigrants also began to arrive. The phenomenal increase in South Asian Muslims eventually led to the immigrants making a stronger effort to form a distinctive American Muslim identity. They came to enhance their professional career with American degrees and to pursue material progress for themselves and their children. Islam was an integral part of their cultural identity and it was not in conflict with their material aspirations. However, very few white Americans converted to Islam until the spread of Sufi Islam in the 70s and 80s.

The Muslim Students Association (MSA) was started in 1963 on the campus of the University of Illinois at Urbana-Champaign (UIUC) by international students.[67] Its initial leadership came from Arab students attached to the Muslim Brotherhood. Among the founders of the MSA in America was Hisham al-Talib, a man who

---

[67] Holton, Christopher, 'The Muslim Brotherhood's Muslim Students' Association: What Americans Need to Know', *Center for Security Policy*, 29 April 2018, https:// tinyurl.com/52uy4mdb. Accessed on 7 September 2023.

later was under FBI investigation for providing funding to al-Qaeda. Another important founder was Jamal Barzingi, who later founded the Dar al-Hijrah mosque in Falls Church, Virginia. It was in this mosque that Islamic terrorists like Anwar al-Awlaki and Nidal Malik Hasan with alleged involvement in the 9/11 attacks were groomed at one time.

According to a *New York Times* report[68], in 2008, right from its inception, the MSA was receiving funds and directions from the Wahhabi-run Muslim World League, the Saudi NGO with a history of ties with jihadist terrorism. The MSA unit of the University of Southern California had invited Taliban diplomat Sayyid Hashmi to speak on its campus just six months before the 9/11 attacks. Khalid Sheikh Mohammad, the 9/11 mastermind, was also a member of the MSA chapter at the North Carolina A&T State University in 1986.

Later, MSA was formed on a number of campuses across the USA and Canada. As an umbrella organization, MSA worked with Muslim students in the universities as well as the Muslim communities in the country. About 80 per cent of the American mosques attached with Sunday schools and community centres are under the Wahhabi–Salafi control. And one of the key Wahhabi ideological agencies in America is called the Council on American–Islamic Relations (CAIR). It has been claimed that about 70 per cent of the American Sunni Muslims wanted Wahhabi teaching in their mosques. Wahhabi control over the mosques implies control of property, buildings, appointments of imams, training of imams and content of the preaching. The literature available in the mosques is distributed from Saudi Arabia.

The Islamic Society of North America (ISNA) is the largest body of Muslims which holds annual conventions at different major cities across the US and Canada. The average attendance in ISNA's

---

[68]MacFarquhar, Neil, 'For Muslim students, a Debate on Inclusion', *The New York Times*, 21 February 2008, https://tinyurl.com/22rhfajf. Accessed on 28 September 2023.

annual convention is more than 50,000 from both Canada and the US. They discuss an entire gamut of Islamic issues and encourage interfaith dialogues, but never discuss how to counter the Wahhabi-led Islamic terrorism and its weaponization. Both ISNA and CAIR maintain a close relationship with the Saudi government. There are more than 1,200 mosques in the US under the Wahhabi control and they receive millions of US dollars in grants from the Saudi government agencies such as Muslim World League and the World Assembly of Muslim Youth. And at one time, they were also the main funders of al-Qaeda.

Make no mistake, a large number of the third generation Muslims in the US, irrespective of their ethnicities, attend the Wahhabi–Salafi mosques and they have become rigidly conservative, keeping their world view within a narrow ideological bandwidth. Subsequent to the 9/11 attacks, the Muslim community, like the larger American society, was polarized along ideological lines. Many Muslims in America, before 9/11, had been celebrating their increasing voice and presence. It was shocking to meet the children of Muslim immigrants, born and raised in the US, twisting their understanding of their own situation to welcome such an outrageous event as payback. It was beyond comprehension how such hatred and contempt had crept into the society in which they had lived all their life.

One of the main factors driving the Muslim youth is their quest for identity. They are often 'different' in terms of the colour of skin, names and religion while comparing to the earlier generation of immigrants. Their Friday sermons are always loaded with strong Wahhabi messages and details of American excesses on the Muslim societies in Middle East and elsewhere. The rhetoric, to a large extent, is based on real-time happenings like the Palestinian siege, the US invasion of Iraq or the bombing in Afghanistan. The simultaneous alienation from American culture as well as the culture of immigrant Muslim parents encourages them to embrace the Internet and social media culture, which pivots individuals to adopt global Islamic militancy.

One of the famous cases of self-radicalized jihadists was of Omar Hammami,[69] son of a Syrian immigrant married to a white American woman, a Southern Baptist Christian, in the town of Daphne, Alabama. In May 2012, Omar uploaded on the Internet the first part of his autobiography—*The Evolution of an American Jihadi: The Case of Omar Hammami*, describing his experiences before and after travelling to the civil war torn Somalia. The first part of the autobiography, in 127 pages, written under the pen name 'Abu Jihad al-Shami', shows how the Salafi brand of Islamic literature available online and in the Salafi mosques is creating havoc in the minds of the Muslim youth.

From his account, one can decipher that he was a smart teenager and had just got elected as president of his sophomore class. He was dating a 'luminous blonde', one of the most 'sought after girls in the high school'.[70] He was a star in the gifted-students programme, with an ambition of becoming a surgeon. For a 15-year-old boy, he had a remarkable amount of charisma. By his junior year, the self-radicalization process had become visible in his character. He changed his dress code and prayed by the flagpole outside the school. Omar Hammami with high grades and ACT scores in the ninety-third percentile, skipped his senior year and directly enrolled at the University of Southern Alabama. There he no longer prayed alone. He could walk to the mosque from the campus; he soon took over as president of the fledgling Muslim Students Association. Omar plunged headlong into Salafism, mastering its nuances and the lexicon. The movement gave him a new sense of brotherhood and discipline. He started wearing his pants above the ankle, a popular look among Salafis. The radicalization went so deep into his psyche that once he even refused to be a part of family photographs. His

---

[69]Mastors, Elena, and Rhea Siers J.D, 'Omar al-Hammami: A Case Study in Radicalization', *Behavioural Sciences and the Law*, Vol. 32, No. 3, 2014, pp. 377-88.
[70]Elliott, Andrea, 'The Jihadist next Door', *The New York Times*, 27 January 2010, https://tinyurl.com/yckj79bk. Accessed on 15 September 2023.

father Shafik Hammami got irritated with his act and ordered him to leave his house. Omar devoted himself to dawah which is the practice of preaching and spreading the Islamic faith. His style of clothing was meant to provoke inquiry. He strolled through shopping malls in robes, attracting questions from strangers. After marrying a Somali girl in Toronto, Canada, Omar moved to Egypt to live and study Islam at the Al-Azhar University.

Somalia, at that time, was consumed by a catastrophic civil war. What was not destroyed by the famine and drought was plundered by pirates and warlords. Amid the chaos, a jihadist movement gave rise to an insurgency that took control of the capital city of Mogadishu in June 2006. The insurgents were led by an al-Qaeda affiliate known as the al-Shabaab, meaning 'youth' in Arabic. Ethiopia, a Christian country alarmed by the Islamic terrorism in their neighbourhood, got prepared to attack Somalia. The Ethiopian troops gathered at the border, backed by the American troops. As news of the conflict resonated in the jihadi chat rooms, Osama bin Laden called all jihadists to move to Somalia for fighting.

From Egypt, Omar closely followed the developments in Somalia. He was mentally prepared and religiously convinced that 'jihad had become an obligation on him'. He wanted to sacrifice his life to save his brothers and sisters in Islam. He had become active on social media sites by then. He then solicited his brothers from the West to join the jihad without naming Somalia. Omar travelled to Mogadishu, and at the airport, he informed the immigration officials that his wife was from Somalia and was visiting her parents. Soon after, thousands of Ethiopian troops invaded Somalia and swiftly gained control of Mogadishu. Leaders of the Islamic Courts Union (ICU) fled the country, while their jihadi wing, al-Shabaab, retreated to the South and mounted a fresh rebellion aimed at driving the Ethiopians out of the country. It was not clear who connected him to the al-Shabaab leadership, however, later in his email to his wife, he wrote that his ultimate wish had been fulfilled, that he had come under the Somali tent of Islamic jihad and that he was 'feeling cool' about it. Within three years, Omar made his way to the top leadership of al-Shabaab. He exercised a powerful role, commanding guerrilla forces, organizing attacks and developing strategies with top al-Shabaab operatives. He soon emerged into something like a jihadi icon, prominently starring in recruitment videos that drew hundreds of foreign fighters to Somalia. It was for the first time that an American national was rising to higher echelons of a terrorist organization. Among the American intelligence communities, there was a wrong perception that Muslim youths in the US, in comparison to their counterparts in the European countries, were upwardly mobile, socially integrated, and therefore, less susceptible to radicalization. On the contrary, the Sunday schools and the Friday sermons in the mosques had already made it possible for any Muslim radical organizations to easily take over its youths. The Salafi literature available on social media had also deeply impacted Muslim youth on campuses across the US.

The presence of American troops in Afghanistan and the invasion of Iraq had doubled down on the psychology of the Muslim youths, who were raised in the West with their one foot in the Muslim world. Through satellite television and the Internet, the distance between here and Yemen, Daphne, Alabama and Somalia had narrowed significantly down. For Omar Hammami, the war in Iraq provided a critical spark as he moved towards an extremist line.

Self-radicalized Islamic terrorists are products of the technology-enabled social media platforms. One such terrorist popped up on 11 December 2017 in Times Square, Subway, Manhattan. Akayed Ullah, a Bangladeshi immigrant and resident of Bangladeshi Enclave in Brooklyn, used to pray in a local Salafi mosque in Brooklyn. He confessed to the investigating officers that he had learned bomb-making online and picked up its components while working as an electrician. Fortunately, his crude pipe bomb could not explode, releasing just smoke but leaving him hurt. He is a good example of how the Wahhabi–Salafi literature, pushed through different Wahhabi organs and Friday sermons, encourages Muslims youths to commit terrorist acts. They are self-radicalized partly by social media and partly by the Wahhabi–Salafi interpretations of the Quran and the Hadith, which have been presented as 'real' Islam.

For the Wahhabi Salafists, their Muslim identity is primarily derived from the frameworks of the Wahhabi interpretation of the Quran and the Hadith. It rejects all cultural elements that diverge from a literal understanding of the Islamic norms. Thus, wearing a dress without a hijab or a full body robe or celebrating the birthday of Prophet Mohammad are heretical innovations (*bidda*) for them. The fact is, almost anything cultural would be a bidda, as there was nothing in Mecca and Medina during the Prophet's times. In fact, even the Prophet had a constant issue with the local settlements because of their rudeness and ignorance.

The Islamic State's exhibitionist violence and apocalyptic ideology are the outcome of Saudi Arabia's decades of sustained and calibrated efforts to transform the peaceful Hanafi Sufi Sunni Islam into a violent and bigoted version of Wahhabi Islam. As the world flattens out further, more and more knowledge, information, news, software, commerce and communities will reside on the World Wide Web. Different generations will interact with each other, with the wider world and with all that resides on the Web without any filters. Social media platforms like Facebook, Twitter, YouTube and WhatsApp have already opened up wide windows for the jihadi Islamists to propagate their twisted version of Islam. If not checked and monitored properly, this social-media-enabled global monster of jihadi Wahhabism would continue to be a hard nut to crack for the rest of the world.

Emergence of New Technology

San Francisco in California, USA, was a hotspot for various socio-cultural, technological and intellectual currents during the late 1960s. There was a technology revolution that began with the growth of military contractors, which soon collaborated with electronic firms, microchip makers, video game designers and computer companies in a process of technological convergence. There also came about a hacker subculture filled with cyber-punks and hobbyists. In due course, with the help of some quasi-academic groups, some smart guys developed the first computer mouse.

There was the Hippie Movement and the countercultural movement of Beat Generation taking the American campuses by storm. The West began to seek personal enlightenment through Zen and the Krishna Cult. Meditation and Yoga became the 'in' thing to do and a lot of young and intelligent people got attracted to various religious and social cults. One of the smartest minds of the twenty-first century, Steve Jobs was a product of this heady confluence of diverse energies thrown out by the time.[71] He adopted a unique culture of eating vegetarian food, meditating in the morning and dreaming of changing the way the world went about. Initially, the Hippies and the technology geeks did not gel with each other well. Many in the counterculture also believed that computers and Pentagon were the new tools of the power structure of American military might. By the early 1970s, however, a dramatic shift was observed in people's mindset, and computers started to be seen as a symbol of individual expression and liberation.

Most of the people who invented the twenty-first century's technological wonders, like the iPhone, Google Search Engine and Microsoft Operating System, which were being increasingly used by the Islamic jihadists, were, in reality, sandal-wearing, pot-smoking free-thinking dropouts from various premier institutes like MIT. That they saw and thought things differently, made them, including Steve Jobs, Larry Page, Mark Zuckerberg and Bill Gates, capable of achieving such enviable feats.

The metaphor of a 'flat world', was first used in a novel context by Thomas Friedman[72] in one of his bestselling books to

---

[71]Isaacson, Walter, *Steve Jobs*, Simon & Schuster, New York, 2011, p. 630.
[72]Friedman, Thomas, *The World is Flat: A Brief History of Twenty-First Century*, Penguin Books, New York, 2005, p. 488.

describe the phenomenon of globalization driven by technology. The telecommunication companies 'wired the world', laying optical fibre cables across the ocean floors, connecting various countries and continents. This excess supply of connectivity meant that the cost of phone calls, Internet connections and data transmission declined substantially. Terrorist organizations like al-Qaeda and ISIS were some of the major beneficiaries of this increased global connectivity. It enabled them to have a big effect even for their small acts like the killings of just a few people. The horrific video of the beheading of the *Wall Street Journal* reporter Daniel Pearl by the al-Qaeda-affiliated militants in Pakistan was transmitted over the world through the Internet. The same videos were also used by these organizations for online recruitments. The flat world made it much easier for the terrorists to transmit their message of terror across the globe in no time.

The ISIS technology wing has proven to be skillful not only at online marketing but also at mining huge volumes of data offered by the World Wide Web to their advantage. They can learn from the Internet about the schedules and locations of potential targets like transportation facilities, nuclear power plants, public buildings and airports. Like many political organizations, the terrorist groups also use the Internet to raise funds. Al-Qaeda always depended heavily on its global fundraising networks. The Islamist terrorist media cells also track visitors to develop consumer profiles and gather information about the users who browse jihadi websites. The visitors who seem to be interested in the jihadi cause and are potential candidates to carry out its works, are then contacted. Recruiters may also use more interactive Internet technology to roam online chat rooms or cyber cafes, looking for receptive young members from the public.

The Islamic State, at one time, had not only captured a large swathe of territory in Iraq and Syria, but also the imagination of a large number of Muslim youths globally. A huge number of young and bright tech-savvy Muslim youths were lured to push the hardline Wahhabi and Salafi agenda in different parts of the world. Thus an architecture of a flat terrorist world was created. Muslim youths under the age of 30 in North America and European countries have already been taught a violent form of Salafi Islam through the Sunday schools and the weekly sermons offered by the imams in the Salafi mosques.

Social Media as Jihadi Platform

The ISIS recognized the power of digital media in the early days, when the Jordan-based al-Qaeda jihadist Abu Musab al-Zarqawi discovered the possibilities of uploading the grainy videos of his jihadist violence on the Internet. As the group evolved and many computer-literate youths got attracted to its fold, ISIS propagandists showed their competitor al-Qaeda that they were quite ahead of the curve. The Islamic State maximized its reach by exploiting a variety of social media platforms like Telegram and Surespot, and content sharing systems like JustPaste.it. As a smart strategy, ISIS decentralized its media operations and kept its feeds flush with content made by autonomous production groups from Mali to Chechnya—a geographical range with cultural diversity, underscoring the fact that Wahhabi Salafism had fully arrived globally. The Islamic State has long taken pride in their flair for developing content that is innovative and offensive in equal measure. Al-Qaeda of Iraq under the leadership of al-Zarqawi had released beheading videos of captives as a propaganda tactic.

Ayman al-Zawahiri, the second most important leader of al-Qaeda, after Osama bin Laden, had however conveyed his strong disapproval of such acts to al-Zarqawi, saying that the display of extreme bloodshed would only damage al-Qaeda's reputation. He had also requested him to refrain from such acts in the future. Nonetheless, al-Zarqawi was killed by an American airstrike in June 2006. And later, al-Qaeda rebranded itself as the ISI (Islamic State of Iraq). The outfit pitched as a dedicated terrorist organization to safeguard Sunni Muslim interests and barreled down to capture maximum lands to create the first Islamic caliphate in the twenty-first century. The ISIS under the leadership of Abu Bakr al-Baghdadi had exploited the sectarian fault lines in Iraq and captured a significant area of northern Iraq, including the second largest city of Mosul.

A clever use of digital media platforms was integral to the fast expansion of ISIS in 2013 and 2014. The group's digital media wing[73] *Al-Furqan* documented every aspect of its offenses, particularly highlighting the grisly fates of Iraqi Shia army who meekly surrendered to the Islamic State fighters. The ISIS propaganda videos called 'Clanging of the Sword Videos' had a telling impact on viewers as in many towns the Iraqi security forces quickly melted away and got scared to fight with ISIS. To lure the Muslim youths from Europe and the US to ISIS caliphate, its production wing selectively put martyrdom videos and literature with similar content emphasizing its utopian aspects and freedom from any trace of religious persecution. They were trying to communicate that the idea of caliphate was no longer abstract or imaginary, but, real and tangible, that one could come and join it.

The Europeans who trekked via Turkey to join ISIS were professionals of high social standing and it helped to provide a new respectability to the jihadi fraternity. The influx of new talents also constituted a valuable addition to the Islamic State media output: advanced action cameras were affixed to AK-47s and sniper rifles, making first-person visuals from the scene of action available for various use of propaganda and publicity. The cockroach-like resilience of the Islamic State social media wing has bewildered the American law enforcement sleuths and the digital honchos from the Silicon Valley. The Islamic State sympathizers were exhorted by its official spokesman, to kill the Western non-believers by any weapon. Those who have been brainwashed by the Islamic State machinery say that they follow Allah and pledge their allegiance to the Islamic State, as a result of it.

---

[73]Whiteside, Craig, 'Lighting the Path: the Evolution of the Islamic State Media Enterprise (2003-2016)', *International Center for Counter-Terrorism*, 15 November 2016, https://tinyurl.com/52x9khwp. Accessed on 7 September 2023.

Earlier, al-Qaeda was more discrete and selective in recruiting their operatives. The reason was that the success of their operation often depended on secrecy, as they always surprised the enemy in the selection of their targets. The recruitments of ISIS, however, were open as they were online, using multiple social media platforms, made available by the American technology. The Islamic State recruitment was primarily aimed at defending the land occupied in Iraq and Syria and establishing the caliphate.

Al-Qaeda prepared a manual called 'A Course in the Art of Recruiting'. The ISIS recruiters followed the same manual to attract fighters to its jihadi base. ISIS preferred to recruit those who were non-practicing or non-devout Muslims. According to the manual, it was easy to indoctrinate and manipulate those who didn't know much about Islam. The manual also advises mailing digital and hard copies of the Wahhabi–Salafi Islamic books and videos to the recruits. The bottom line is that the recruiters have to be in constant contact with potential jihadis. They (the recruits) should get to know most of the Hadith on jihad and martyrdom, until he or she desires deeply for it.

The grandiose plan of ISIS leadership was to unite the global Muslim community and build a caliphate in the large swathe of land captured in Iraq and Syria. ISIS started to govern its captured territory according to a strict interpretation of the Sharia law and convinced its new recruits to move to the promised caliphate. They maintained that the promised caliphate was under attack by the Iraqi and Kurdish ground forces, backed by the American air force; and in Syria, under the Bashar al-Assad forces, Irani volunteers and Hezbollah ground forces, backed by Russian air force.

In the meantime, the heart of the Middle East imploded following the euphoria of the Arab Spring. Al-Qaeda's toxic narratives complemented and enhanced the growth of the Islamic State, forcing fighters to enter the chaos in Syria, Iraq, Libya, Egypt and Yemen. By 2015, hundreds of young American and European Muslims joined the Islamic State. The Soufan Group, a global security research and analysis agency, estimated that between 27,000 and 31,000 volunteers, including women and white converts from the West, had travelled to Iraq and Syria to join ISIS caliphate. French, German and British citizens constituted the majority of the European fighters as they were raised on the Wahhabi–Salafi jihadist narratives of Islam. In 2015, the Internet was fast taking over the conventional forms of media, such as books, magazines and television. Social media outlets allowed anyone to enter the mainstream. Most social media platforms are also very easy to use, costing very little for their users.

Contrary to the popular perception, most of the young people who got radicalized online, were not devout Muslims. Many, in fact, even did not seek it; rather, it found them. Online radicalization occurs in all economic classes. The common denominator seems to be that everyone who is radicalized and recruited online feels sympathetic towards the ISIS cause and their anti-West narratives. Radicalization is more widespread in those communities, where inequality and political frustrations prevail. It often takes root among the people who empathize with the oppressed and wish to show their solidarity. When they watch the YouTube videos of the atrocities in Palestine and Iraq, it ignites a spark in their mind. Once that strong spark of empathy was aroused, then it was observed that the majority of youths get soon inclined to learn more about it and slowly walk into the jihadist trap.

Islamic Extremism in Cyberspace

Cyber magazines are a signature communication tool for both the al-Qaeda and the Islamic State. *Inspire* is a magazine originally developed by the al-Qaeda to disseminate inspirational and terror-related knowledge, including bomb-making and organization of attacks. Published in English to reach a wide Western audience, it was widely available on the Internet as early as 2010. The magazine was successful and inspired many to commit terrorist acts. The two brothers involved in the famous Boston Marathon bombing, Tamerlan and Dzhokhar Tsarnaev, had reportedly fabricated the bombs in a pressure cooker, using a recipe from the *Inspire* magazine. The IT advisers of the Islamic State had very early understood the extraordinary reach of social media platforms like Facebook and Twitter globally. The average age of Facebook users was 30 in 2014.[74] The online social network had roughly 1.3 billion active accounts. It was used as an effective platform for spreading the message of Islamic jihadism and as a gateway to a wider extremist network linking with different radical groups and discussion forums.

Twitter was also used extensively to disseminate violence-ridden video content,[75] to promote its ideology and make direct connections with prospective recruits. It enabled them to assess feedback and reactions from the opponents of IS, since many in the Middle East also did not support the Islamic State. The outfit could use this data to their advantage in different ways. The twitterati brigades of the Islamic State used to put out fake news stories to entice the followers and win their sympathy. Many times, their tweets were picked up by the mainstream media as breaking news. A notable incident occurred in April 2013, when the *Associated Press* twitter account was hacked by the Islamic State and an ominous message was posted: 'Breaking News: two explosions in the White House, Barack Obama injured.' Within minutes of this false Twitter report trending, stocks on Wall Street plummeted. When Twitter closed some accounts suspected to be operated by Islamic terrorists, the group opened another account to be instantly accepted by a large number of followers. The same tactic was adopted by other terrorist organizations as well, as they change names and get back to business again.

YouTube is another medium that these terrorists use effectively. This immensely popular platform receives hundreds and thousands

---

[74]'How Old Are Facebook Users?,' *Gemius Global*, 4 February 2015, https://tinyurl.com/5cwrxayr. Accessed on 24 September 2023.
[75]Bodine-Baron, Elizabeth, 'Fighting the Islamic State on Social Media', *The RAND Blog*, 11 October 2016, https://tinyurl.com/yc25ks6s. Accessed on 8 September 2023.

of new videos daily and millions of users watch them every day, making content monitoring extremely difficult. According to statistics released by YouTube, about 300 hours of videos are uploaded to the site every minute. Because of the sheer volumes added to it each day, YouTube struggles to filter the content. The intelligence communities in the Western countries are in a fix as the trade-off is between the vital information the jihadist videos divulge and the damage they can do to the youths. It is imperative for the media platforms such as YouTube, Google, Twitter and Facebook to use algorithms to detect violent language and content, as much as they use them to ferret out content in child pornography and prevent them from being posted.

Video Game Technology (VGT) too is being widely used by the terrorist groups. The Global Islamic Media Front, a radical organization with ties to al-Qaeda and ISIS always look for 'a computer-savvy, media-saturated, video-game-addicted generation'. Once a website featured a video game titled 'Quest for Bush', in which players fight 'Americans' and proceed to different levels including 'jihad growing up' and 'America's Hell'. The video game technology is smartly used for jihadi recruitment. It is often done by adapting the style of the most popular video games like 'Grand Theft Auto' with little modifications, so that players can roleplay as members of ISIS, engaged in combat. Specific modifications made to the game include ISIS fighters killing law enforcement officers and attacking the US military convoys with explosives and ISIS snipers shooting down the American soldiers. A bunch of smart Muslim boys constitute the core of ISIS technology cell in Raqqa, ISIS headquarters in Syria.

The US army also developed video games in 2002, to reach out to the younger generation for recruitment. America's army claims that video games are very effective in their recruitment drive. ISIS is well aware of the video game success of the US army's marketing campaign. ISIS appropriated the idea and boosted its recruitment campaign in the Western countries. In a flat world, the terrorist groups also learn tactics from one another. The video game technology is an effective tool to reach out to a larger audience of vulnerable Muslim youths who in their growing age had been exposed to the Wahhabi–Salafi narrative of Islam from the neighbourhood mosques. ISIS also uses social media to launch cyber attacks. These attacks known as 'denial of service' are done simply by scrambling the cyber networks and inundating the system with enormous 'pings' to create a flood of unwanted messages. A ping is a data packet that allows an attacker to determine whether a given system is active on the network. Once a flood of pings is transmitted to a targeted site, the pings saturate the victim's bandwidth and fill up the system's memory space, causing the network to hang or crash. ISIS still attracts technologically smart young recruits, who possess tremendous hacking skills, particularly from the US.

ISIS has devised a strategy to recruit women from the West, as they have to grow ranks in the long-term. It also needed a cadre of women to give birth to the next generation of jihadi fighters. Muslim women raised in the West are prime targets for recruitment. The Islamic State women sympathizers, some of whom are also recruiters, have created dozens of social media accounts, urging women to move to the 'Land of the caliphate'. Travel manuals and other guidance are made available online for travellers to Syria and other destinations.

To lure smart young women to the organization, photographs of women with full armoury of weapons are posted on its websites. The ISIS also put up fake tweets of women who earlier had joined the Islamic State in Syria. The tweets give flowery descriptions of positive environments where they had been embraced by the promised Islamic caliphate. The truth, however, was horrendous, as women who escaped from the hell of its captivity give details of how they were mistreated, exploited and used as sex slaves by the jihadi fighters.

The French police had prepared an internal report after the November 2016 terror attacks in the country, for its Ministry of the Interior. One of the chilling facts in the report is that at least 90 'suicide bombers' could be freely roaming in the European Union.

The report also mentions how ISIS was mastering the encryption and bomb-making techniques to plan an attack of their choice.

The planning of Paris terror attacks was very precisely worked out as top-level bomb-makers were flown from Syria to France. They used easily available material to make the bombs, but it required special training, suggesting that a skilled person was available in Paris before the attacks.

The obvious question is how to stem this growing threat of radicalization through online platforms and new technologies. Software and social media giants like Facebook, YouTube, Twitter and Microsoft collectively announced formation of the Global Internet Forum to Counter Terrorism (GIFCT). They said that the collaboration would focus on technological solutions for the problem, through research and partnership with the government and civil groups. The tech firms' CEOs long struggled to balance their mission of supporting free speech and the need to prevent online terrorist content. The companies were seriously worried about how the flat world technologies were being used by regressive forces to spread violent and hateful messages online. The companies through the new forum decided to share new practices regarding the 'content detection and classification techniques using machine learning' and 'define the standard transparency reporting methods for terrorist content removals.' They also decided to develop a robust partnership with the United Nations' Counter Terrorism Committee to 'identify how best to counter extremism and online hate, while respecting freedom of expression and privacy.' Facebook also invested in software to stop extremist content before it is published on its site through a proactive screening.

The smart techies working with ISIS, however, found ways to bypass these barriers and continue to post content. Britain recently renewed its campaign against online terrorism with a crackdown on social media platforms, which failed to take action against terrorist propaganda. French President Emmanuel Macron has also maintained that they would explore new legal measures against those tech companies that fail to remove hateful content. The popular encrypted text messaging app, Telegram, however, remained uncooperative.

Fall of ISIS Capital

Raqqa, the so-called capital of the Islamic State in the Euphrates river valley in eastern Syria, was liberated on 17 October 2017 by the SDF, backed by the US forces. The ISIS was using suicide bombers to stop the advance of the coalition forces during the last days of its fall. Earlier, the outfit had seized the ancient ruins of Palmyra in Syria and of Hatra in Iraq. Its fighters also destroyed some of the important historical monuments there, as they found them against the Wahhabi interpretation of Islam.

Analysts say that ISIS was preparing for a new phase of morphing back into a kind of underground insurgency. It is well-known that no ideology can be defeated and eradicated just like that. It can only be controlled steadily and intelligently. It had taken roots among the disaffected Sunni population that was willing to tolerate and embrace an ultra-conservative brand of Islam, without fully understanding the consequences. The ousting of the Islamic State militants from Raqqa also had some symbolic dimensions to it as it was the de facto capital of the self-declared caliphate. Now, it has fallen from their grasp. It was home to over 300,000 people once. But tens and thousands of people fled the region when the militants solidified control over the city, early in 2014. Those who were unwilling to buy their strict interpretation of Islam were publicly hanged or imprisoned in the stadium complex. During the last two years only 20,000 residents remained in the once sprawling and affluent city. It is feared that more than 8,000 Islamic State fighters from France, Belgium, Holland, Germany and Britain had escaped from Raqqa before the fall and they were likely going elsewhere, instead of returning to their home countries. They had been brainwashed with so much hatred that it would be very difficult to reform them. The edifice of the Islamic State might have crumbled in all the places, including Raqqa, Mosul, Tikrit and Deir al-Zour, but its ideology is very much alive and visible on social media. In many cases it also continues to inspire the lone-wolf attackers, as seen on 1 November 2017 in Lower Manhattan, New York City.

The Uzbek immigrant Sayfullo Saipov, 29, rammed a truck into the crowd killing nine people and wounding a couple of dozens. He was a voracious consumer of ISIS propaganda on social media. During the FBI interrogation, he admitted that he was spurred by an ISIS video to attack Americans as revenge for the killing of Muslims in Iraq. The FBI agents also found about 90 videos on his cellphone, including of ISIS fighters killing prisoners, giving instructions for making explosive devices and Abu Bakr al-Baghdadi in action. Saipov confessed that he was particularly inspired by a video of al-Baghdadi in which he questioned the Muslims elsewhere in the world—what were the Muslims in the US and elsewhere doing in response to the killing of Muslims in Iraq?

Lone Wolf Terrorists

The term 'lone wolf' was popularized by two white supremacists, Tom Metzger and Alex Curtis, in the late 1990s, as part of the efforts to encourage fellow racists to act alone in committing violent crimes for tactical reasons. Similar tactics were advanced by the Islamic State media managers as part of motivating Muslim youths globally to follow the path of jihad and act individually. Any such acts committed by individuals independently are done without taking the Islamic State in the loop. The Islamic State leadership, however, owns it and lionizes the 'martyrs'. Usually, the lone wolf terrorists share an ideological or philosophical identification with an extremist group, but would not communicate with the group. While the lone wolf's actions are motivated to advance the goal of a certain group, the tactics and the methods are conceived and executed solely by the individual, without taking commands or directions from anybody outside. Because of this lack of personal contact with any larger group, lone wolf terrorism often poses serious problems to the state authorities as well as the agencies dealing with counter-terrorism.

Self-radicalization of Muslim youths through neighbourhood mosques, social media platforms, or extremist Islamic organizations could be some of the reasons for the phenomenal growth of lone wolf terrorism. The real threat comes from the single individual, the 'lone wolf', residing next door. He could be radicalized on the Internet, motivated by messages on social media or inspired by the imams at the local mosques even to fabricate bombs and plot strikes at famous landmarks in the city. Acts of lone wolf terrorism have been reported in the US, UK, France, Germany, Belgium, Russia and Sweden. The 2009 shooting rampage on the Fort Hood army base in Texas, the attack on the music concert in Manchester and the London Bridge attack are only some of them. These attackers pose a big challenge to the police and the intelligence communities, as it is extremely difficult to detect and defeat them before the act. Sometimes, even two brothers or members of the same family are complicit in the planning and execution of the crime, as we have seen in Spain, France and Sri Lanka.

There are about 30 million Muslims spread across Europe (excluding Russia), the US, Canada, Australia and New Zealand. The majority of them follow the one-dimensional, regressive, rigid and ultra-conservative Wahhabi–Salafi brand of Islam with strict practices including in dress code, which keep them away from modernity. If they would like to catch up with modernity while keeping the Islamic traditions and practices intact, then they will have to be first weaned off from the venomous Wahhabism and led to the progressive and peaceful traditions of Islam practised by the Hanafi and Sufi Sunni sects. This was the Islam once peacefully practised around the world, including in Saudi Arabia.

6

THE INTERNET OF JIHADI MOBILIZATION

The Internet is a vast cyberspace that provides opportunities to all. It has become a powerful channel, giving access to diverse sources of information to the entire world, allowing everyone to transmit his or her thoughts and opinions in various ways: one to one, one to many and many to one. It is an indispensable technological wonder, where knowledge and information flow freely. But, like any other technology, it can be used or abused to cause devastating damage to the entire society. There is an incredible growth in the number of people using social media every year. As in 2019, there were around 2.77 billion people using social media. With the smartphone technology and Internet connectivity becoming cheaper and the access easier, these numbers are expected to grow even higher and in a short time, it is projected to cross 3 billion.[76]

Jihadi Armies in Cyberspace

The followers of Wahhabi Salafism use social media platforms very smartly. They have 'cyber armies' to recruit and radicalize Muslim youths globally. Cyber magazines have been a signature communication platform for al-Qaeda and the Islamic State.[77] It is a vital tool for recruiting new members, raising funds and publishing

---

[76] Aldashov, Andrey, *The Role of the Internet in the Mobilization of Grassroot Social Movements: Analysis of the Russian Case*, 2010, Central European University, MPhil thesis.
[77] Berton, Beatrice, and Patryk Pawlak, 'Cyber Jihadists and Their Web', *Briefs* (European Union Institute for Security Studies), No. 2, 2015.

content to inspire young and impressionable minds. Even in the early days, al-Qaeda had shown its capability to use the Internet for various propaganda purposes. Its first website, Azzam.com, was created in the late 1990s.

Inspire, al-Qaeda's online magazine, was published in English to reach out to a vast Western audience. True to its name, the magazine succeeded in inspiring the youths to take up the cause of jihad very effectively. Several editions of *Inspire* provided elaborate instructions on how to make bombs in one's own kitchen and execute attacks, to cause maximum damage.

Like al-Qaeda, the Islamic State also has an online magazine called *Dabiq*.[78] The Islamic State supports its content, by effectively using a decentralized content production method towards a single goal, led by its central operatives. Aimed at recruitment and promotion, it produced two special issues of the magazine in July 2014. *Dabiq* is meant for a global audience, and it was released in different languages including French, German and Russian. The magazine was designed with three important objectives: religious, military and political. The first issue of *Dabiq* called Muslims to join the caliphate in Syria. The magazine is named after a small town near Aleppo, which is cited in the Hadith, where one of the greatest battles between Muslims and the Crusaders took place. The first two issues of the magazine opened with a quote from Abu Musab al-Zarqawi, the founder of al-Qaeda in Iraq (AQI). It said, 'The spark has been lit here in Iraq, and its light will continue to spread.' In the second issue, which was titled 'The Flood', a picture of the Noah's Ark was given and an article described the battle for the Islamic State as the flood. The Islamic caliphate was imagined as the 'ark' and the rest of the world was to be swept away soon.

Besides its theological and religious indoctrinations, *Dabiq* also powerfully described the outfit's military achievements. It is often

---

[78]Kibble, David G., 'Dabiq, the Islamic State's Magazine: A Critical Analysis', *Middle East Policy Council*, Vol. 23, No. 3, 2016, pp. 133–43.

used as a powerful tool for recruitment. Its content was planned and designed to win the backing of different tribes in different areas and support of various Sunni sects. It graphically portrayed many excesses committed by the Assad regime in Syria on its innocent civilian population, especially women and children, belonging to the Sunni sects.

The Islamic State's social media platforms often project the outfit as a 'winning brand', and convince the young men and women that they are on the 'winning side'. The third issue of *Dabiq* came out with the cover story 'A Call to Hijrah', referring to the journey the prophet made from Mecca to Medina for establishing Islam. Muslims were advised to hasten the migration from the Western European countries before the windows were closed. The magazine was also meant to attract all types of volunteers and fighters to protect the twenty-first-century Islamic caliphate, which was becoming a reality. A call was given through the magazine to scholars, judges, physicians, engineers and people with military background, to migrate to the Caliphate and serve the Islamic State. *Dabiq* outlined the front's future vision of liberating key places like Jerusalem from heretics.

The magazine was brought out in an impressive way with high quality of production. Its articles were arguably of high quality, legitimizing the ideology of the Islamic State and sufficiently supported by the Quran and the Hadith. The articles in various editions encouraged Muslims to get involve in the fight to establish and expand the Islamic State. For example, volume eight of *Dabiq*, with the lead 'Abandon the Lands of Shirk and Come to the Land of Islam', gives as many as five Hadiths to support its call. Two of them are as follows: 'Whoever gathers and lives with a mushrik [polytheist], is like him', and 'Allah does not accept any deed from a person until he parts ways with the mushriks and goes to Muslims.' The article trashes the pluralism of the West and argues that Western schools teach the value of tolerating other faiths, whereas the Quran teaches that Islam is the one true faith. In fact, it's a totally twisted interpretation of the Quran. The historical reality is that, in the first Islamic state of Medina, Jews and Christians lived side by side with members of the Muslim community. The magazine, however, excelled in publishing highly motivating articles and pieces praising the exceptional role played by the Islamic State. Radicalization and the online recruitments were a continuous process in which *Dabiq* played a crucial role. The Islamic State also used all other social media platforms to radicalize and recruit young Muslims to the organization. It could perhaps be the only terrorist organization, which uses all the new technologies smartly and effectively to its benefit. Its marketing campaign, which happens on a massive scale, is truly mind-boggling and impressive.

Cyber-jihadists also widely use the Internet to attack Western governments and institutions. They encourage Muslims to hack important Western websites and urge them to read documents like 'The 39 Principles of Jihad'. The jiahdist army is growing both in numbers and sophistication. The IS-affiliated British group, Cyber caliphate, led by the British hacker known as Abu Hussain al-Britani, who left for Syria, had hacked and taken control of both the Twitter and YouTube accounts of the US Central Command. In the aftermath of the 2015 terrorist attack in France, the jihadist army hacked about 20,000 websites in the country.

In the UL, the Counter Terrorism Internet Referral Unit (CTIRU) in cooperation with various social media platforms removed about 72,000 pieces of terrorist or extremist content that were in breach of the company's own terms and conditions. Similarly, many European and Arab countries joined hands with America to establish an information coalition to reduce the growing menace of jihadi terrorism. The late Jamal Khashoggi, general manager of the Al-Arab news channel, had suggested that, part of the reason for the growth of the IS, was the lack of human rights protection and democracy in the Arab world, together with failed governments and failed education and social justice[79] systems.

---

[79]Welby, Justin, 'What Should We Do About ISIS?', *Prospect*, 14 October 2014,

Osama bin Laden was one of the first Islamic terrorists to embrace new technologies for attaining his goals as early as in 1997. He had fully realized the value of harnessing 'new media' for pushing his global jihadi agenda. He used the Internet well before 9/11 to broadcast his messages worldwide and to recruit potential jihadist volunteers to his organization. The extremist outfits also used the Internet for operational purposes.

It is now in public domain that much of the planning activities of the 9/11 attacks were done using online platforms. The attackers communicated with one another through the Internet and researched their targets online. The al-Qaeda leader Ayman al-Zawahiri stated in 2005 that 'we are in battle and more than half of this battle is in the new media. In the Internet battle, we are in the race for the hearts and minds of our Ummah.'[80]

Today, the Islamic State has brought cyber jihad to a whole new level. From static websites, chat forums and online magazines, it has evolved significantly to make effective use of the latest interactive and fast-paced social media platforms. Al-Qaeda and its affiliates see the Internet as a great domain to disseminate information and anonymously interact with one another.

The Islamic jihadists in Syria, Iraq and beyond use all types of social media applications to their advantage. The Islamic State is an active user of blogs, instant messaging apps, video sharing sites, Twitter, Facebook, Instagram and WhatsApp. Nonetheless, Twitter is the most widely used platform, as it is less expensive and cellphone-friendly. Their posts may contain images, texts and links to other platforms, and the incoming tweets could be forwarded to everyone in the address list. The IS's website volunteers are very smart as they integrate the twitter feeds of dedicated fighters or followers with other social media platforms and disseminate their messages to a wider audience. The website volunteers most often are a radicalized

---

https://tinyurl.com/bdffehjs. Accessed on 9 September 2023.
[80]*Media Operative, You Are a Mujahid, Too*, Himma Library, April 2016.

person's wife or other young women sympathizers of the Islamic State, stationed anywhere in the world.

The Internet Indoctrination

The radical preacher and Yemeni-American cleric Anwar al-Awlaki, was on the run in Yemen once. The US intelligence experts, who were stationed in Yemen, had spotted him in Shabwa Province, a stronghold of al-Qaeda in southern Yemen, where he was on a mission to recruit young Yemenis to the jihadi army. He was hiding in the village Abdan, and when a pickup carrying him left the village, the vehicles were fired at three times by a drone mid-air. He was incredibly lucky that all three shots missed the target.

Awlaki spent his last two years in physical hiding, but he was visible online, firing emails and posting web videos. His English sermons were sold in multiple CD collections.[81] They were recorded in the late 1990s when he was a respected leader of the mosque Al-Ribat al-Islami, in San Diego. The theme of his sermons was against the foreign and domestic policies of the US. He believed that all the US policies were controlled by 'the strong Jewish lobbyists'. He was a radical hero of the Muslim youths as he used to weave his sermons around brave Islamic characters. He used to run blogs and videos on YouTube until they were shut down. He used to say that jihad was obligatory for every capable Muslim. He inspired dozens of people in the US, the UK, France and Canada to conduct lone wolf terrorist attacks in their own countries.

Many studies have shown that social media can be a powerful tool to bend impressionable young minds by using motivational content. It is often done by indoctrinating the Wahhabi interpretation of the Quran and the Hadith. It can easily make a young practicing Muslim

---

[81]IPT News, 'Awlaki's US Sermons Foreshadow Role as Terrorist Mentor', *Investigative Project on Terrorism*, 26 July 2010, https://tinyurl.com/396e96hr. Accessed on 23 September 2023.

more intolerant and rigid in dealing with other faiths. Open forums and chat rooms act as engines of transformation as they can help to validate existing beliefs and facilitate support from like-minded people. Today, jihadist and extremist sympathizers freely post videos, tutorials and highly intolerant religious propaganda material online with the aim of recruiting and cultivating partnership for terror activities.

The Muslim youths today, like anybody else grow up with the Internet, and they live and socialize online. Many studies on the processes of radicalization have shown that the extremist content online, by itself, does not radicalize or recruit people. Instead, they complement the offline efforts to radicalize, enhance the ability of recruiters and self-identified extremists to accelerate the processes, and, finally, to commit the act of terror.

Today, young Muslims in their early teens, living anywhere in the world, are thinking of knowing more about the Islamic State ideology. He or she can go online and find a jihadi *ulema* or preacher to talk about the virtues of Islamic jihad. On finding it interesting, they could very well go ahead in that direction even without their parents knowing about it, as the parents too would be leading a very insular, detached life. They can engage on social networking sites like ASKfm or be linked to the offline resources in the neighbourhood mosques, where they could interact with the local ulama who is programmed to motivate youths to do jihad in the service of Islam.

Many scholars argue that a growing number of Muslims today, whether they live in a Muslim-majority country or in a minority one, like in Western democracies, suffer from a kind of identity crisis unlike ever experienced throughout Islamic history. They are being often looked down upon and face intense scrutiny because of their religion. News channels are always rife with reports of suicide bombers creating mayhem in multicultural or multi-religious societies. In the Muslim-majority countries, like Yemen, Pakistan, Mali and Syria, suicide bombing and killing are done, but on the sectarian lines. This has driven a large numbers of Muslim youths to look inward and ask the question of what does it mean to be a Muslim in an interconnected, globalized twenty-first-century world. They, in fact, are also seeking an answer to what constitutes the difference between culture and religion.

In 2011, following the Arab Spring, a sense of frustration and anger became a daily experience of people in various countries of the Arabian Peninsula. The Middle East became more fragmented on sectarian lines. Their rulers began to be driven by more extreme ideologies than at any time since the collapse of the Ottoman Empire. Instability and war in countries like Iraq, Syria, Yemen and Somalia triggered massive migration within the Middle East and to the European countries. Recruiters were busy targeting young and vulnerable youth in the refugee camps. They looked for fighters from the insurgencies of Iraq, Chechnya, Libya and Syria. There is no shortage of angry young men in the Muslim world. In Western countries, the Islamic State targeted the Muslim diaspora that has never acclimatized to the mainstream society and faced Islamophobia. It was offered a brotherhood, compensation for their work and a caliphate.

Bigotry and barbarity of the Islamic State, which has its roots in Wahhabism, was nothing new. In 1744, after signing the historic deal with Muhammad ibn Abd al-Wahhab, the Saudi emir, Ibn Saud had set out to propagate their new interpretation of Islam—Wahhabism, which was named after Abd al-Wahhab. The settlements in Najd were brutalized by the combined might of Wahhab's ideology and the Al Saud's fighters. All the Muslims were coerced to accept the rigid and intolerant brand of 'Desert Islam'.

On 28 June 2014, the first day of Ramadan, the spokesperson of the Islamic State Abu Mohammad al-Adnani declared the creation of the Islamic caliphate of the twenty-first century. On 4 July, the leader of Islamic State Abu Bakr al-Baghdadi, calling himself the 'Caliph Ibrahim', gave a surprise sermon in the historic ninth-century Al-Nuri mosque in Mosul which now lay in ruins. He set himself up as a ruler 'by the order of God', designating himself as the 'commander of the faithful' and the caliph of Islam. His images of giving the Friday sermon and declaring the caliphate appeared on Twitter, before its full-length video was uploaded on YouTube, which led to the global media covering the story.

The Islamic State media campaign was overseen by Abu Amr al-Shami, a Syrian, born in Saudi Arabia, who was previously leader of the Islamic State in Aleppo. The ability to decentralize its social media operations[82] has always been one of the key strengths of the Islamic State, which allowed its supporters to operate their own ministries of information. Decentralization is, in fact, essential to the survival of the leaders of terror organizations. The Islamic State is no longer identified by any of its top leaders, but its ideology is spread across a large section of Islamic believers globally. This is the perfect testimony of its decentralization. The Islamic State and its ideology is brand new and anyone can be a part of it. No participant is expected to travel to any place to take the blessings of its leader. It is now functioning as a bottom-up organization.

The Keyboard Warriors

Hundreds and thousands of Islamic State volunteers across the world embrace Internet forums and social media platforms to create a virtual or wireless caliphate—fighting enemies on the ground as well as on the Internet. They may be called the 'keyboard warriors' of the organization. They abuse, threaten and the worst of all, takfir (the act of declaring a fellow Muslim a non-believer) those who are not like them or speak against them.

These keyboard warriors[83] are very smart, capable of tweeting terror before their boots hit the ground. Chat rooms and discussion

---

[82]Pace, Nicholas B., 'Decentralization: The Future of ISIS', *Small Wars Journal*, 11 May 2015.

[83]Snow, Deborah, and Rachel Olding, 'Muslim Leaders Need "Keyboard Warriors" to Help Fight Islamic State', *Sunday Morning Herald*, 27 January 2015.

forums were widely used by these groups in the early 2000, while many extremist groups act now in the dark world of the Internet, where membership, authentication and passwords are required. Pathways to the chat rooms can be found on social media accounts of the extremists groups and their supporters. Younger users end up in these forums through social media. Most social media platforms also allow users to post their comments, which provide a common space for the extremist exchange to take place.

Al-Furqan is the official media wing of ISIS, which posts messages from its leadership besides retweets and snippets from its supporters and affiliates. The global reach and exposure of these social media communications is mind-boggling and cannot be underestimated. Facebook has more than 2.6 billion monthly active users as of the first quarter of 2020. It has become a hub of decentralized information distribution and a medium to show support, protest and solidarity. Its pages are used by foreign fighters in Syria to invite and recruit their friends to join the IS. Twitter, which has been used widely by the Islamic State and its supporters across the world, had more than 330 million monthly active users and 145 million daily active users in May 2020. Jihadists are also using Twitter to engage in real time discussions, to organize debates, provoke and stage protests. Their Twitter feeds are written in perfect English, sometimes bilingual, and at times paired with feeds in other languages so as to reach a wider audience.

The Islamic State distinguishes itself from other groups on Twitter through hashtags with its own identity and they also hijack trendy twitter topics sometimes to its advantage. During the 2014 World Cup Football, hashtags like '#Brazil_2014' were attached to the Islamic State propaganda material as a part of the smart strategy to expand their audience base. Besides developing a complex coding system, it even has created its own apps such as the Twitter-based app called 'Dawn of Glad Tidings', which was available through Google Play Store. The app allowed a centralized body to post tweets from the subscribers' personal twitter accounts, connecting them with all its supporters. The tweets were dictated by an Islamic State social media manager and they were posted along with other links, hashtags and images. To avoid triggering of spam detection algorithms, the centralized tweets were properly spaced out in time. IS fighters live-tweet during fighting, reporting deaths, injuries and victories.

There are several categories of accounts, such as official, unofficial and regional, to which designated individuals give live information from their respective territories. The Islamic State is a unique terrorist outfit that has unleashed the world's first social media war, in which some participants post more than 250 times a day, attracting tens of thousands of followers.

The Islamic State groups use the social network platforms like Twitter[84] to their complete advantage. With it, they get free publicity in real time. The targets usually are Western institutions, electronic news media and anyone who reacts to a well-timed jihadist tweet. Jihadists also use Twitter to put fake news stories to entice followers and win their sympathy. There have been many instances of the mainstream media mistaking the terrorist-originated tweets as legitimate sources of breaking news.

It is known that the Islamic State loves Twitter. For several years, its followers have been hijacking the platform under the pretext of free speech to freely promote their content with very little or no interference at all. Strangely, lack of action from Twitter promoters has resulted in a strong pro-IS presence on its platform. Twitter argues that a case has to be made for removing the content or the online accounts of the cyber jihadists. Since the middle of 2015, Twitter has suspended more than 125,000 accounts 'for promoting terrorist acts' in violation of twitter rules. The company maintained that all the accounts were 'primarily related to the IS'. Each time that happens, they have to rebuild their audience, which causes disruption

---

[84]Reilly, Ryan J, 'Twitter Had to Staff Up to Fight the Islamic State's Keyboard Warriors', *Huffington Post*, 2 February 2016, https://tinyurl.com/b3f5anpk. Accessed on 7 September 2023.

to their activities. On the other hand, the Islamic State tweets can also provide information to the intelligence communities.

The US intelligence officials describe the site as a 'gold mine' of information about the foreign fighters networks. In fact, the State Department itself uses Twitter for a counter propaganda campaign titled 'Think Again Turn Away'. It tries to misguide the Islamic State and neutralize its recruiting initiatives. The site's rules prohibit threat of violence, harassments and other abuses, and the government agencies and law enforcement officials may request the removal of any objectionable content that appears on its page.

In recent years, Twitter has cracked down on some of its account holders, including those sharing macabre images or videos of violence. It may be said that Twitter is like a town square, a free megaphone to reach out to a mass audience, easily accessible on smartphones and largely not monitored.

The Islamic State also uses YouTube effectively. The online video-sharing platform is attractive and makes it easy for its links to be copied to other platforms. It is watched by more than 2 billion Internet users worldwide. However, it is impossible to monitor all the videos uploaded every day, as an incredibly high number of videos are uploaded to the site every minute. The video platform, which is a subsidiary of Google, maintains that it is not possible to filter the entire content; sometimes jihadist material are removed but immediately replaced by new ones, they say.

Video games are just another way for the jihadists to make a difference to their recruitment drive. Adapting the most popular video game of 2012, Grand Theft Auto,[85] the Islamic State created a game of its own, so that players could roleplay as its fighter members and vicariously engage in combat against its enemies. However, it is ironic that the Islamic State is using Western video games to demonstrate its hatred towards them.

---

[85]Crompton, Paul, 'Grand Theft Auto: Militants Reveal Video Game', *Al Arabiya News*, 20 September 2014.

The first European conference on intelligence and security bioinformatics, held in Esbjerg, Denmark, in 2008, observed that 50 per cent of jihadist videos contained 'martyrs virtues' and another 30 per cent footages of suicide bombings. The rest, it said, was focussed on the Wahhabi and Salafi literature and inviting the believers to jihad.

The Al-Hayat Media Center is the media wing of the Islamic State, which produces video content for the IS. In July 2014, before the group launched its attack on Mosul, a city of 1.5 million people, it released a film called *The Clanging of the Sword IV*. The smartly produced film with slow motion graphics and aerial drone footage was meant to demoralize the Iraqi soldiers before the assault commenced. Visuals of huge black flags flying were also used to scare and compel the enemies to flee. The video was uploaded on Justpaste.it, and it was instantly posted to several accounts on YouTube. Al-Hayat smartly posted more than 40,000 tweets in a single day as the Islamic State fighters marched towards Mosul, the second most important city of Iraq, and captured it. The media centre also produced several attractive material aimed at recruitment. It produced an HD propaganda series called 'Mujatweets', which portrayed the daily life of fighters in Iraq and Syria in a realistic but inspiring way. It also included very positive testimonies by European fighters who were already there.

In September 2014, an Islamic State-style video game emerged. In the game, which was modelled on the popular Grand Theft Auto Series, the players were seen dressed like Islamic State fighters and tasked with shooting the police and blowing up military targets. A lengthy video by the outfit was released in September 2014, showing the final assault on Tabqa Air Base in Syria, in which the Islamic State fighters were seen firing automatic weapons at hundreds of Syrian soldiers who were fleeing the base over an open territory. At the end of the video, several hundreds of these soldiers were shown being marched across the Raqqa desert to a clearing, where all of them were shot dead at point-blank range. In another video, released in October, showing the beheading of the British hostage Alan Henning, titled 'Another Message to America and Its Allies', Henning was shown reading from an Islamic State statement: 'Because of our parliament's decision to attack the Islamic State, I as a member of British civil society, will now pay the price.' In one of the earlier videos, 'Jihadi John' was featured speaking in a British accent, 'The blood of David Haines was on your hands, Cameron. Alan Henning will also be slaughtered, but his blood is on the hands of the British Parliament.' Earlier in September, the British Parliament had approved the airstrikes against the Islamic State in Iraq. Consequently, the Islamic State shocked and embarrassed the Western powers by executing four of their foreign hostages—two American and two British—in an appallingly brutal way.

They further embarrassed the world through mass displacements of Yazidis in northern Iraq and through other widespread war crimes including 'sexually motivated campaigns' against the Yazidi women and children, which continued to flood the Internet, print and television networks. The young Yazidi girls were used as sex slaves by IS fighters.

An edition of *Dabiq*, the Islamic State magazine, published on 12 October 2014 portrayed Yazidis as mushrik (non-believers) and, hence, open for enslavement, including as concubines. Another chilling video of the Islamic State became viral; it showed fighters stopping three large trucks on the Syria–Iraq highway. The Islamic State fighters at the check post were shown checking the drivers' IDs and asking them, 'You are all Shia?' To which they replied, 'No, we are Sunni from Homs.' The video continued to show the Islamic State men putting them through a test to see if they were Sunnis or not. The gunmen, at last, find them as Alawite Shias from Syria and shoot them at point-blank range at the roadside. Such mindless cruelties clearly displayed the pervasive hatred of the Jihadi Salafists for Shias or any other sects of Muslims other than the Wahhabi Sunnis.

Jihadi Women Power

In October 2014, the Islamic State formed Zhora Foundation and the Al-Khansa Brigade, aimed at luring young women volunteers[86] to its fold with a special manifesto of its own. The Islamic State claimed that women have an important role to play in the organization, including as doctors and nurses. They play a crucial role in building the Caliphate, as they practice Islam and support their husbands by rearing their 'Lion Cubs'. They recruited women the same way as they did with men—by identifying those who lost their way and were desperately seeking a sense of belonging and identity.

Intelligence sources estimated that more than 800 women had travelled to Iraq and Syria to the IS-occupied areas along with their husbands, or parents or, in some cases, brothers. Most of them are lured into believing that they are the part of a humanitarian mission towards the goal of establishing the Islamic caliphate. Some were also offered financial incentives, in case their husbands die in the service of Islam. They would be provided a financial package besides the adulations of an Islamic martyr. The largest number of female recruits came from countries like France, Britain, Germany, Belgium and Spain. Twitter was the favourite media platform for the recruiters to connect with the 'Umm', a honorific title used to address the women recruits, which in Arabic means 'mother'. The recruitment websites usually have the right mix of ideological indoctrination as well as elements of seduction for those fighters seeking to marry after coming to the caliphate. The network also provides nursing and cooking advice for those wives who want to keep the jihadists happy. Information on Sharia law is provided besides tips on using weapons and social media tools so that they too can contribute by attracting even more women recruits to the force. Majority of girls attracted to the IS are between the age of

---

[86]Kfir, Issac, 'The Role of Women in Islamic State-led Terrorism', *The Strategist*, Australian Strategic Policy Institute (ASPI), 2017.

16 and 24; some reports also suggest that girls as young as 13 have also been charmed by its propaganda machines. Women are told to populate the Islamic caliphate by setting an example of stability and normality. The women brigade is also expected to do moral policing in the occupied areas, such as Mosul and Raqqa, for the strict interpretation of Sharia law.

The Islamic State propaganda is sleekly designed in such a way that it appears to give women and girls a sense of empowerment. The propaganda carefully omits the harsh realities of the Sharia rules to be followed in the Caliphate, including public stoning, compulsory dress codes and material hardships. However, the reality on the ground is different. A marriage bureau was opened for those women who want to marry jihadist fighters. Under the face of the bureau, the fighters were committing horrific sexual violence on a seemingly industrial scale.[87] The UN has estimated that in August 2014, ISIS forced more than 1,500 women, teenage girls and boys into sexual slavery.

The amazing story of two American women, who met and befriended each other at Baghouz, the final land pocket of the Islamic State caliphate, is telling and revealing. Baghouz is a tiny enclave on the banks of the Euphrates river. It was the final scrap of territory left to the extremists group that in 2014 controlled a vast stretch of territory across Syria and Iraq. It aspired to create an extended jihadi state, which by January 2019, however, was reduced to less than six square miles.

The journey of the American women, which ended up in a despicable tent in Baghouz, started in 2014, after they got brainwashed and groomed online to be the 'jihadi brides' of the Islamic State fighters. Muthana, daughter of Yemeni immigrants, was born and brought up in Hoover, Alabama, and graduated from the University of Alabama at Birmingham. She grew up in an ultra-conservative household—no partying, no boyfriends and no cell phone. When

---

[87]Sherwood, Harriet, 'Young Western Women Among Jihadis', *The Hindu*, 1 October 2014, https://tinyurl.com/2jjfshrs. Accessed on 27 September 2023.

she finished high school, her father gave her a phone as a graduation gift. It soon became her portal to the world of an extreme Islam. She was drawn to the Islamic State through social media site Twitter.

In 2014, an online contact walked her through the steps of joining the Islamic State. She dropped out from the semester and used the money given by her father as course fees to buy a ticket to Turkey. She told her parents that she was travelling to Atlanta for academic purposes. She was smuggled across the Syrian border in November 2014 and taken to a female dormitory, which was packed by hundreds of single women from around the world. Every day, an Islamic State official would roam the dormitory carrying a list of young fighters looking for brides. The young ladies were not allowed to leave the dormitory until one got married. After a month, she acquiesced to meet Suhan Rehman, an Australian fighter from Melbourne. He used the name of Abu Jihad, meaning 'father of jihad'. They met in a room with a chaperone. After a brief conversation, they agreed to marry, and he took her home. She took the name Umm Jihad, meaning 'mother of jihad'. She actively propagated jihad on social media and, through her tweets, incited hatred against the West, including America.

After three months, her husband was killed in battle. Her second husband was killed in Mosul and the third in Raqqa. She was lucky to escape the bombing and move from one Islamic State controlled enclave to another along the Euphrates river valley.

Similar was the fate of Kimberly Polman, the Canadian–American woman who converted to Islam and soon came in touch with the online jihadi recruiters and eventually ended up in the Islamic caliphate in Syria in the early 2005. She had basic nursing skills and soon got married to a fighter. By 2005, the world had come to know about the heinous crimes committed by the Islamic State forces, including the beheading of journalists and the enslavement and rape of women from the Yazidi community in the Mosul region of Iraq. Polman tried to escape from their captivity once but was unlucky and got caught by them. Later, in a prison, she was raped and beaten by Islamic State men many times, which was also done to scare others who attempted to escape from their camp.

She survived the bombing many times as the enclaves of the Islamic State continued to shrink over the years. Both American women, Muthana and Polman, finally moved to the small IS-held enclave in Baghouz, which was liberated in January 2019. Encircled by the American forces, the last six-square-mile enclave, faced severe shortages. When groceries and food were hard to come by, both of them, along with others, collected grass from crevices of pavements, boiled it and ate it. Both of them, at last, managed to escape the last Islamic State enclave along with the civilian families and eventually found themselves surrounded by the US forces, who separated them from the stranded civilians and put them in a camp with other 'jihadi brides' where they shared their personal journeys with *The New York Times*.

In 2011, President Obama and his security team were convinced that the Internet had become an effective tool for the Islamic State terrorists. The White House interacted with the Silicon Valley leadership on how to restrict the use of Internet by the jihadists without compromising on the basic freedom of expression and liberty of people. The US created its first Countering Violent Extremism (CVE) strategy in 2011, which revolved around countering the radicalization of all types of potential terrorist with a 'strategic implementation of plan for empowering local partners to prevent violent extremism'. The US State Department in 2011 also created the Center for Strategic Counter-terrorism Communications (CSCC), which attempts to engage violent extremists in online debates and contest their claims in an attempt to dissuade others from joining Islamic State. It also established the twitter account 'Think Again Turn Away' with the same purpose, where it planned to engage in debate with jihadi fighters and their supporters.

The Organization of Islamic Countries (OIC), representing about 1.6 billion Muslims in 57 countries passed a resolution against the IS, stating that the 'IS has nothing to do with Islam' and it had committed crimes that cannot be justified or tolerated. More than

120 Muslim scholars wrote to Abu Bakr al-Baghdadi that he had misconstrued Islam, since he had ignored the context of the Quran as well as the Hadith. In fact, what al-Baghdadi was following was a version of Islam, rebooted by the eighteenth-century radical cleric Muhammad ibn Abd al-Wahhab and is aggressively pursued by the religious establishment of Saudi Arabia.

The global Muslims were being lured and forced to follow this version of intolerant and bigoted Islam as it was hard-pushed by the kingdom of Saudi Arabia's Ministry of Religious Affairs on the strength of enormous financial resources post 1979. Another religious body of the kingdom, the Council of Senior Scholars, had also given an extremely intolerant and regressive Wahhabi–Salafi interpretation to the Holy Quran, meant to be promoted across the globe, through various cultural and religious arms of the kingdom, using its huge riches from the Arabian petrodollar.

The Saudi Crown Prince MBS, however, is now thinking of reverting back to the devotional or moderate version of Islam, which he attempted through a list of measures by terming it as part of an effort to 'restore Islam'. The Crown Prince is strongly advocating for a 'moderate and balanced Islam' that is open to the world and to all religions and traditions. However, enforcing a change would require a major overhauling of the Kingdom's sprawling religious bureaucracy, which fears that the kingdom is forsaking its centuries old principles.

The Saudi clerics have long been subservient to the royal family, but the ascendency of the young prince has seriously eroded their independence. Crown Prince MBS has said categorically that 'serious measures would be taken to stamp out the uglier part of Salafism that permeate Islam around the World; it could usher in an era of peace and prosperity.'[88] What he is precisely doing is making an attempt to replace Wahhabism with a less rigid and aggressive form

---

[88]Hubbard, Ben, 'Saudi Prince, Asserting Power, Brings Clerics to Heel', *The New York Times*, 5 November 2017, https://tinyurl.com/2p8fd9ns. Accessed on 23 September 2023.

of Islam that would accommodate the secular Saudi nationalism, with a strong anti-Iran/Persian/Shiite tenor. Nonetheless, if the prince is bent on pursuing an anti-Qatar and anti-Iranian stand, it is likely that he may find himself in a very tight spot soon.

Virtual Caliphate

The term 'virtual caliphate' has grown in popularity as a way of describing the future trajectory of the Islamic State.[89] The physical defeat of the Islamic State in Iraq and Syria was important as far as putting the brakes on the ever-growing monster of Wahhabi Salafism in the Muslim world. Many Arab fighters who escaped from the Euphrates river valley in Syria during the last days of the war, have, since then, taken shelter in Yemen and Libya. Reports indicate that some fighters who had gone underground in Syria earlier are now emerging and forming sleeper cells to resume the fight. Virtual caliphate is a stratified community of Muslims who subscribe to the Sharia law and are located in the global territory of cyberspace.

The radicalization process usually develops gradually over many years, but in some youths, it occurs within a short period of time. Many recent cases of the 'lone wolf' or the 'virtual pack of wolves' extremist attacks in the West raise the question whether these may be exclusively attributed to the open access to social media outlets. Someone looking for confirmation of his or her ideas will find the Internet as an echo-chamber of their already existing ideology.

The Internet has contributed greatly to the quick radicalization of the present-day youths in the Western countries thanks to their tech-savvy nature and a good command over the English language. All the terrorist groups, led by the Islamic State, are specifically using social media platforms to target vulnerable youths and radicalize them with smartly crafted messages and fancy videos. The jihadist

---

[89]Votel, Joseph L., et al, '#Virtual Caliphate: Defeating ISIL on the Physical Battlefield Is Not Enough', Center for New American Security, Washington, DC, 2017.

groups use social media for multiple purposes including propaganda works and activities like live-reporting of the lone wolf attacks from the place of action. Those who died for their cause are honoured as martyrs and eulogies are placed on social media platforms to be circulated widely on the Internet.

More susceptible to radicalization are those who feel left out by the system or feel discriminated against by the society for one or the other reason. Radicalization is more widespread among Muslims in Western countries, where they lead an isolated and insular social life.[90] It often takes root easily in those who sympathize with the oppressed and wish to show their solidarity with them. Radicalized men and women often go through despair, humiliation and outrage over the injustice and hardly find any options for bringing about a change. A brief moment of intense emotion evoked in them while watching a video of some innocent Muslim being brutalized somewhere may trigger a spark in them to act violently. Once an individual is mobilized, the next steps vary. Usually, many start browsing various jihadi sites and educating themselves with the Islamic ideology even further, imbibing it more deeply. In order to fully convince themselves, they look for some interpretation of the Quran and the Hadith which justifies and encourages jihad, invariably ending up with some Salafi literature. A potential candidate for recruitment may come to the group's attention as he or she makes a small financial donation, downloads some jihadist literature, enters a jihadi chat room, or visits a radical page on Facebook. Technology enables them to accomplish all the jihadi jobs online. Facebook claims that any profile, page or group related to the jihadist organization will be shut down and any content celebrating the Islamic jihad will be removed. There is no place for terrorists on Facebook, says its official spokesman. It seems to be working broadly, as Facebook is quick to delete posts or any extremist content once they are posted on its page.

---

[90]*Radicalization Dynamics: A Primer*, American Civil Liberties Union, June 2012, https://tinyurl.com/4tezcx2k. Accessed on 26 September 2023.

The very characteristic of the Internet and social media explains why it is so effectively used by terrorist organizations. First of all, it is very cost-effective and user-friendly. One can easily hide behind fake identities, and thus spread the messages anonymously to reach a large group of target audience. They can be one-to-one or one-to-many and highly interactive at the same time. The messages may be used for 'narrowcasting', to communicate between a specific target group, which was effectively used by the outfit al-Shabaab, during the Westgate shopping mall attack in Nairobi in September 2013. Who knows, if the next generation of computers with all the artificial intelligence-enabled features, would make the job easier for the extremist organizations to expand their influence among the target audience and execute attacks in different parts of the world.

Preventing Online Extremism

Tech companies and social media giants are finally taking action to prevent the online radicalization. Researchers specializing in online extremism say that blocking certain accounts or content may work to temporarily disrupt the groups, but it eventually drives them underground. The problem lies in the global nature of social media, the reliance on self-policing by users to identify objectionable content, and the fact that many of those banned accounts simply open fresh accounts and continue posting their hatred once they are banned. A blanket policy of banning anything that may be seen as inciting violence could lead to questions of censorship, as one person's hateful propaganda could be another's free speech.

The physical defeat of Islamic State is not sufficient. According to the head of the US military operations commander in the Middle East, the Islamic State's loss of territory does not mean that the ideology is defeated. The group continues to coordinate and inspire attacks from a 'virtual caliphate' present online. Twitter has suspended more than 635,000 accounts linked to the Islamic State since 2015. Facebook, YouTube and other social media companies regularly remove jihadi content from their sites. Despite the enhanced global surveillance by social media companies, the Islamic State still publishes its monthly online magazines in ten languages. Amaq News Agency, a news outlet linked to the Islamic State in Iraq and Syria, still posts videos that are widely shared on Twitter, Telegram and other platforms.

The Islamic State extensively uses foreign-born operatives to communicate online with potential sympathizers abroad. After the initial conversation, they move to some encrypted messaging apps like Telegram to avoid detection. In Paris, a jihadi recently used his Telegram channel 'Sabre de Lumiere' which means 'Sword of Light', to communicate with the Islamic State sympathizers in France. Four French Muslim women were arrested when they were allegedly heeding to his directive to 'fill a car with gas cylinders, sprinkle petrol on it and park in a busy street' to be set ablaze later, according to a message intercepted by the French police. The Peugeot parked near the famous Notre Dame Cathedral in Paris, however, failed to explode.

The father of a Paris attack victim, Reynaldo Gonzales, filed a lawsuit against three of the largest social media companies—Google, Facebook and Twitter—for the death of his daughter Nohemi Gonzalez during the unfortunate Paris attack in 2015. He accused the companies of facilitating terrorists to communicate and share unlawful information on their platforms. The media giants were forced to take action, including by removing all jihadi content from their platforms. It is always a tough task for the companies to strike a balance between restricting objectionable content and, at the same time, allowing the users to enjoy their freedom of expression. Under the US law, the Internet companies are exempt from liability for the content users post on their networks. Even with strict laws, jihadists always find new ways and strategies to be present on social media platforms.

The covert Russian messaging app Telegram, which provides complete anonymity to its users and relies on client–server, server–client encryption, is said to be a favourite of many extremist outfits.

The success of the Islamic State Twitter campaign can be attributed to its use of the platform as a 'radicalization echo-chamber', namely the sharing and spreading of jihadist propaganda for continued consumption by its supporters or potential supporters. The chamber comprises three user groups—nodes, amplifiers and shout-outs—that may be understood as a tier-like system. The nodes, which is the first tier, are by and far the loudest and most authoritative voices of the jihadi realm on social media, tweeting out videos, news, articles, etc. The amplifiers then engage with the content further by re-tweeting it. While not presenting any new material and propaganda, they actively use nodes' Twitter accounts. An average Islamic State Twitter account will have 1,000 followers and the echo-chamber process is an integral part of ensuring the continued success of the accounts.

It is a fact that the Islamic State has faced a decisive defeat in Iraq and Syria physically, which has forced it to retreat to a virtual safe haven, from which it continues to coordinate and inspire attacks in the real world, as well as build a support base for it. These virtual warriors of the outfit are the least predictable people. They are the ones who get radicalized online and nurse a range of grievances or deep personal grudges with no direct contact with the group's hierarchy. But Islamic State will lose no time in declaring them as 'Soldiers of the caliphate'.

Whether Islamic State or something similar will be born from its ashes and will survive in its heartland is unclear and depends on various aspects. It depends on how Iraqis handle its Sunni–Shia fault lines and purge Salafism from the Sunni mosques. The Islamic State has great skill of exploiting sectarian tensions and terrorizing communities into submission. The Iraqi ruling dispensation has to go extra miles in its sectarian and ethnic peace-building efforts. All the forces, including the US, who are fighting against the extremist forces, should know that even though the Islamic State flag is shredded in Raqqa, Mosul and other parts of the region, its ability to inflict terror and take advantage of the ungoverned countries by exploiting the simmering ethnic and sectarian hatred, is far from being fully extinguished.

7

EVOLUTION AND EXPANSION OF THE ISLAMIC STATE IN IRAQ AND SYRIA

Ahmed Fadil al-Nazal al-Khalayleh, popularly known as Abu Musab al-Zarqawi, was the founder and patriarch of the Islamic State.[91] In 1999, he was released from the detention of Jordan along with Abu Muhammad al-Maqdisi, an Arab jihadi ideologue. Al-Zarqawi parted ways with al-Maqdisi and travelled to Afghanistan, with the recommendation of a London-based jihadist Abu Qatada al-Filistini, who advised him to connect with the al-Qaeda's leadership. He was given a special grant of US$200,000 to set up a jihadist training facility in Herat, close to Afghan's western border with Iran.

Al-Zarqawi established the training camp on land granted by the Mullah Omar government. Once the work was over, he brought many jihadist trainees from Jordan and formed an organization called Jamaat al-Tawhid wal-Jihad (JTWJ).[92] This organization received international media attention when jihadis, trained by al-Zarqawi carried out attacks on the Radisson Hotel and several other popular tourist sites in Jordan. The US named it as a terrorist organization and listed it for international sanctions by the UN 1267 Committee for its links to al-Qaeda. The group's main goal was to undermine the establishment of a free and pluralistic Iraqi state by fomenting

---

[91] Lister, Charles R., *The Syrian Jihad: Al-Qaeda, the Islamic State and the Evolution of an Insurgency*, Pentagon Press, 2015, pp. 500.
[92] US Department of State, *Foreign Terrorist Organization: Designation of Jama'at al-Tawhid wa'al-Jihad and Aliases*, 15 October 2004, Press release.

a sectarian war in Iraq.

The US invasion of Afghanistan post 9/11 forced al-Zarqawi and his group to abandon his facility in Herat and flee to Iran. He was protected by the jihadist organization Hizb-e-Islami Gulbuddin in Iran. Sometime in 2002, al-Zarqawi and his followers moved out of Iran and entered northern Iraq to set up a camp in the Kurdish north. Here, al-Zarqawi came in contact with another jihadist organization Ansar al-Islam,[93] which adhered to a rigid Salafi ideology. It was operating in the rebellious Kurdish region and was indirectly supported by the Saddam Hussein regime to control the dynamics of Kurdish territories.

Al-Zarqawi's impeccable al-Qaeda credentials made it easier for him to be a part of the core group of Ansar al-Islam leadership. This led to the US intelligence falsely believing that Saddam Hussein had an al-Qaeda connection, and the conspiracy theorists in Washington, DC, connected the dots to link Saddam Hussein with the 9/11 attacks. In 2002, Ansar al-Islam was actively fighting the Kurdish militia. Saddam used to get intelligence from its senior operational structure, which was of great value to the regime. Despite being a non-practicing Muslim with a strong Baathist secular ideology, Saddam had exploited Islamic conservatism as a strategic counterweight to the growing influence of the Muslim Brotherhood since the early 1990s.

Rise of the Islamic State

The Islamic State of Iraq and the Levant (ISIL) is also known as the Islamic State of Iraq and Syria (ISIS) al-Sham and more popularly, known as the Islamic State or IS. It is also known by its Arabic language acronym Daesh. Islamic State is a militant group that follows

---

[93]Gregory, Kathryn, 'Ansar al-Islam (Iraq, Islamists/Kurdish Separatists), Ansar al-Sunnah', *Council on Foreign Relations*, 5 November 2008, https://tinyurl.com/4zvmz839. Accessed on 12 September 2023.

a fundamentalist, Salafi jihadist ideology of the Sunni Islam.[94] In late 2004, Abu Musab al-Zarqawi joined al-Qaeda and established it in Iraq (AQI) after pledging allegiance to Osama bin Laden. His organization JTWJ had also set up a jihadist training camp in the northern province of Sulaymaniyah. It was one of the camps the US had targeted during the early days of its Iraqi invasion, thus bringing al-Zarqawi into direct conflict with the US, which would later define his ideology.

During the very early months of the invasion, al-Zarqawi's JTWJ demonstrated the organization's intent. In a professional and planned way, al-Zarqawi detonated a series of car and suicide bombs on a chain of high-value targets in the city of Baghdad and caused maximum casualty. He had crafted his terrorist roadmap very meticulously to hit the Jordanian interests, the international community and its supporting establishments, and the Shia Muslims. An important Shia symbol was targeted in the southern city of Najaf, where the Imam Ali Mosque was hit by a car bomb, killing more than 90 worshippers, including, Ayatollah Mohammad Baqir al-Hakim, a senior Iraqi Shia cleric.

Al-Zarqawi also expanded the JTWJ across Iraq and planned the destruction of the Golden Mosque of Samara by a suicide bomber on 22 February 2006. It contained tombs of some of the holiest imams of the Shia Islamic pantheon from the ninth century, one being of Imam Hasan al-Askari, father of the 'Hidden Imam'. Only someone with an intense hatred for Shia Muslims could destroy such a sacred mosque that had withstood some of the bloodiest conquerors like the Mongols. Al-Zarqawi established a robust network in Syria, to present himself as a defender of Sunni honour and supremacy. He was determined to spin it into an anti-Shia revolution both in Iraq and Syria. At that time, al-Zarqawi was working towards establishing

---

[94]Comerford, Milo, Mubaraz Ahmed and Daniel Sleat, 'The Rise and Fall of ISIS', *Tony Blair Institute of Global Change*, 13 June 2017, https://tinyurl.com/y9hxbrku. Accessed on 12 September 2023.

ISIS, with a caliph and the Sharia law to rule it.

Between 2004 and 2006, al-Zarqawi was consistent in his fight against the Allied forces in Iraq's urban centres. He penetrated into local Sunni communities in rural areas and influenced the local tribal leadership. Al-Zarqawi also became notorious for kidnapping Americans and uploading their beheading videos on YouTube. The combo visuals of beheading and the assembly line of suicide bombers had made the JTWJ the most brutal terrorist organization of the time. Al-Zarqawi was a smart and tactical person. He had intentionally never pledged allegiance to the al-Qaeda or the Taliban leadership in Afghanistan. In 2004, the central leadership of al-Qaeda had negotiated to bring his JTWJ under the al-Qaeda tent. After back and forth negotiations between Osama bin Laden, Ayman al-Zawahiri and al-Zarqawi, an agreement was reached to rename the JTWJ as the al-Qaeda in Mesopotamia, or simply, the al-Qaeda in Iraq (AQI). The overtly sectarian strategy pursued by the AQI was, in many respects, at odds with al-Qaeda's central leadership. The brutal beheading videos and the continuous mass killings of innocent people by suicide bombers at public places were matters of great concern for the al-Qaeda central leadership. The AQI under al-Zarqawi charted its own trajectory for Iraq, notwithstanding the central leadership. In January 2006, five smaller jihadi groups merged with the AQI after protracted negotiations and formed the Majlis Shura al-Mujahideen (MSM) in Iraq. United under a big umbrella, the al-Zarqawi leadership worked towards uniting the Sunni heartlands of Iraq and levelling the playing field towards the establishment of an Islamic State.

Apparently, al-Zarqawi wanted to be seen as a defender of the Sunni honour and supremacy. By trying to get the US-led coalition forces rid of Iraq and triggering a civil war, dominated by sectarian hostilities, he was fantasizing a Sunni-led regime to come to power once again. Al-Zarqawi's vision of the endgame was to establish the Islamic State that would take root in Iraq and later in Syria.

Even during Saddam's time, the Iraqi society was deeply sectarian. All the Islamic State predecessor organizations were anti-Shias, and al-Zarqawi's own personal hatred of the Shia faith had doubled down on the overall Sunni–Shia matrix. His public statements and personal writings were obsessively hostile to the Shia faith. In one of the addresses, he had said: 'The Muslims or Sunnis will have no victory over the aggressive infidels such as Jews and Christians, until there is total annihilation of those under them, such as the apostate agents headed by the *rafida* [another word for Shias].'[95] Six years after al-Zarqawi's death, the Islamic State operational strategy and modus operandi continued to be dominated by sectarianism and anti-Shia motivations. His hostility to the Shias remained the most authoritative narrative in the Sunni camps thereafter.

Al-Zarqawi's primary political objective was sectarian: to empower Sunni Islam and violently attack, suppress and uproot Shia Islam.[96] While anti-Shiism was a long-standing orthodox Sunni fixation, it was aggravated by the Khomeinist revival of Shiism in 1997 and the Wahhabi Salafists' opposition to it. Al-Zarqawi's anti-Shiism was fanatical, obsessive, and characterized by demonization against Islam considering them more dangerous than Americans.

Ultrasectarianism, uncompromising violence and a focus on the immediate creation of an Islamic State as a base for the return of the Islamic caliphate defined al-Zarqawi. He popularized the perception that Shias were the single greatest threat to the very existence of Sunnis. To reinforce his opinion, he described Shias as mass murderers who indulged in widespread atrocities. He even articulated the genocidal 'Final Solution' doctrine towards them. Middle East experts observed that he maintained a fundamental Islamic State premise through his existence. In the global jihadist circles, it was he who introduced the barbaric use of social media

---

[95]Lister, Charles R., 'Lasting and Expanding', *The Islamic State: A Brief Introduction*, Brookings Institution Press, 2015, p. 8.
[96]Hunt, Emily, 'Al-Zarqawi's "Total War" on Iraq Shiites Exposes a Divide among Sunni Jihadists', *The Washington Institute for Near East Policy*, 15 November 2005, https://tinyurl.com/bdfespby. Accessed on 12 September 2023.

for displaying the grotesque spectacle of beheadings, terror-inducing coercions and other acts of brutal violence.

His consistent anti-Shia rhetoric, however, upset his Jordanian mentor Abu Muhmmad al-Maqdisi, who questioned his blaming and targeting of Shia Muslims for all the evils. Maqdisi, through his website, www.almaqdese.com, and interviews on television channels, criticized al-Zarqawi's acts and said that he did not consider ordinary Shiaes as non-Muslims and they should not be equated with Americans. Maqdisi strongly objected to attacks on Muslim civilians and places of worship. Many al-Qaeda senior leaders in Afghanistan also maintained that al-Zarqawi's actions in Iraq and Syria 'seriously damaged the reputation of Islam'.

US Blunders in Iraq

The mindless decision by Paul Bremer, chief administrator of the US-led Coalition Provisional Authority (CPA), to dissolve the entire Iraqi military, security and intelligence apparatus meant that Iraq's 400,000 security forces cease, to function overnight.[97] The American political scientist and legal scholar James P. Pfiffner, in an article in the *Intelligence and National Security* journal in 2010, has succinctly catalogued the US blunders in Iraq. The decision, according to him, had fuelled the insurgency, alienating thousands of ordinary Iraqis who could not support their families. It disrupted normal social and economic activities. It brought about a general feeling of insecurity and extreme anger against the US among the people, many of whom had weapons and trained to use them.[98] The patrols by the British and American special operation forces were restricted to main urban areas. The disbanding threw thousands out of work and created a

---

[97]Fetouri, Mustafa, 'Paul Bremer's Legacy in Iraq Is Being Expanded across the Arab World', *Middle East Monitor*, 23 May 2019, https://tinyurl.com/25t7xu7k. Accessed on 12 September 2023.
[98]Pfiffner, James P., 'US Blunders in Iraq: De-Baathification and Disbanding the Army', *Intelligence and National Security*, Vol. 25, No.1, 2010, pp. 76–85.

large pool of unemployed and armed men who felt cheated and humiliated by the US occupiers.

The irony was that Paul Bremer had no experience in the military or in Middle Eastern politics or administration; this was his first stint in Iraq and he had spent only 10 days in the country when he issued the order. The CPA orders had been a matter of many heated discussions, deliberations and controversies among the retired army officers, politicians and administrators thereafter. President Bush had later told his biographer Roger Draper that 'the policy was to keep the army intact. How the decision was reversed is a mystery to me.'[99] It was possible that Bremer made the decision entirely on his own. But it seems unlikely that Bush or the White House would allow this to happen. Bremer, when locked in an argument with retired army lieutenant general Jay Garner had said that he was only following the President's orders. Maybe the Secretary of Defense Rumsfeld could also be the man responsible for this chaos in Iraq. This one decision, however, had provided a huge opportunity for the jihadist groups, both local and foreign, to recruit the jobless Iraqi army officers to the networks of the Islamic State and other extremist organizations. Many independent recruiting centres mushroomed in the Sunni-majority towns of Iraq and in the eastern part of Syria between 2003 and 2005 to attract foreign fighters and Iraq veterans.

It was a young Iraqi from Mosul, Abu Ghadiya, who was appointed by al-Zarqawi, the al-Qaeda representative in Iraq, as the chief of logistics. He controlled the flow of funds, weapons and fighters through Syria into Iraq. He set up an office in Damascus to provide passports to foreign fighters who were arriving by air at the Damascus International Airport and by land from Jordan to the south, Lebanon to the west and Turkey to the north. The Damascus office, with laptops connected to high-speed Internet, managed the database of foreign fighters. The volunteers would brief the new

---

[99] Kaplan, Fred, 'Who Made the Worst Decision of the Iraq War?', *Slate*, 27 March 2018, https://tinyurl.com/mr367jys. Accessed on 20 September 2023.

arrivals and provide them information in hard copies about their stay and travel to Iraq and to whom they should meet once they arrive in the Sunni-dominated Iraqi neighbourhoods.

Earlier, all the Syrian Baathist, Iraqi Baathist and the al-Qaeda forces had come together as they all believed and practised the same Sunni–Wahhabi–Salafi ideology and considered Shias as heretics. The strategic calculus in Syria, however, slowly changed under intense US and international diplomatic pressure to shut all foreign fighters recruitment centres operating on its territory. By early 2005, the Syrian security establishment also shifted its earlier soft position and began arresting all the middle level al-Qaeda operatives, linked to their facilitators in Aleppo, Damascus and Deir ez Zor. The number of foreign fighters coming through Syria decreased considerably and the fighters then started taking the Turkish and Lebanese routes.

All the predecessor organizations of the ISI had been deeply sectarian, and it was part of the strategic narrative related to the emerging Sunni–Shia fault lines. This also had a reinforcing effect on al-Zarqawi's personal hatred towards Shia Islam, as he was raised on the Saudi Salafism, which considered followers of Shia and Sufi Islam as apostates and heretics. His hatred was so pervasive that he even dispatched his father-in-law to bomb the Shia shrine in Najaf. His final public address before he was killed by the US bombing on 7 June 2006 stands testimony to this hate. Five days after al-Zarqawi's death, the AQI named as its new emir Abu Ayyub al-Masri, who renamed the AQI as the Islamic State in Iraq (ISI) on 15 October 2006. Shortly after that, Abu Omar al-Baghdadi was named the leader of the re-named outfit.

In a video uploaded on the Internet by the AQI the following day, it claimed that the intended 'state' would include Iraq's existing provinces of Baghdad, Anbar, Kirkuk, Saladin and parts of Babil, and will be governed by the Sharia law. The ISI formation statement named Abu Omar al-Baghdadi as the caliph, who was given the title of Emir al-Muminin—normally reserved for the first four caliphs of Islam. Abu Omar al-Baghdadi was a member of the Quraish tribe, from which the next caliph would emerge according to Islamic traditions. However, Abu Omar was killed along with the AQI leader Abu Hamza al-Muhajir in April 2010 during a US raid. He was immediately replaced by another prominent ISI emir belonging to the same tribe: Abu Bakr al-Baghdadi.

Between 2012-13 and 20 the Islamic State fighters attacked the US-run military prisons. They carried out several bombing attacks and were successful in freeing jihadists from as many as eight prisons. Following the withdrawal of the US forces in 2011, all the jihadi organizations came together as one group to materialize their dream. Fully loaded with the Salafi ideology and motivated by the thought of reclaiming the lost space of Sunni Islam in Iraq, the group launched its own jihadi surge. The political frustrations, sparked by the proliferation of the Arab Spring and the discriminatory attitude towards Sunnis by the Shia-dominated regime installed by the US interim administration, were rightly exploited by this group. By the summer of 2014, the Iraq and Syria moved closer to disintegration as their diverse communities—Shias, Sunnis, Kurds, Alawites and Christians, found that they were fighting for their own existence.

The Islamic State increased the frequency of attacks, targeting southern Shia areas of Iraq and the Kurdish north. In the meantime, senior commanders were sent to Syria to establish a joint front with al-Nusra, an affiliate of the al-Qaeda in Syria. The Islamic State leaders were focussing on the Iraq Shia government to stop the unprecedented suppression of the Sunni communities by launching coordinated suicide and car bomb attacks in Baghdad and other important locations. The bombs went off almost daily and gunfire was a steady background noise of Baghdad. The mounting civilian casualties and the widespread mayhem shook the central Iraqi government and it also destroyed the morale of the security forces.

Between 2012-14 and 20 the Islamic State expanded its operational network considerably by collecting intelligence on the local community dynamics and the armed and security forces. The ISI increased 'spot assassinations' of the city's security officers. A study was conducted by the 'jihadists think tank' to test the resolve of the Iraqi security apparatus and to identify the security holes before the Islamic State would make its soft entry. The Sunni tribal leadership was connected to the Islamic State equation to blunt any attempt by the Shia government to make a reconciliation with the Sunni communities.

Role of Foreign Fighters

The ISI had become heavily influenced by the role of foreign fighters,[100] of which a majority was coming from the Arab states. Tunisians, Saudis and Jordanians continued to outnumber other foreign nationals. It was suggestive of the fact that there were compelling Islamic reasons for the fighters to voluntarily join the organization. The majority of foreign fighters used to go to Syria. Then March 2003 happened, and the neighbouring Iraq was invaded by the coalition army led by the US ground forces. The anti-American jihadists in Aleppo, Deraa and elsewhere began to adopt a strident and overt public profile. Iraq provided an opportunity to the Syrian jihadists to organize groups to give resistance to the coalition forces. During the early days of the invasion, busloads of jihadists drove across Syria to the eastern city of Deir ez Zor, where the border guards willingly waved them through 'open gates' to Iraq. Many reports suggested that within 11 days of the invasion, more than 5,000 volunteers had travelled to Iraq via Syria.

The Islamic Jihad Movement of Palestine had sent more than 1,000 volunteers, many of who had signed up as suicide bombers. The British Special Air Services commandos even detained four busloads of potential suicide bombers with Syrian passports, who were going to the Sunni-dominated western Anbar province. This was the beginning of a mass migration of Syrian and other jihadists

---

[100]Barrett, Richard et al., *Foreign Fighters in Syria*, The Soufan Center, 2014, https://tinyurl.com/mtcvkzkv. Accessed on 12 September 2023.

to Iraq to fight the American-led coalition forces. Paradoxically enough, the movement was facilitated by the Syrian security forces, despite Bashar al-Assad giving his unqualified support to the US president in their 'war on terror'. Eastern Syria has a 605-km-long border with Iraq, which is tribally dominated, largely deserted and sparsely populated. After the Iraq invasion, the global jihadists used the porous border as a transit point to enter Iraq. The Iraqi recruiters brought European and Arab jihadists through the crossing point of Deir ez Zor.

The dynamics of Syrian revolution were still taking shape in late 2012 as the public surge pivoted in favour of the opposition and the government's area of influence shrank very fast. The government forces were compelled to redeploy in the front areas as border crossings were beginning to fall off government controls. Regime army, security and police officers were continuing to defect in dozens, while more senior officers were also beginning to quit. In the fast-developing conflict, the small jihadist group al-Nusra had established its active presence in different parts of Syria with its recently acquired capabilities for carrying out sophisticated and sustained guerilla type campaigns. It was doing fine to bolster the opposition to the regime. But some also viewed it as a body created by an agent of the regime. This was the perception and not the reality on the ground. The winter of 2012–13 set the stage for a gradual Islamization of the northern insurgency, which itself encouraged tensions between the Islamic factions and the groups aligned with the Free Syrian Army (FSA).

Abu Bakr al-Baghdadi, the Islamic State supremo in Iraq, had formally approved the relationship with the al-Nusra, to pitch against the regime forces. Al-Zawahiri, the Pakistan-based al-Qaeda leader, however, was not pleased with the development, as his intent was to keep his identity separate from Syria's al-Nusra. He also abhorred the emerging leadership of Abu Bakr al-Baghdadi. Ayman al-Zawahiri was blaming ISIS for sparking a 'political disaster' in Syria as fighting intensity was increasing in the oil city of Deir ez Zor. Raqqa was emerging as the de facto capital of ISIS. With the intra-jihadist relations at an all-time low, ISIS fighters had already begun targeting the al-Nusra fighters and other smaller Syrian jihadi groups. Slowly, the balance was tipping in favour of ISIS and the news agency Reuters reported that ISIS was killing more al-Nusra fighters every week than the pro-regime forces. Al-Zawahiri was very upset about the developments. He dissociated himself from ISIS and blamed them for causing divisions within the mujahideen in Syria. He was very critical of Abu Bakr al-Baghdadi and even maintained that he was not part of al-Qaeda in Iraq.

After months of allegations surrounding their roles in the conflict, Iran, Hezbollah and other foreign militias[101] all began to emerge as active players in the Syrian power game. They started by advising, training and helping the forces in support of the regime. Iranian military advisors and Hezbollah had been reinforced by other Shia militants, primarily from Afghanistan, Iraq and Pakistan. The original aim was to defend the holy sites of Shias, as they believed that Sunnis would destroy them if the Bashar al-Assad regime toppled. Syria is Iran's main ally in the Arab world, and Tehran entered the conflict fearing that any successor to the Assad regime, led by the country's Sunni majority, would align itself with Saudi Arabia.

A decision was made to create a nationwide paramilitary force, known as the National Defense Force. Syrian jihadist groups and the foreign fighters continued to increase their role in the insurgent operations after forming different coalitions. Subsequently, the Syrian jihadist groups coalesced into two large fronts, the Syrian Islamic Liberation Front (SILF) and those with more Wahhabi strain as the Syrian Islamic Front (SIF). It was reported that in early 2013, at least 3,000 foreign fighters joined the Syrian jihad and some of them were former Guantanamo Bay detainees. In March 2013, the jihadists, along with other smaller villages and towns in the Euphrates river valley, captured the northern city of Raqqa. The European and North

---

[101] Laub, Zachary, 'Who's Who in Syria's Civil War', *Council on Foreign Relations*, 2017.

American Salafi jihadists with an international outlook were gaining stature in northern Syria and Damascus.

Another new actor emerging on the other side of the fence was the Islamic Revolutionary Guard Corps. They were set to fight alongside Hezbollah and other Shia militias in favour of the Assad regime. The Syrian regime had started employing helicopter gunships and fighter jets in confronting the opposition and its civilian supporters. The Syrian army had even fired short-range unguided Scud Ballistic Missiles into populated areas. The Palestinian and Kurdish fighters also entered the scene to complicate the situation further. The FSA, whose leadership was based in Turkey, had virtually ceased to exist as an organization. Its place was taken by autonomous small 'rebel units' across Syria. During the winter of 2013, the opposition groups led by Wahhabi–Salafi jihadists had captured many towns and rampaged them by enforcing the strict Sharia laws. For the first time, the Assad Presidency came under serious threat from the opposition, as the fighting capabilities of the government forces were depleting fast. But a new reality was to emerge in Syria soon.

The visible presence of pro-regime militias and the Iranian-backed paramilitary irregulars was beginning to herald a potential strategic rebalancing in the country by the early months of 2013. The regime and pro-regime forces were able to stabilize parts of Damascus, the southern city of Homs and the Alawite heartlands. The support provided by Iran and Hezbollah to the regime strengthened the president and his fighters, who directly locked in with the opposition. Northern Syria, however, was increasingly dominated by the opposition groups, and it was slowly turning into safe havens of jihadis. The various tribes in Deir ez Zor had formed a working relationship with the al-Nusra front and captured the oil field facilities there.

In 2006, a prominent Iraqi tribal leader, Sheikh Rishawi, announced the formation of the Anbar Awakening Council, which would restrict the territorial control of ISIS in the western Sunni-dominated Iraq. This bottom-up tribal initiative came at the behest of the US forces with their funds and weaponry. It actually came up in response to ISIS's imposition of a strict Sharia law, which included banning women from purchasing supposedly sexually suggestive cucumbers and prohibiting production and sale of ice cream as it 'represented the American imperialism'.

In the year 2007, the Syrian administration came under scrutiny as the US intelligence had informed the White House that about 90 per cent of foreign fighters were transiting through Syria, to Iraq. They suspected that a section of the Syrian security forces were complicit with jihadi elements in the regime. In Iraq, the ISI was under intense pressure from the security forces, backed by the coalition troops and the Iraqi Sunni society, all acting in tandem to defeat the ISI. The US Secretary of State Condoleezza Rice also asked the Syrian foreign ministry to stop the cross-border network of foreign fighters. Syria's apparent role in backing ISIS in Iraq came to light with the confession of a Saudi fighter who had divulged that he had received training from a camp run by al-Qaeda, which was protected by the Syrian intelligence services. The camp was known to the Syrian intelligence apparatus. ISIS militants had launched many daring attacks from Syria to the border towns of Anbar Province. In 2009–10, ISIS suicide bombers were bombing at their will. And they had created an unprecedented mayhem in Iraq. Most of the time, the targets were Iraqi Shias or the security forces, which were dominated by Shias.

The foreign fighters' jihadi romance with Iraq and Syria was truly global. Volunteers from at least from 86 countries travelled to Syria to fight alongside the Islamic State. The recruiting power of its social media platforms was amazing. Over 5,000 fighters from four European countries alone—France, the UK, Germany and Belgium— joined the outfit. There was a big concern in the European capitals regarding the security implications of their possible return to these countries. In North African countries like Libya and Tunisia, foreign fighters' hubs were very active. It was in the Libyan cities of Benghazi and Derna, where they gathered for recruitment. In Tunisia, the city of Ben Gardane provided the largest number of fighters. There, the tradition of jihad was so strong that once al-Zarqawi even remarked, 'If Ben Gardane had been located next to Fallujah, we would have liberated Iraq very easily.'[102] There were about 600 fighters from the South Asian countries, mainly Indonesia and Malaysia. Those who were already in Saudi Arabia for studies had also joined the force. According to the FBI director James Comey, more than 150 Americans and as many Canadians travelled to Syria as of September 2015.[103]

Historically speaking, Saudi Arabia had played a major role in making the jihadi fighters amply available for recruitment from different parts of the world for the last several decades. Starting from the early 1980s, the kingdom has been spreading across the globe, the extremely intolerant, bigoted and regressive ideology of Wahhabi Salafism, based on a literal and fundamental interpretation of the Quran and the Hadith, using its massive wealth from the oil. This aggressive export of the ideology was made possible through different socio-cultural and religious arms of the kingdom, including the Muslim World League.

In 2014, ISIS posted a video of the foreign jihadists burning their passports to demonstrate their permanent commitment to jihad and the cause of the Islamic State. The video was professionally shot as each jihadi ripped up his passport and threw it into flames, as they made a declaration of their faith and promise to fight against the ruler of the country. A Canadian was also seen, in the video, making a short speech in English, before he switched over to Arabic, targeting America and Canada saying, 'We are coming and we will destroy you.'[104] Jihadis from countries like Saudi, Egypt, Jordan and

---

[102]Bryant, Lisa, 'Inside Tunisia's Extremist Breeding Ground', *VOA*, 6 June 2016, https://tinyurl.com/yrbsmhvw. Accessed on 25 September 2023.
[103]U.S. Government Publishing Office, 'Countering Violent Islamist Extremism: The Urgent Threat of Foreign Fighters and Home-Grown Terror'. 11 February 2015, https://tinyurl.com/2x4xy8rk. Accessed on 26 September 2023.
[104]Mayer, Andre, 'John Maguire ISIS Video Is "Silly," Say Radicalization

Chechnya were also seen making short speeches to declare their lifelong commitment to ISIS in the video. The whole of the Euphrates river valley through western Iraq, eastern Syria and right up to the Turkish border was under ISIS rule in 2015. The entire swathe was estimated to be equal to the size of Britain. The Syrian-Iraqi border largely ceased to exist. In Iraq, all the Sunni areas, about a quarter of the country, were once under the control of ISIS.

A Moroccan-Swedish national, Abu Qaswarah al-Maghrib, who had earlier learned the jihadist craft in Afghanistan, was assigned the responsibility of managing the affairs in the city of Mosul. After his death in 2008, a Syrian national, Abu Mohammed al-Jolani, was given the responsibility. The US Special Forces, in 2009, increased their attacks on the Islamic State, and many senior leaders of the outfit were killed. Nevertheless, the edges made by the US-led coalition forces tapered off following the withdrawal process of the forces from mid-2009 to August 2010. President Obama made some sincere efforts to end the combat mission and negotiate a protocol with Nouri al-Maliki's Shia government in Baghdad. He proposed to maintain the US bases, with 50,000 troops in the country to ensure internal security, beyond December 2010. The Iraqi parliament, however, rejected the US proposal under Iranian pressure, ignoring the developing Sunni insurgency led by the Islamic State. Later, President Obama glossed over the rejection, describing it as Iraq shaping its own future.

The Syrian security forces brutally crushed the uprisings and protests during the Arab Spring in the country by killing the young, old and children on its streets. The ordinary citizen was appalled across Syria. Using the Internet, they posted videos of the excesses by the security forces. They mobilized the crowds and encouraged escalation of protest, and by, and by the birth of a revolution happened. In the beginning, people raised issues like liberty, freedom,

---

Experts', *CBC*, 9 December 2014, https://tinyurl.com/4982b6pz. Accessed on 25 September 2023.

anti-corruption and the participation of people in governance. The entire family, from grandparents to grandchildren, used to participate in peaceful marches, hoping that the mass movement would end up getting some concession from the Assad regime. Continued and harsh response from the security forces brought all the opposition groups together and they formed many self-protection militias, which by the summer of 2011 gave rise to the FSA. In the meantime, jihadists released from the prisons since March had begun to merge together and form a slightly more Islamists-minded resistance force.

In the late 1990s, Hafez al-Assad, father of Bashar al-Assad, had taken a conscious decision to allow the practice of a more overt form of Wahhabi Salafism in Syria. Consequently, dozens of new mosques, Islamic schools, and Quranic centres were opened across the country, funded by the Muslim World League of Saudi Arabia. Wahhabi–Salafi-inspired Islamic literature and interpretation of the Quran were introduced to all the Sunni mosques and madrasas by marginalizing the traditional Hanafi Sufi Islam, formerly followed by majority of the Syrian Sunnis. These institutions became the hub of a strident strain of conservative, intolerant, Salafi Islam. The sense of moderation, derived from the Sufi Sunni Islamic traditions declined all over Syria. Unfortunately, Bashar al-Assad also was supportive of these jihadists in the early years of his rule with a mistaken hope that they would extend support to his rule. On the flip side, the Wahhabi influence was slowly growing strong and their presence was becoming visible in the Sunni majority southern city of Deraa, and the northern city of Aleppo.

An important preacher was Mahmoud Ouul al-Ghassi, who was operating from the al-Sahour Mosque in Aleppo. At that time, the Palestinian issue with renewed conflicts was dominating the news. For the emerging Syrian jihadists, the events of 9/11 in the US, were a great inspiration, and all the Wahhabi Sunni jihadists were celebrating the victory of Osama bin Laden and its al-Qaeda organization. A section of Syrian society always followed the anti-American and anti-Israel narratives. It was not surprising that after

9/11, isolated celebratory functions were held in different parts of the country. The powerful security apparatus, built by the Baath party and Hafez al-Assad was able to arrest the offenders and give unequivocal support to the US in its fight against the jihadis. Aleppo, which was traditionally a Sunni-dominated Islamic urban centre, had slowly been converted to a centre of Wahhabi–Salafi strain of Islam, attracting many jihadists to it from other parts of Syria. Abu al-Qaqa's Ghuraba al-Sham movement was growing in strength, and it soon became dominant in Aleppo. Even the security forces were no longer able to restrain it. Soon, more than a thousand volunteers tried to enforce strict Sharia laws on the outlying residential areas of Aleppo. During nighttime, the jihadi moral police started patrolling and intimidating the people, who were used to Syria's traditional liberal lifestyles.

According to the Austrian Ministry of Interior, 230 identified individuals had left for Syria and Iraq from the country to join ISIS. The departing Austrians were predominantly of Chechen, Turkish and Balkan origin. They were all second- or third-generation immigrants in the age group of 18 to 35. Most recent estimates from the official sources suggested that 515 jihadis went from Belgium, of which 47 were females. According to Danish Security and Intelligence Service (PET), at least 125 people had left Denmark to Syria and Iraq. French security agencies maintained that more than 900 individuals left for Syria and Iraq from France. They constitute the largest numbers of European jihadists, mostly second and third generations immigrants from Morocco, Tunisia, Algeria and Senegal. Of this, about 23 per cent were converts. According to sources from the Federal Prosecutor of Germany, 750 people in the age group of 20 to 30 had left for jihad from the country. About 12 percent of the group were converts and mostly employed in the low-paid skilled sector. Based on the official records, around 220 jihadist under the age of 25 had left the Netherlands to join ISIS. The majority were from the lower middle class socio-economic backgrounds having Moroccan, Somali, Antillean and Turkish ethnic origins. Most of them were deeply frustrated of their own societal positions or were faced with discrimination because of their ethnicity.

Spain, another European country with a sizable Muslim population, saw 139 jihadi fighters in their mid-20s travelling to Syria and Iraq as a part of the aggressive mobilization from Western countries. According to the UK Office for Security and Counter-Terrorism (OSCT), approximately 700 British-born youths between the age of 18 and 30 had left for jihad. They were mainly Arabs, South Asian ethnic groups and converts from Africa. The recruitment videos and messages on social media were so effective that ISIS had attracted jihadi fighters from countries like Croatia, Czech Republic, Estonia, Finland, Ireland, Italy, Latvia, Luxembourg, Malta, Poland, Portugal, Romania, Slovakia, Slovenia and Denmark. By the early 2016, an estimated 43,000 jihadis under the age of 35 had left Europe to fight for the Islamic State. The Netherlands-based international Centre for Counter Terrorism (CCT) reported that 2015 witnessed the largest exodus of Muslim jihadis from the European Union to Syria and Iraq. A compelling reason, it said, was the announcement regarding the soon-to-be established Islamic caliphate in Syria.

President Bashar al-Assad had completed his 10 years in power in Syria by 2010. In politics, he was continuing his father's strategy. By August 2011, several jihadist insurgent groups were established in Damascus and northern Syria with a senior commander of ISIS dispatched to establish a Syria-based wing of the outfit. As violence across Syria reached a certain level by the end of the year, ISIS carried out its first suicide attack outside the Syrian military intelligence facilities in Damascus. As the anti-government violence gained momentum in Homs, Aleppo, Damascus, Deir ez Zor and Raqqa, the security forces crushed them brutally, including through aerial bombing. President Bashar al-Assad labelled the unrest as a foreign conspiracy. The fight was getting intense. Many senior Syrian army officers belonging to Sunni sects were deserting the security forces and joining the foreign fighters front led by ISIS. The morale of the Syrian army was at its lowest point as the news spread of the proliferating numbers of defections. The officers were refusing orders to shoot at innocent civilians. Strangely enough, President Assad then signed a decree, which gave official amnesty to Muslim Brotherhood and other political detainees. This allowed a large number of jihadists prisoners to find themselves released. Many of them took an active role in the ongoing revolution. The unrelenting air bombing and killing of civilians in Homs and Aleppo convinced all Syrian watchers that President Assad had adopted a security-focussed solution to the revolution.

Mohammed al-Jolani, a Syrian-born jihadi from the Golan Heights region had travelled to Iraq during the occupation and joined the al-Qaeda there. He was asked by Abu Bakr al-Baghdadi to travel back to Syria to organize ISIS linked cells. In 2008, he served in Mosul and, after the death of al-Zarqawi in 2006, rose in the hierarchy. In October 2011, Jabhat al-Nusra was formed. The Iraq-based ISIS had agreed to provide it with financial support. In the initial meetings, Jolani and others had designed its ideological foundation and the religio-political objectives very clearly. Soon other prominent ISIS fighters joined. The al-Nusra did not officially announce its existence till early 2012. Its main mission was to focus on Syria. Although the core members of the al-Nusra had strong links with ISIS, they never declared it publicly. In order to implement the planned strategy, the al-Nusra attacked targets in Aleppo and Homs to cause maximum damage to security forces of the Assad regime. Then came reports of 'massacre' of civilians, seemingly committed by the pro-regime militia in the Sunni neighbourhoods.

Role of Other Arab Nations

The governments of both Saudi Arabia and Qatar were early supporters of the political and military uprising in Syria. The private financial support from individuals and institutions out of Kuwait, however, played a key role in sustaining the insurgency. The fundraising efforts by the Kuwaiti Salafists, under the Islamic

Heritage Society, was commendable. At this point, a large majority of funds was sent to groups affiliated to the FSA. In early 2012, the al-Qaeda leader al-Zawahiri called for jihad in Syria against the regime, and appealed to all jihadists to travel to Syria and support the Islamic revolution. In mid-2012, Syria was fast moving towards civil war, as foreign fighters continued to arrive in an organized way. By the end of July, there were hundreds of non-Syrian fighters in the ranks of armed insurgency with the al-Nusra and FSA tags.

Saudi Arabia was important in the Middle East not just because of its vast oil wealth. The fact that it was the global epicentre of Wahhabi Salafism, the extremely fundamentalist ideology, made it all the more important. It was from there that the scary version of Islam, with a strict Sharia law and an intense hate for non-Sunni sects and non-Muslims, was being exported to different parts of the world. This religious intolerance and political authoritarianism, promoted by Wahhabi Islam with its callous readiness to use violence, has many similarities with European fascism of the 1930s. Amazingly, Wahhabism had almost completely taken over the mainstream Sunni Islam globally in recent decades. In one country after the other, Saudi Arabia has been investing hugely for training imams, building mosques and establishing the Islamic study centres to promote Wahhabism. As a result, sectarian strife between Sunnis and Shias has grown vigorously with the latter finding themselves targeted with unprecedented viciousness, from Los Angeles to Tokyo and from Alaska to Cape Town.

Sectarianism continues to poison the relationship between the sects in every small or large Muslim community. A Muslim friend in New York observed: 'Go through the address books of any Sunni or Shia person, you will find very few names outside their own sect.' In fact, even Saudi Arabia, Jordan and Turkey are frightened by the monster they themselves have helped to create by promoting Wahhabi Salafism. It is beyond comprehension for many why the US and its Western allies are still siding with the theocratic absolute monarchy of Saudi Arabia, which is the global promoter of Wahhabism. The resurgent al-Qaeda and the Islamic State are growing because the intolerant and exclusive Salafism has taken strong roots within the Muslim communities over the years. And, thanks to none other than Saudi Arabia, ISIS has smartly globalized and weaponized a section of Muslims across the world.

Besides the global spread of Wahhabism post 1979, another important factor that is contributing to the radicalization of the Muslim community is the Middle East policy of Western countries, which is hegemonic, exploitative and insensitive towards a lot of socio-religious factors. The lack of integration of Muslim communities with the European societies is always keeping them away from the mainstream. The surrounding social structure and their family's insistence on following a strict Salafi way of life make them lonely and force them to spend more time on the Internet. The isolation makes them depressed, frustrated and alienated from the cultural realities of the host country, making them more vulnerable to the instigative sermons of the jihadi imams and the online radicalization taking place on the Internet.

By the fall of 2014, the Islamic State had gone through over 15 years of evolution, surviving the US invasion of Afghanistan and its military might in Iraq. If the jihadi movement has to transform its concept into reality, it has to first build a viable state somewhere and smartly incorporate the operational architecture to it before giving it a chance to stand alone. The summer of 2014 was dramatic for ISIS and for the entire international jihadi movement. The events in Iraq were directly affecting the future trajectory of the Syrian conflict. The military success of ISIS in capturing a large swathe of territory, stretching across 670 km of Syria and Iraq, was groundbreaking, and it was all set to revolutionize the future of jihadist militants around the world.

Capture of Mosul

By 9 June 2014, ISIS had captured many important landmarks of the city, like the headquarters of the Federal Police Division, the international airport and the provincial council buildings. The ISIS suicide bombers were effectively used to hit the army depots and other resistance points. The Islamic State fighters fully captured the city of Mosul[105] on 10 June by defeating a 30,000 strong Iraqi army and another 30,000 federal police force in a fierce fight of six days. They captured huge ammunition, all kinds of military vehicles, including a large number of Humvees. A vast amount of cash was in the local banks when Mosul fell. ISIS took out approximately over US $2 billion from various banks in the city. Before invading Mosul, they were in virtual control of Raqqa, part of the Deir ez-Zor province. The city's main prison, Badush, was emptied and over 1,500 detainees were set free. More than 600 Shia Iraqi soldiers, recruited after the US invasion, were executed in a nearby desert ravine. After stabilizing its authority in Mosul, ISIS attacked and captured other Sunni strongholds like Fallujah. Later, they also captured Kirkuk, Zab, Ninawa, Rishad, and Hawija. Then, they headed directly along Highway I into the northern city of Saldin. The ISIS fighters after encircling Tikrit sparked great panic in the nearby Air Academy, where 3,000 soldiers shed their military uniforms and fled on foot in fear of the impending attack.

The ISIS fighters were not alone in their advances and routing of the Iraqi armed forces. In fact, a large number of Sunni armed militia groups, drawn from many organizations, were contributing to this armed rebellion. In addition to the capture and the subsequent execution of hundreds of prisoners, most of them Shias, ISIS also attacked and kidnapped many Turkish truck drivers outside Mosul and attacked the Turkish consulates in the city. The Sunni extremists were moving towards the north in the Kurdish territory. But, they were resisted by the Peshmerga forces and the Kurdish army. Iraq was fast splitting along sectarian and ethnic lines, with Kurds seeking their

---

[105]Cockburn, Patrick, 'Iraq Crisis: Capture of Mosul Ushers in the Birth of Sunni caliphate', *The Independent*, 11 June 2014, https://tinyurl.com/4ecyy2j5. Accessed on 8 September 2023.

authority in the north and the vast majority of Sunnis supporting the revolution. The Shia-led Nouri al-Maliki government continuously ignored the legitimate demands of the Sunni population. The government forces were in great trouble and fast losing space and manpower.

The rout of Iraqi forces was led by their commanding officers. In the town of Baiji, home to Iraq's largest refinery, they gave up without resistance, as they did in Tikrit. At both the places, commanding officers were rescued by helicopters. In Tikrit, soldiers who surrendered were divided into two groups—Sunni and Shia— and all the Shia soldiers were machine-gunned as they stood in front of a trench. Their execution was recorded on video to intimidate the remaining units of the Iraqi security forces. The US reported that five army and police divisions out of 18 had disintegrated during the fall of Mosul and other areas in northern Iraq. The defeat was mostly due to disbelief and panic in the highest echelons of the government as most of the commanding officers were hand picked by the prime minister himself. People were frightened by the abject surrender of the security forces. Rumours were afloat that soon ISIS would attack Baghdad, which was only an hour's drive away from Tikrit and Fallija. The Sunni neighbourhoods in Baghdad, like Adhamiya on the east bank of Tigris, appeared to be deserted. ISIS was desperate to seize even parts of Baghdad, one of the great Arab capitals and former seat of the caliphate, as it would attract great media attention and give huge credibility to its claim of founding the new Islamic State.

The fall of Mosul had changed the balance of power between Iraq's three main communities: Shia, Sunni and Kurds. Shia rule in the non-Shia areas received a blow from which it would become difficult to recover; Kurdish dominance in mixed Kurdish-Arab areas expanded and the 5 or 6 million Sunni Arabs would never be marginalized again. It is just not in Iraq that the balance of power was changing. The Iraq-Syria border no longer existed for most practical purposes. In Syria, ISIS forces were becoming more powerful because of the weapons and money from its newly conquered territories in Iraq.

To salvage the deteriorating situation, the Grand Ayatollah Ali al-Sistani, Iraq's leading Shia cleric, was compelled to announce a passionate appeal during his Friday sermons on 13 June 2014 that all the able-bodied Iraqis should come forward to defend their holy land from ISIS terrorists. That evening, thousands of Shia volunteers congregated in Taji to receive the basic training to fight the Sunni insurgency, which was coming like a tsunami across Iraq and Syria. There were reports that the whole of the Anbar, the giant Sunni province, with a population of 1.5 million, had fallen. It was at that time that the US entered the chaotic scene of the sectarian war, with President Obama approving the deployment of 275 military personnel to Iraq. ISIS was rampaging through Iraq by capturing town after town and executing soldiers. Its extraordinary success had bewildered the Arab watchers around the world. ISIS, after capturing Mosul, had transferred huge amounts arms, ammunition and Humvees to eastern Syria to strengthen its attacks there. The Al-Hayat Media Center, the media wing of ISIS, released an HD video titled 'There Is no Life Without Jihad' on 19 June 2014, inviting English-speaking Muslims in Western countries for jihad. A large number of recruits were attracted from Australia, Britain, the USA and Canada. As a result of this, more than 700 fighters joined the force from Australia and Britain alone. The ISIS leadership in Iraq and Syria was upbeat by their remarkable success in capturing a large swathe of land both in northern Iraq and eastern Syria. The checkpoints on the border between Iraq and Syria were controlled by ISIS fighters.

For Iraq, the declaration of a new caliphate by Abu Bakr al-Baghdadi, replacing the one abolished by Mustafa Kemal Ataturk in Turkey in 1924, was a declaration of war. For the people in Baghdad, a city of 7 million, mostly Shias, the expansion of the Islamic State was a nightmare. Al-Baghdadi moved into Mosul in a convoy, like a head of the state, led by horses carrying ISIS flags, with four motorcycle riders on either side of the swanky SUVs.[106] Similar parade was taken

---

[106]Lafta, R. et al., 'Living in Mosul during the Time of ISIS and the Military

out in Raqqa, the de facto capital of ISIS in Syria. Al-Baghdadi issued a video on 1 July 2014, in which he stressed upon the Islamic values of his organization and the establishment of the caliphate as an idea, which needed to be supported and consolidated by all Muslims. In his words, it was a mechanism for the reassertion of honour and power of the Sunni Muslims in the world.

The Islamic State was structured like a pyramid, with Abu Bakr al-Baghdadi at the top as the Emir al-Muminin (Leader of the Muslim world), and under him, two deputies—one for Syria and one for Iraq. Below that stood a 10-man cabinet of ministers, a row of *walis* (governors) and a 12-man military council. They did not officially call it a 'state' but behaved like it was one and designed its internal structure accordingly. Following al-Baghdadi's assumption of control in 2010 and his phenomenal rise in importance, ISIS underwent a process of 'Iraqi-zation', whereby high-ranking positions were given to those who had held senior positions in Saddam Hussein's Baath government. The Islamic State's total income was estimated to be US $1–3 million per month, which made it the wealthiest terrorist organization in the world. The funds were used to pay salaries and run the local governments in occupied territories. Some US dollars were also used to buy tribal loyalties. The governance was based on a strict Sharia law, under which harsh punishments were given to offenders. The Islamic State, structurally, was always a jihadist organization undergirded by Salafism. They thrive amidst chaos and survive under immense pressure, so as to fight another day.

Capturing and ruling a large swathe of land across Iraq and Syria, ISIS showed that its administration could be ideologically sustainable. It is true, nonetheless, that the Islamic State's Salafist ideology would not have succeeded had the Shia-dominated Nouri al-Maliki government in Baghdad been more sensitive towards the concerns of the Sunni communities. Another factor that played a big

---

Liberation: Results from a 40-Cluster Household Survey', *Conflict and Health*, Vol. 12, No. 1, 2018, https://tinyurl.com/2pmbjcej. Accessed on 28 September 2023.

role in turning people against the regime was the brutal suppression of the popular uprising by the authorities in Syria during the early stage of the revolution.

By December 2014, the Islamic State fighters defeated the Iraqi army, the Syrian army, the Syrian rebels and the Kurdish Peshmerga. It almost established a state stretching from Mosul to Fallujah, and from Aleppo in Syria's northern border to the desert of Iraq in the south. Numerically, small ethnic and religious groups like the Yazidis of Sinjar and the Chaldean Christians of Mosul, become victims of ISIS brutalities. In its expansion plan to push the boundaries into Syria, the Syrian-Kurdish town Kobani came under its siege. Despite reservations by Turkey, the US air force came to rescue Kurdish defenders and started hitting targets with the ground information provided by Kurdish fighters. Subsequently, reinforcements came in the form of Peshmerga fighters and Kobani was saved.

The ISIS military successes have been helped not just by the incompetence of its enemies but also by the divisions between them. When the US air force bombing began in Syria, President Obama announced that Saudi Arabia, Jordan, the UAE, Qatar, Bahrain and Turkey were all joining the US as military partners against ISIS. But, as the Americans knew very well, these were all Sunni states, promoters of Salafism, which had historically played a vital role in fostering the jihadis in Syria and Iraq. This was a huge political problem for the US security establishment. Vice President Joe Biden, in a lecture at the Kennedy School at Harvard University, had said that Turkey, Saudi Arabia and the UAE had promoted 'a proxy Sunni-Shia war' in Syria and poured hundreds of millions of dollars and tens of thousands of weapons to anyone who fights against Bashar al-Assad. Weapons and dollars had been made available to jihadist organizations like the al-Nusra and al-Qaeda.

Turkey changed sides since the first uprising against Assad in 2011. When Bashar al-Assad dug his heels in and did not go the way Gaddafi did in Libya, Turkey decided to lend its full support to the jihadist groups led by ISIS, just as Pakistan had supported Taliban in Afghanistan before 9/11. During 2012–13, over 12,000 foreign jihadi fighters from Europe, Middle East, North Africa and North America transited through Turkey to the Syrian border; global media called it 'the jihadi highway'. The US was concerned and put pressure on Turkey to close its border with Syria. Later, Turkey complied and the flow turned into a trickle.

The relationship between Turkish intelligence services and ISIS was cloudy, but Turkey could secure the release of its consulate staff who were kept in Raqqa in exchange for the ISIS fighters held in Turkey. The news started trickling down from Mosul and other ISIS-held areas that life was hell even for the Sunni Arabs. The ISIS fighters had blown all the mosques in the city belonging to the followers of the Hanafi Sufi Sunni and Shia Islam as ISIS denounced them as places for apostasy, not prayer. The religion of Yazidis, who were living in poverty, is a blend of various religious traditions, including the veneration of fire from Zoroastrianism, baptisms from Christianity and circumcision from Islam. A large number of Yazidis were killed, raped and expelled from their lands during ISIS raids. Across their captured territories in Iraq and Syria, columns of ISIS fighters launched blitzkrieg attacks to catch their enemies by surprise. They came in captured US-made Humvees and trucks with swaying black flags. In a strategy of demoralizing the opposition forces even before the first shots were fired, jihadi social media experts would upload the HD videos of ISIS atrocities on the Internet. They were specialized in the use of suicide bombers, either moving or on foot or travelling in vehicles.

Prime Minister Haider al-Abadi's government, which took over in 2015, was more inclusive than that of his predecessor, Nouri al-Maliki. The Sunni Arabs, by this time were also totally fatigued by ISIS atrocities and the implementation of the strict Sharia law. The international community lauded the new government for its non-sectarian stance; Arab Sunnis hoped that they would face less day-to-day repression.

After the liberation of Mosul in July and Raqqa in October 2017, ISIS was severely weakened as a military threat. Together, Mosul and Raqqa became the twin symbols of ISIS's self-declared state, its base for operation and the destination for foreign recruits from around the world.[107] Air strikes by the US-led military coalition devastated both the cities. When the Syrian Democratic Forces announced the liberation of Raqqa, it marked the end of the Islamic State's global centre. It was here that the outfit had its first consolidated control on an urban population, before it went sweeping over the Iraqi border, capturing the city of Mosul and coming strikingly close to Baghdad. Abu Bakr al-Baghdadi had claimed that the Caliphate virtually extended over to the entire Sunni Muslims globally.

In the end, however, more than 8,000 of its fighters slipped off the battlefield to blend into the local population or moved to failed nations like Libya, Somalia, Yemen and Afghanistan. They left the entire region in total ruins, including the great cities of Mosul, Aleppo, Homs and world heritage sites like Palmyra. The images were reminiscent of the devastation caused to Frankfurt and Germany after the Second World War.

The anti-ISIS coalition, in the meantime, got fractured again, reviving divisions and creating conditions to allow the jihadists to regroup once again. The ISIS thought of taking advantage of the recent face off between the Peshmerga forces in northern Iraq and the Iraqi government forces over the independence of the semi-autonomous Kurdish region. Similarly, the US-backed Kurdish forces in western Syria fought against ISIS with their demand for a separate Kurdish region in Syria. The US security establishment and the State Department had no plans to stabilize the situation or capitalize on their military success. The semi-autonomous region of Kurdistan, which until recently was Iraq's anchor, was a big concern. Its future

---

[107]Cronk, Terri Moon, 'Raqqa, Mosul Liberations Progress as ISIL Loses Resources to Fight', *DOD News: US Department of Defense*, 6 December 2016, https://tinyurl.com/yck7uedt. Accessed on 23 September 2023.

as a unified Iraq was in danger. The US, Turkey and Iran—the main allies of the Kurds—did not like an independence referendum held in September 2017. The separation would undermine the unity of the anti-ISIS forces. The US prevailed upon the Iraqi government in sharing the oil revenue and maintaining the semi-autonomous status of Kurdistan. Meanwhile, Russia and Iran expanded its influence. Iran, being a Shia-majority state, has a leverage with Shia-ruled Iraq while keeping close relations with the Shia militias in Syria. Iran provided troops and arms along with Russian jet fighters and kept Bashar al-Assad in power. And in turn, it helped Tehran's goal of establishing a corridor linking Iran's Hezbollah in Lebanon with Damascus. In fact, Syrian forces were in a race to take control of the remaining ISIS pockets from the control of the US-backed forces as part of strengthening their hands in the future negotiations over Syria's political settlement.

Once the fighting was done, there was no way to force Russia and Iran to leave Syria. But the US smartly chiselled out a way to negotiate the limits of power of the two countries in post-war Syria. Another big challenge was an old one: persuading the Shiite-led government in Iraq to integrate the Sunni minority into the governing structure so that Sunnis too get to have a stake in the country's future. Chronic mistreatment of the Sunnis always created a fertile ground for ISIS recruiters.

Leaders of Turkey, Iran and Russia met at the Black Sea resort in Sochi on 22 November 2017 and underscored the influential role played by Russia in determining the outcome of the war. The meeting was aimed at impressing the US and the world that Russia was the new power broker in the Middle East and would play an important role in framing 'the future structure' of the Syrian state.

The US leaving Syria and Iraq without a proper recovery plan encompassing reconstruction, security and improved governance was creating conditions for ISIS to return. Having decimated the very land that they once occupied and where they set up a caliphate, the US and its partners were now required to show the militants as well as the overwhelmingly young population of the Middle East that the future did not lie with the extremists but with the people who love peace and prosperity.

After the retreat of the Islamic State fighters from the towns and villages of Iraq and Syria in 2017, a media outlet linked to the Syrian military said that the Islamic State of Abu Bakr al-Baghdadi may be holed up an ISIS pocket in the eastern town of Boukamel, which is located on the Iraqi border and was said to be its last stronghold in Syria. The pro-Syrian government media, however, reported that the town was liberated; a journalist of the Arabic news channel *Al-Ikhbariya* reported joyfully, breaking out on camera that 'Daesh is finished. Live.'

Many incidents, such as the ferocious attack on the Sufi al-Rawdah mosque in Bir al-Abed in the Sinai region of Egypt on 25 November 2017, however, showed that ISIS was not done yet. They are portable like Islam. After the collapse of Raqqa and Mosul, the fighters joined the ISIS sleeper groups in the Sinai desert. For decades, Egypt has seen Sinai through a military prism, taking an aggressive approach to an alienated local community. The military has engaged in summary executions and the destruction of entire village communities along with their leadership. The region faced deep socio-economic issues, including chronic unemployment, illiteracy and no access to health care. The dysfunctional region of Sinai is an ideal sanctuary for the runaway Islamic State fighters. It is a vast terrain of desert and mountains, with long shorelines and semi-porous back doors across the border into Gaza, which has been controlled by Hamas.

The collapse of Libya in 2011 has ensured a steady flow of weapons ever since the death of Muammar Gaddafi. After the collapse of the Islamic caliphate in Syria and Iraq, there was a large influx of Islamic fighters—some estimate more than 8,000—from Raqqa and Mosul. The recent attack on the Sufi mosque in Egypt could be an extension of ISIS's act based on the Salafist hatred for Sufi Sunni and Shia Islam. Nevertheless, the Islamic Brotherhood ideology, which is pitched against the Wahhabi Salafism of Saudi Arabia, is the most popular form of Islam in Egypt. President El-Sisi pretends that the attack on the mosque in Egypt, killing over 300 Sufi Sunni Muslims, is an economic and law and order issue. In reality, it is a layered and complex Islamic ideological issue with far-reaching implications to the future of Islam and world peace.

In the post-Islamic State scenario, Washington is trying to ramp down the escalating tensions between the Kurdish militia and Turkey in Syria, and between the Iraqi government and the Kurdistan Regional Government in Iraq. In Syria, the US operation forces fought with the Kurdish militia under the Syrian Democratic forces and comprehensively defeated the Islamic State. In Iraq, the combined strength of Peshmerga forces and the Iraqi army, backed by the US air power, defeated the Islamic State and liberated Mosul and other cities.

The small riverside Syrian town Baghuz, on the border with Iraq in the picturesque Euphrates river valley, was the stronghold of ISIS after Raqqa was finally liberated on 23 March 2019. The Syrian Democratic Forces, with American air cover, fought fiercely and liberated it from ISIS control. Thousands of foreign fighters surrendered. They were kept in camps along with the SDF and the American Special Forces. About 10,000 'jihadi brides' married to the fighters and their children were also captured and housed in separate camps in northern Syria. This was a big moment for the entire world to show that ISIS was finally finished. But ISIS is a global phenomenon, with many of its affiliates still present in different parts of the world, like Afghanistan, the Philippines, Nigeria and Bangladesh. It is also very much present virtually as faceless insurgents who command thousands of followers in cyberspace. They pop up and show their presence by attacking Shias, Sufi Sunni and other religious minorities like Sikhs in Afghanistan. One may say that the al-Baghdadi era of ISIS ended when he was killed in the US raid in northern Syria on 26 October 2019. But ISIS is like a seed that has gone to the wind.

Killing the terrorists is not enough. Defeating and discrediting the ideology behind them is more important. The Wahhabi ideology, which is the inspiration behind most of the Islamic extremism, has to be discredited through concerted efforts by the global Muslims as well as followers of other faiths. To begin with, all the Wahhabi literature and interpretations of the Quran and the Hadith done at the behest of Saudi Arabia from the Wahhabi–Salafi perspective have to be banned. Among other things, efforts should also be taken to purge the priests from all the Sunni mosques that follow the Wahhabi–Salafi strain of Islam, if peace is to prevail in the long run.

8

REVIVING SUFI TRADITIONS TO RESTORE PEACE IN THE ISLAMIC WORLD

The famous American academic and public intellectual Samuel Huntington wrote about the 'clash of civilizations' in 1993. He believed that the world was categorized along cultural lines—Christians, Muslims, Buddhists, Hindus, etc.—and argued that future wars would be fought not between countries but between cultures. But what he may not have seen is that there exists a universal civilization,[108] or say, a global culture that unifies people despite the differences in caste, religion, colour and ethnicity. This universal language undergirded by love, peace, tolerance and togetherness is what Sufism has come to represent since many centuries.

There is disagreement among religious scholars and Sufis themselves about the origin of Sufism. The traditional view is that it is the inward dimension or the mystical form of Islam It had its origin in the centuries following the life of Prophet Mohammad. Some of the early converts to the Islamic faith and the close companions of Mohammad were also inclined towards the deepest possible expression and fulfillment of their love for God.

The guidance that forms the basis of Sufi practices is found in the Quran and in the teachings of the Prophet. For example, the practice of silently remembering the divine was taught by the Prophet to his companion Abu Bakr as the two sought refuge in

---

[108] Acim, Rachid, 'The Reception of Sufism in the West: The Physical Experiences of America and European Converts', *Journal of Muslim Minority Affairs*, Vol. 38, No.1, 2018, pp. 57-72.

a cave during their migration from Mecca to Medina. The famous *miraj*, or the night journey of the Prophet, has long inspired mystics as a metaphor for the spiritual journey. The Prophet was physically transported by God from Mecca to Jerusalem, from Jerusalem up to seven heavens, and finally close to God by 'two-bow lengths'. The Sufi aspirants strive to transcend the physical limitations of space and time and to draw closer to the divine. Many such examples demonstrate that there was a strong mystical element in the life of Prophet Mohammad, who seems to be the first Sufi communicating directly with God.

Sufism is the branch of Islam, which accommodates local practices and makes it culturally relevant to the believers, without compromising on its core. Sufism also is very missional, attracting a lot of people globally into the fold of Islam. Alexander Dknysh, professor at the University of Michigan and an expert on Sufism, describes it as a 'very wide amorphous movement', practised in both Sunni and Shia traditions.[109] Sufism has shaped literature and art for centuries, and in reality, the 'golden age' of Islam was driven by Sufism between the eighth and thirteenth centuries. In modern times, the predominant view of Sufi Islam is of love, peace and tolerance. Similar sentiments were expressed by people like Imam Feisal Abdul Rauf, an American Sufi cleric of Egyptian descent who preached in the New York City for many years and founded the Cordoba House, meant to promote a moderate image of Islam in the West.

Marginalization of Sufism

Tasawwuf, regarded as the science of soul, has always been considered an integral part of orthodox Islam. Ibn Taymiyyah, the fourteenth-century Syrian Hanbalite jurist, is believed to be the originator of Salafism. He began practicing the Salafist ideology by demolishing

---

[109]Dknysh, Alexander, 'Sufism: A New History of Islamic Mysticism', *Journal of Islamic Studies*, Vol. 30, No. 1, 2017, pp. 97-103.

the tombs and other structures that had come up around the graves of the Prophet's companions in the holy cities of Mecca and Medina. Nevertheless, he stressed the primacy of Sharia as the soundest tradition in tasawwuf. Ibn Abdul Wahhab, the eighteenth-century reformist, who was hugely inspired by Ibn Taymiyyah, however, had great reverence for Sufis like Abdul-Qadir Gilani. He even wrote eloquently on the subject of Sufism in his commentary on Gilani's book *Futuh al-Ghayb* and considered tasawwuf essential in the life of the Islamic community.

The marginalization of Sufism can be attributed mainly to the emergence of Wahhabi Salafism in the eighteenth-century Najd, which eventually became the official religion of Saudi Arabia.[110] The reformist school of Abd al-Wahhab, known as Wahhabi Salafism, preached against Sufi practices by reinterpreting the earlier Islamic sources. The ultra-conservative Wahhabi movement, which derived most of its religious knowledge from a literal reading of the Islamic scriptures, aimed much of its criticism at the Sufi orders for allegedly 'distorting' the Islamic practices. Like other conservative sects, the Wahhabi Salafis condemned many of the Sufi practices, including the pilgrimage to Sufi shrines, metaphysical interpretation of the Quran and other ritualistic ceremonies of Sufis.

According to Salafism, such practices are equal to idolatry or what is generically called *bida* in Islam—a crime that carries serious punishment. All social forms of modernity have been rejected by Salafis. They view Sufi thoughts and practice as new inventions and accuse them of committing blasphemy, often leading to the act of takfir or excommunication for alleged deviations from the core values of Islam as they perceive it.

The Sufi Sunni traditions, which encompass metaphysics, ethical disciplines, devotional practices, music, poetry and mystical

---

[110] Armstrong, Karen, 'Wahhabism to ISIS: How Saudi Arabia Exported the Main Source of Global Terrorism', *New Statesman*, 27 November 2014, https://tinyurl.com/yz337be9. Accessed on 23 September 2023.

experiences, are not recognized as being compatible with Salafism, which strives to purge Islam of beliefs and practices with no mention in the Quran or the Hadith. During the fourteenth and fifteenth centuries, many Syrian and Indian ulamas, like Shah Waliullah, combined orthodox Sufism with a Salafi spirit. Most of the founders and early leaders of Tablighi Jamaat, the Sunni Islamic missionary movement, had strong family connections with different Sufi orders. They even practised some Sufi devotions privately, but the movement firmly rejected Sufism as it existed in South Asia, especially the venerations of saints.

Sufism, known as tasawwuf in the Arabic-speaking Muslim world, is a form of Islamic mysticism that emphasizes on self-introspection and spiritual closeness to divinity. It is not a sect but a stream solidly grounded in mainstream Islam. It is always associated with the spiritual dimension of the faith. There have always been individuals whose deep yearning and inner restlessness have driven them to spend time in contemplation, meditation and prayer. Sufism mostly focusses on the renunciation of worldly things, purification of the soul and the mystical contemplation of God's nature. One such person was Prophet Mohammad himself, who, before receiving prophetic revelations, would often withdraw to a cave outside Mecca to worship God.

Between the years 622–632, Prophet Mohammad established a community in Medina based on the Islamic principles of equity, justice, piety and a sensitive leadership. After his death, the first four successors followed his teachings closely. They governed judiciously in the rapidly expanding territories in accordance with the teaching of the Quran and the Sunnah. By pledging allegiance to the Prophet, the *sahabah* (companions of the Prophet) had committed themselves to the service of God. According to Islamic belief, by pledging allegiance to the Prophet, the sahabah have been pledging allegiance to God. According to the Holy Quran (48:10), 'Those who gave pledge to Allah, the hand of Allah is over their hands. Then, whoever breaks his pledge, breaks it only to his own harm, and whosoever fulfills what he has covenanted with Allah, He will bestow on him great reward.'

Sufis believe that by pledging allegiance to a legitimate Sufi, one is pledging allegiance to the Prophet, and, therefore, a spiritual connection between the seeker and the Prophet is established. It is through the Prophet that Sufis aim to learn about, understand and connect with God. Ali is regarded as one of the major figures among the sahabah. Since Sahabah have directly pledged allegiance to the Prophet, Sufis maintain that the knowledge about the Prophet and a connection with him may be attained through Ali. This may be supported by the Hadith, which Sufis regard to be authentic, in which the Prophet had said, 'I am the city of knowledge and Ali is its gate.' Ali's deep knowledge of tasawwuf is generally agreed upon by Muslims.

Some practitioners believe that Sufism is the strict emulation of the way in which Prophet Mohammad's heart was strengthened through direct connection with the divine. Many assert that Sufism is unique within the confines of Islam as it strongly follows Prophet's Sunnah, including its dining and dress codes. By and large, Sufism is the mystical aspect of Islam that deals with the purification of the inner self.

In the seventh century, Sufism had no strictly codified or organized method, practice or structure. Gradually it began to be structured into different orders, which continued to the present day. All these orders were founded by important Islamic saints; some of the largest and most popular are the Qadiriyya (named after Abdul Qadir Gilani), the Rifaiyyah (after Ahmed al-Rifai), the Chishtiya (after Moinuddin Chisti), the Shadhiliyya (after Abul Hasan ash-Shadhili) and the Naqshbandiyya (after Bahauddin Naqshband Bukhari). The founders of these orders were followers of the orthodox Sunni Islam, attached to any one of the four orthodox legal schools of Sunni Islam.

The Qadiriyya order followed the Hanbali school as its founder was a renowned Hanbali jurist. The Chishtiya was Hanafi; the Shadhiliyya, Maliki; and the Naqshbandiyya, too, was Hanafi.

Interestingly, some of the most eminent defenders of Islamic orthodoxy, including Abdul-Qadir Gilani, Imam al-Ghazali and Sultan Saladin were connected to Sufism. Turkey and Persia together have been major centre for many Sufi lineages and orders. Apparently, Sufism was not any distinct form of faith, but it merged with the orthodox Sunni Islam and enriched it with tasawwuf.

Al-Ghazali (1058–1111), the famous religious scholar and Sufi mystic, was born in Tabaran, near Khorasan, in present-day Iran. Orphaned at an early age, he was raised by Sufis. He, in his many writings, has discussed the concept of self and the causes of misery and happiness. He also argued that Sufism originated from the Quran, and thus, was compatible with mainstream Islamic thought and did not in any way contradict the Islamic law. It, instead, is necessary for its total fulfillment. He further argued that only the Sufi emphasis on the inner devotion can fulfil the strict demands of the Quran.

Al-Ghazali's arguments did much to relieve the hostility and suspicion that had developed between the ulama and Sufis. The acceptance of Sufism into the fold of orthodoxy had monumental consequences. Islam acquired a more popular character and a new power to attract followers. Some scholars credit Sufism for the success of Islam in establishing itself beyond the Middle East. Historically, Sufism is one of the most important aspects of Islam and the Muslim life in the Islamic civilization starting from the early medieval ages to present day. Slowly, it permeated into every aspect of the Sunni Islamic life in the regions stretching from India, Iraq to the Balkans, Senegal and Morocco.

The expansion of the Islamic civilization coincided strongly with the spread of Sufi philosophy in Islam. The spread of Sufism helped the spread of Islam and the creation of a distinct Islamic culture, especially in Africa and Asia. The Senussi tribes of Libya and Sudan are some of the strongest followers of Sufi Islam. Sufi poets and philosophers like Rumi have greatly helped in spreading Islam in Central and South Asia. It was the guiding philosophy of the Ottoman Empire. When Ibn Abd al-Wahhab rebooted Islam in the eighteenth century with puritan rigidities and branded Sufis as heretics, it was the Ottoman rulers of Saudi Arabia who ordered to kill the followers of the Abd al-Wahhab–Ibn Saud combined, who were pushing the new strand of Wahhabi Islam as the real Sunni Islam in lieu of the traditional Sufi Sunni Islam.

Sufism produced a flourishing intellectual culture throughout the Islamic world between the eighth and thirteenth centuries. Remnants of the socio-cultural and scientific achievements of that period, also called the 'golden age' of Islam, survive even today. Sufism continued to be a crucial part of global Islamic life until the twentieth century, when its historical influence upon the Islamic civilization began to be undermined by the tsunami of Wahhabi Salafism, propelled by the petrodollar power of Saudi Arabia.

The relationship between Saudi Arabia and Qatar, two Arab Sunni nations, began to be particularly strained after the Arab Spring that spread across much of the Arab world in the early 2010s. A fierce diplomatic conflict between these countries, sometimes referred to as the Second Arab Cold War, drove Qatar closer to Turkey and Iran in a move that could potentially alter the Middle Eastern politics and make the revival of a traditional Sufi Sunni Islam possible. Turkey and Iran have come together in a strategic non-formal alliance of Sunni and Shia countries to protect the tiny emirate of Qatar from the threat of an alliance led by Saudi Arabia. Following the spat, Turkey established a military base in Qatar, and Tehran opened its airspace and sea and ground transport links with Qatar, to counter the belligerent attitude of the Saudi-led group of Gulf nations. Historically, Turks have long been exposed to the Persian culture and have inherited certain indelible religious and cultural legacies. Iran is home to a large Turkish minority, as it was once ruled by the Turkish royal families such as the Safavids and the Qajars from the early sixteenth century.

The Ottoman–Safavid wars through the sixteenth and nineteenth centuries, were, essentially, a rivalry of two Turkish dynasties that, respectively, carried the banners of Sufi Sunni Islam and the Shia

Sufi dynasties. The theological orientation of Sufism, with its inward search for God and spirituality, was such that its followers often shied away from political forms of Islam. Some Sufi leaders, particularly in the Muslim world, have allied themselves with political forces, but never with their militant causes. Many Sufi orders put great emphasis on Sharia and a strict observance of the orthodox requirements in the areas of worship and social spheres.

Organizations like the Islamic State and al-Qaeda, which are strong followers of Wahhabi Salafism, target Sufis because they believe that only their form of Islam is valid. Many fundamentalists see the reverence for saints, which is a common trait of Sufism and Shiite Islam, as a form of idolatry. They view it as a form of worship towards something other than the singular god. Many scholars have written that Ahmed ibn-Taymiyyah, who is said to be the father of Salafism, was reportedly a member of the Qadiriyya Sufi order. Until recently, it would have been unthinkable for students of Islamic studies to consider Sufism as anything other than an integral part of a holistic Islamic education. In fact, it is the essence of theology, religious practice and spirituality.

Sufism in the West

Many academics, thinkers and philosophers from the US and Europe have embraced Sufism and Sufi stalwarts like Rumi (1207–1273), Hafez (1325–1389) and Ibn Arabi (1165–1240). For them, Sufism is the symbol of tolerance, dignity and respect for all humans, cutting across caste, colour and creed. Edward Said, the famous Palestinian intellectual, used to acknowledge Hafez, the Persian mystic and spiritual poet, as one of his role models. After the civil right movement of the 1960s, a large number of African Americans were attracted to the Sufi Sunni Islam, which had arrived in the West through Moroccans and Tunisians. The first Arab country to establish an embassy in Washington, DC, was Tunisia. The Western fascination for the East lies in its mystic heritage. It is well known fact that a huge number of Western immigrants to America got attracted to Islam through Sufism, and now, the West is distrustful of Islam because of Wahhabi Salafism, which propagates nothing but extremism, intolerance and hatred for other faiths.[111]

Many American converts to Islam in the 1970s have confessed that they embraced Islam because of its Sufi values. Chishti Sufis are among the oldest in America. There are different Sufi groups in the US. Some are of Turkish-Persian and South Asian descent, while some others are of Moroccan origin.

After the American Civil War (1861–1865), the traumatized American society took to Sufism in a big way, as it was therapeutic and soothing. They found Sufis as a safe space, wherein they could be relieved and comforted. It remains to be a puzzling question why the US did not invoke Sufism among American Muslim communities after the traumatic incidents of 9/11. Presently, they are fully consumed by the Wahhabi–Salafi ideology of hate and bigotry.

The American Sufi Sunni Muslims were among the first responders in the aftermath of 9/11 to promote peace and non-violence. They came forward to organize interfaith dialogues and build bridges to reach out to people of other faiths. Sufi poet Rumi had called all religions to be a manifestation of the same divine reality. In the late 1970s, the Rifai Order made its presence in America and established a modest centre in Washington, DC. Subsequently, the order expanded in the 1980s and 1990s and opened centres in New York, Staten Island, Cleveland, Chicago and Toronto.

There are 6 million Muslims in France (8 per cent of the country's population), with many Sufi followers. Not all of the Sufi orders present in the country are a result of the recent migration of Muslims. For example, France's North and West African communities follow Tijani and Muridi orders. There are other, more contemporary-looking Sufi orders. Faouzi Skali, a Sorbonne-educated anthropologist, who oversees a branch of Qadiri order in France, has succeeded in making

---

[111]Malik, J., *Sufism in the West*, Routledge, New York, 2006.

Sufism attractive to an urban, modern-educated, middle- and upper-class audience. He has also successfully marketed Moroccan Sufism through different cultural events and festivals in the country and abroad. Sufism spreads among intellectuals and thinkers who follow the philosophy and the spirit of seeking something bigger, with an inclination for inner transformation.

The hard push of Salafism by Saudi Arabia starting from the early 1980s has resulted in many problems, including the ubiquitous terrorist attacks in different parts of the world. As a consequence, Muslim communities are facing different kinds of social isolation. It has triggered Islamophobia that as reached its peak across Europe in recent years. The good news is that the revival of Sufi Sunni Islam is helping, at least slowly, to bring back faith and acceptability for Muslims in the French society, as it is totally against radicalization and extremism. The famous French rapper Abdel Malik, belonging to Qadiria order, powerfully demonstrated that Sufism is able to build individuals, sharpen their artistic skills, block negative thoughts and enhance love for other people.

The Muslim population of present-day Britain comprises South Asians, Africans, Arabs, Balkan people and Central Asians, with a small percentage of white converts.[112] Broadly speaking, they are of two distinct Islamic identities. One is that of the Wahhabi–Salafi Muslims, who believe that the individual should choose to be either Muslim or British. They argue that the national values differ from religious norms. The other group calls themselves as believers of Sufi Sunni Islam. They believe that one can be both Muslim and British at the same time, and there is no contradiction involved. They argue that the nationality and faith can be combined in Muslims who reside in Britain. Both the groups legitimize their interpretation with the help of the Quran and the Hadith, the primary sources in Islam.

---

[112]Fuad, Ai Fatimah Nur, 'Muslims in Britain: Questioning Islamic and National Identity', *Indonesian Journal of Islam & Muslim Societies*, Vol. 2, No. 2, 2012, pp. 215–40.

Unfortunately, no one is refereeing the debate among the Muslim communities.

Muslim immigrants arrived in Britain in large numbers as settlers in the 1960s and 1970s, and almost all of them were believers of Sufi Sunni Islam. However, the Salafi ideas started getting traction in the 80s with the organized push from Saudi Arabia. An institution namely JIMAS (Jamiyat Ihya Minhaj al-Sunnah) was solely focussed on promoting and spreading Salafism in Britain. The promoters also call it 'the society for the revival of the prophetic ways'.

In the early 1990s, Salafis came out openly promoting the ideology through mosques like Green Lane Mosque and Salafi Institute in Birmingham, Ibn Taymiyyah Mosque in Brixton and the Luton Islamic Centre. Their vision was promoted not only through different institutions, but also through individuals, mostly Western converts. Among other groups settled in Britain pushing the Wahhabi–Salafi ideology are Jamaat-e-Islami, Ahle Quran, Ahle Hadith and Tablighi Jamaat. They describe themselves as non-political organizations. However, a common characteristic of all these groups was that they all oppose Sufism.

All radical movements like Hizb ut-Tahrir are influenced by Wahhabi Salafism. They believe that God called upon all Muslims to fight against infidels. It rejects Western values like democracy, liberalism and secularism. They perceive that these ideas are incompatible with Islamic values and Sharia laws. The religious dress code of Salafists among men and women are more visible today than in 1970s. At that time they were adherents of the traditional Sufi Sunni Islam, which never prescribed a stringent dress code. This is one reason why the largest contingent of youth, who joined the Islamic State in Syria were from Britain. Both fundamentalists and the modernists believe that Islam can not be ignored from their social lives.

It is in the beginning of the twentieth century[113] that Albania

---

[113] Alexe, Dan, 'The Influence of Sufi Islam in the Balkans', *EUobserver*, 1 December 2010, https://tinyurl.com/mvxzvw6s. Accessed on 21 September 2023.

and Kosovo gained independent from the Ottoman. The Sufis of the Ottoman enriched the Balkans enormously to the development of an Islamic intellectual and aesthetic culture. One of the first Sufis to have come in the area was the Bektashi Saint Sari Saltik (Mehmed Buhari) in the fourteenth century. His shrines are found in a number of countries in regions like Bosnia, Romania, Macedonia and Albania.

The believers percent in the Balkan region traditionally followed a tolerant and mystical form of Islam. Luckily, Sufism is still the main form of Islam in these regions and the penetration of Wahhabi Salafism is not widespread, unlike in Western European countries. A large percentage of Muslims here still follows the Hanafi Sufi Islam traditions, and it is particularly so in Kosovo and Macedonia. The majority of Roma ethnic groups in Macedonia, Kosovo, Bosnia and southern Serbia are Muslims, and most of them belong to one or the other Sufi orders. Sufi orders, such as Bektashis of Albania, Bulgaria and Macedonia, have been present since the Middle Ages. The Islamic cultures of Muslim communities in the Balkans have largely been shaped by the legacy of Sufism. Regardless of their ethnicities, Sufi orders are deeply embedded in the cultures of Muslim communities in Europe. Sometimes it is even difficult to distinguish what ethnic groups they come from.

Sufism in South Asia

After the spread of Islam across the Indian subcontinent in the Middle Ages, many Sufi saints belonging to different orders started coming to India from the twelfth century. In the beginning of the thirteenth century, three well-known Sufi orders were established in India almost simultaneously, namely Chishti, Suhrawardi and Firdausi.

The fifteenth century witnessed the introduction of Qadiri, Shattari and Naqshbandiyya orders on the subcontinent. These Sufis established their hospices or *khanqah*s in different parts of the country as social and cultural centres. They did not differentiate between the rich and poor or discriminate between different castes, which was prevalent in the Hindu society. Soon, their acceptability surged and they became very popular among the marginalized communities of different faiths.

Hazarat Nizamuddin Auliya (1235–1325) sent his other disciple, Zar Zari Zar-Baksh (giver of gold), along with hundreds of disciples to settle in Khuldabad near present-day city of Aurangabad. He died there in 1309. It is believed that Sai Baba of Shirdi was a disciple of Zar Zari Zar-Baksh. When he was 22, he meditated in the same cave where Zar-Baksh used to meditate. The religious identity of Sai Baba was foggy, as no one ever knew whether he was a Muslim or a Hindu by birth. There were strong elements of non-duality in all of what he said in his unique manner. Whether he was a Sufi saint or a man of Advaita Vedanta did not concern millions of his Hindu, Muslim and Sikh devotees across India. His life was a striking example of the convergence of different faiths.

The Indian subcontinent is historically a land of great seers and saints. The first great Sufi saint to have come to India was Ali al-Hujwiri (1009–1072), popularly known as Data Ganj Bakhsh, who settled in Lahore, now in Pakistan. He was born in Ghazna, Afghanistan. During his travels to Syria and other major countries of the Middle East, he deliberated with many renowned Sufis. His master asked him to travel to India and settle in Lahore. Initially he was reluctant to travel to Lahore as his co-disciple Sheikh Hassan Zanjani was already there. On insistence of his master, he travelled to Lahore, but on reaching, came to know that Sheikh Zanjani had passed away. He settled near Bhatti Gate outside Lahore, where his tomb is now situated.

The most popular and outstanding among the Sufi saints in India was Khwaja Moinuddin Chishti (1143–1234), who was born in Tajikistan. Orphaned at the young age of 12, he travelled to Samarkand in Uzbekistan and received his early education there. He then travelled to Nishapur, where he became a disciple of Khwaja Uthman Chishti. After receiving training in the Chishtia order for seven years, he was inducted in that order. From Nishapur, he travelled to Baghdad, where he met may renowned saints of his time, including, Shaykh Abdul Qadir Gilani (the founder of Qadiri order), Abu Najib Suhrawardi of the Suhurawardi order, Shaykh Abu Yusuf Hamdani of Naqshbandiyya order, and Sheikh Shamsuddin Tabrizi, mentor and spiritual master of Jalaluddin Rumi. In Isfahan, he met Khwaja Qutubuddin, who became his disciple, and later successor, in Delhi.

Khwaja Moinuddin Chishti first went to Lahore, where he visited the tomb of Ali al-Hujwiri. From there, he travelled to Ajmer through Multan, and to Delhi in 1165 –66 where he spent the rest of his life. He introduced the Chishtia order in India and acquired an iconic status after Emperor Akbar reached Ajmer on 14 January 1562 with a small retinue and prayed at his dargah. After distributing alms, Akbar also ordered the ladies of the palace to be brought to the dargah to pay homage to the saint. This was the beginning of his annual pilgrimage and reverence to the Sufi saint.

Being without a heir till he was 27, Akbar prayed at the dargah to invoke the blessings of Khawaja for a son with a vow that he would walk barefoot from Agra to Ajmer if a son was born to him. When Akbar's wife, princess of Amber, gave birth to a male child in the Fatehpur Sikri Palace on 30 August 1569, Akbar left for pilgrimage to the shrine. He left for Ajmer from Agra on foot on 20 January 1570 to reach the shrine on 5 February, travelling 10 to 12 miles per day. The dargah of Moinuddin Chishti or Garib Nawaz became a famous pilgrimage centre for people of all religions, since the time of Mughals.

All Sufi saints were regarded highly by most of the Mughal rulers. Sheikh Qutbuddin Bakhtiar Kaki was the disciple and spiritual successor of Moinuddin Chishti. He was born in 1186 at Farghana in Isfahan, where he had the fortune of meeting Khwaja Moinuddin Chishti when he was on his way to India. Sheikh Fariduddin, popularly known as Baba Farid, spiritually succeeded Sheikh Qutbuddin Kaki. Baba Farid lived a life of severe austerity and piety. He married the daughter of King Balban of Delhi. Baba Farid died in 1266 at the age of 93. One of the most renowned and revered Sufi saints, Hazrat Nizamuddin Auliya, was a disciple and chief successor of Baba Farid. Credit goes, to a large extent, to Hazrat Nizamuddin Auliya and his disciple Hazrat Amir Khusro for taking Sufism to every nook and corner of India.

Hazrat Nizamuddin Auliya was born in Badaun, present-day Uttar Pradesh, in 1236. He was born in a very poor family and lost his father at the age of five. When his mother had no food to offer, she used to tell him that 'today we are guests of God'. Her trust in God was so extraordinary that the young Nizamuddin imbibed all the great qualities from her at a very young age. At the age of 20, Nizamuddin joined Baba Farid as a disciple. Later, Baba Farid sent Sheikh Nizamuddin as the viceroy to Delhi. In Delhi, public reverence come up for Hazrat Nizamuddin Auliya. The ruling monarch of Delhi at the time, Mubarak Khilji, used to hold public durbar on the appearance of the new moon and expected Sheikh Nizamuddin to be there. But Sheikh Nizamuddin refused to pay obeisance, and that irked the king, who ordered him to leave Delhi. Before the appearance of the next new moon, the ruler Mubarak Khilji was assassinated and replaced by Ghiyasuddin Tughlaq. Like his predecessor, he also ordered Hazrat Nizamuddin to leave Delhi and the former immediately left for Bengal. When the royal command was read out to Sheikh Nizamuddin Auliya, he uttered, *'Hanooz dilli dur ast,'* which meant Delhi is still far off. On his return journey from Bengal, Tughlaq could not make it to Delhi, as a pavilion erected for his reception at Tughlakabad near Delhi accidently fell on him and the ruler died.

Hazrat Amir Khusro was a devoted disciple of Hazrat Nizamuddin. He too was a famous poet who, for the first time, used Urdu, the common mans language, to compose songs, riddles and rhymes for them to reach the masses. Amir Khusro, after the death of Sheikh Nizamuddin Auliya, spent his entire life near the grave of his master in grief.

Hazrat Nizamuddin Auliya was succeeded by another of his disciple Sheikh Nasiruddin, more popularly known as 'Chiragh-e-Dehlavi'. Muhammad Gesu Daraz, popularly known as 'Bande Nawaz' succeeded him. Though he was born in Delhi, his father took him to Daulatabad. Later, he came back to Delhi and was initiated by Sheikh Nasiruddin. In 1398, he moved to Deccan, where Sultan Firoz Shah Bahmani received him with great respect. Sheikh Gesu Daraz died in 1422 in Gulbarga in Karnataka, where his tomb is situated. During his lifetime, he wrote a number of books on Sufism and Islam.

Naqshbandi Sufi order was among the last to enter the Indian subcontinent. The order was named after Muhammad Bahauddin Shah Naqshband, a renowned Sufi master. Towards the latter part of seventeenth century, another great Sufi saint, Bulleh Shah, spread the message of love and spirituality beyond the barriers of caste, creed and religion in India. He was a disciple of the Sufi saint Bahauddin Zakariya of the Suhrawardi order. Bulleh Shah's father Shah Muhammad Darwaish, was a greatly knowledgeable person and scholar of Arabic and Persian languages with a good understanding of the Quran.

The process of assimilation of Indian and Perso-Arabic music started under the famous Suhrawardi Sufi saint, Sheikh Bahauddin Zakariya (1191–1267), whose hospices would host musical concerts, where singers would attempt the aforesaid assimilation. It is said that Multani, one of the most popular ragas in Hindustani classical music, was created by Bahauddin Zakariya. During the thirteenth century, Delhi began to emerge as a great centre of the Chishtia order of Sufism.

Amir Khusro (1253–1325), was born in Patiyali, in present-day Uttar Pradesh. His father, Amir Saifuddin Mahmud, before migrating to India, was the chief of a clan called 'Lachin' in Turkistan during the reign of Changez Khan. In India, he got a job as an official in the court of Sultan Shamsuddin Iltutmish. A Sufi musician, poet and a multifaceted scholar, he played an important role in the development of many musical instruments and forms of music, of which *qawwali* became the most popular under the reign of Delhi sultans.

Different musical genres like *qaul, naqash, tarana, nigar* and ghazal became part of the repertoire of Indian singers. The qawwali became an integral part of the royal courts as well as of the Sufi centres in the country. Qawwals also came to be known as Delhi singers. They based their singing on *raga–ragini*s as well as on folk music, thus creating a wonderful musical amalgam that goes very well with the syncretism of the Sufi saints. It is said that Hazrat Nizamuddin Auliya was fond of Raga Poorvi and that he would want to listen to it every day. A *khayal bandish* composed by Amir Khusro in his honour is still sung by Hindustani classical vocalists in Raga Poorvi. Qawwali is similar to Hindu *kirtan*s and became very popular among masses of all faiths in North India. Sufis of various orders were attracted to the qawwali concerts called *sama* and to different Indian classical music varieties. Samas gatherings were considered beneficial for spiritual nourishment.

It is believed that Amir Khusro invented the musical instrument sitar and several melodies played on it, by blending Persian and Indian notes. Popular melodies like qaul and tarana were designed by him to provide novelty to the sama rituals. The Vaishnavite devotional songs, thus, became the part of the Samas. All the Sufi orders in North India, came into contact with Hindu ascetics—yogis, *bairagi*s and *nathpanthi*s. Sufis adopted the language of the common people and metaphors popular among the Hindu ascetics. They adopted the medieval Sanskrit text, Amrit Kund, expounding the teachings of Yoga Shastra. It was translated into Persian, and later into Arabic. All the Sufis in the Indian subcontinent venerate the basic tenets of Islam. They usually accept the path of Sharia, the oneness of God (Tawhid), the necessity of prophet-hood and its culmination in Prophet Mohammad. In their personal lives, Sufis remain devoted to Islam, and in public, their concern for humanity is all pervasive.

Muslim mystics or Sufis have made highly important and enduring contributions to the development of the composite Indian culture. They show great respect for the beliefs and traditions of the majority Hindu community, ranging from openness, love, and tolerance. They have contributed to the country's composite ethos by influencing the hearts and minds of many Hindu and Muslim leaders, intellectuals and poets, who played significant roles in shaping the destiny of the country. Raja Ram Mohan Roy, a famous Bengali public intellectual, was greatly influenced by Islamic mysticism, so much so that he tried to bring in a synthesis of Vedanta philosophy and Sufism. Similarly, Rabindranath Tagore's poetry imbibed a great deal from the Baul Sufi singers of Bengal. His father, a scholar in Persian, used to recite to the young Tagore poetry of the great Persian poet Hafiz. Beginning in the twelfth century, Sufism was the mainstay of the social order of the Islamic civilization, and since then, it spread throughout the Muslim world, including in China, West Africa, the US, and South and Central Asia. As it spread, Sufism naturally adopted the local culture, as is seen in India, making it popular among the people.

The famous Bhakti movement originated in the seventh century in the southern parts of India, which later spread towards North India. It reached its peak between the fifteenth and seventeenth centuries. Bhakti saints like Sankara, Ramanuja, Madhava, Surdas, Mirabai, Tulsidas, Kabir and Guru Nanak were engaged in breaking down the barriers within Hinduism. The intellectual interaction between the early Bhakti movements and Sufism laid the foundation for a more liberal understanding and a composite culture in the Indian society. Both Kabir and Guru Nanak had preached a non-sectarian religion based on a tolerant society. The Sufis believed in the concept of *Wahdat-ul-Wajud* (the unity of being), popularized by the famous Sufi mystic Ibn Arabi (1165–1240). He said that all the religions were identical in caring for the poor and downtrodden. One of the core beliefs in Sufism is the devotion to God in the service of mankind. They never differentiated on the basis of faith but treated all humans alike. The Islamic emphasis on equality was respected far more strongly by the Sufis than ulamas or any other factions in Islam.

In the fourteenth century, Ibn Taymiyyah became one of the first Islamic scholars to attack the 'devotional Islam' practised by the Sufis. A few centuries later, another scholar from Arabia, Muhammad ibn Abd al-Wahhab got inspired by Ibn Taymiyya's ideology with far-reaching consequences. When the ruthless orthodoxy preached by Abd al-Wahhab gained traction in the tribal Saudi settlements during the eighteenth century, the orthodox ulamas blamed the Sufi orders for moving away from the original principles of the Quran. This battle between the orthodox and liberal elements continues till date, where the Wahhabi elements stand to destroy the soft nuances of Islam and transform it into a militant jihadi brand, promoted by Saudi Arabia.

In the subcontinent, the Bhakti saints and Sufis contributed enormously to the growth of regional literature. Most of the Sufi saints were poets who chose to write in the local languages. Baba Farid recommended as a Punjabi language for religious writings. Before him, Sheikh Hamiduddin wrote in Hindawi. His verses are the best examples of the early translation of Persian mystical poetry into Hindawi. Sheikh Gesu Daraz was the first writer of Deccani Hindi. He found Hindi more expressive than Persian to explain mysticism. A number of works were also written in Bengali.

Different Sufi orders got established in the Deccan region. Some of them came from North India while some others from outside India, including Baghdad, Iran and Syria. Among the North Indian orders were Chishti, Junaidi and Shattari. The orders from the Middle East and Central Asia operated under a separate set-up at Bidar, Bijapur and Aurangabad and included the Qadiri, Nimatullahi and Naqshbandi. Hagiographical writings show that Sufis were present at Khuldabad (Daulatabad), Gulbarga and Bijapur even before the year 1300. However, only vague information is available about their personalities, ideas, orders and methods of functioning.

Some scholars were of the view that some Sufis accompanied the early Muslim conquerors like Alauddin Khilji. By the beginning of the fourteenth century, Deccan assumed importance and was often talked about in the assemblies of Sheikh Nizamuddin Auliya in Delhi.

In the sixteenth century, the Sufi order of Naqshbandi also reached the Deccan region. They openly championed the cause of Islam. In the caste-ridden society of Deccan, Sufis of different orders adhering to their respective principles like generosity, affection, hospitality, love and equality not only adjusted well with the society, but also found ready acceptance among the masses. After interacting with the local communities, the behavioural pattern of Sufis changed with the passage of time. Their khanqahs became the hub of spiritual and intellectual activities blended with the local culture. They kept a distance from the ruling elite and enjoyed their independence. By the end of seventeenth century, khanqahs were replaced by the dargah, the *pir*s by the *pirzada*s and, thus, the high intellectual and spiritual exercise passed into the hands of illiterate masses that were seeking blessings from the tombs and not spiritual affinity to God.

Kashmir and Sufism

Sufism in Kashmir Valley, throughout its history, has integrated the soul of its people and guided the Kashmiri society.[114] Kashmiri Sufism is unique in the sense that it incorporates the mystical philosophies of the Islamic teachings with the Tantric traditions of Buddhism and Hindu Shaivite philosophies. Since the medieval times, the traditional Sufi orders that have taken roots in Kashmir were mainly Suhrawardy, Qadiri and Naqshbandiyya orders. The Sufi orders that took root in Kashmir had Hindu–Muslim syncretism as their main feature. Rishis and Sufis from both Pandit and Muslim communities came to spread the message of love and peaceful coexistence. They strived to reach out to God through both the Quran and the Hadiths as well as the Hindu Vedas and philosophies. This secular and indigenous

---

[114]Beigh, Javed, 'The Joining of Hindu and Muslim in Kashmir Sufism', *Kashmir Reader*, 16 August 2020, https://tinyurl.com/5n882k32. Accessed on 19 September 2023.

character of the Kashmiri Sufism was the foundation upon which the Kashmiri Pandit and Kashmiri Muslim collectively built the syncretic traditions of '*Kashmiriyat*'.

Sufism reached Kashmir simultaneously with the spread of Muslim rule in 1320. Nonetheless, continuous Sufi activities like the establishment of khanqahs and *silsila*s began only towards the end of the fourteenth century. The Sufi orders like Suhrawardi, Kubarawi, Naqshbandi and Qadiri took strong roots among the Kashmiris by the end of sixteenth century. The Sufis who came to Kashmir from Persia and Central Asia had the purpose of spreading the message of Islam. They established khanqahs in different localities of the valley. In the early days, the khanqahs were used for feeding the poor. The attached madrasas were used for teaching purposes. The madrasas established by Sheikh Ismail Kubrawi, attracted students from even Afghanistan and central Asia.

Some of the Sufi orders like Suharwardi also laid greater emphasis on women's education and opened madrasas for them. The Kashmiri literature also got influenced by Sufism, and many Hindu scholars learned Persian language, producing excellent poetry and prose in it. There is no doubt that Sufism had played a major role in shaping the life, attitude and religious convictions of the people of Kashmir. Unfortunately after the 1990s, the fault lines between Sufism and Wahhabi Salafism, the orthodox and rigid form of Islam, got sharply widened.

The Rishi and Other Orders

The Rishi order is an indigenous tradition of mystical teachings and spiritual practices, established in the Kashmir Valley in the fifteenth century as part of the 'Rishi Sufi' movement, led by saints like Baba Hyder Reshi, also known as Resh Mir Sahib and Sheikh Nooruddin (1378–1439), popularly known as 'Nund Rishi'. Sheikh Nooruddin was a great mystic who had risen above the courts and the socio-religious institutions of his time. The simplicity and purity of his life had greatly impressed the people of Kashmir. Some rulers even made coins in his name. The Rishi practices a philosophy of life different in many ways from those of the other Muslim saints of Kashmir.

The attitude of Sufis on the whole was of empathy and consideration for others. Their ethical standards and moral values were examples for the all Kashmiris in diverse aspects of social life. The mystical worldview of Sufis had a deeper impact on the individual and collective life of Kashmiris. The gradual imbibing of the mystical influence by the people was a process that stretched over many centuries. For example, the prayer 'Aurad-ul-Fatiha', has been chanted by the faithful in Kashmiri mosques since the fourteenth century, when saint Mir Syed Ali Hamdani was alive.[115] He first introduced the practice and popularized it among the masses. He introduced the anthology of Quranic verses and the Prophet's saying as chanting in the mosques, similar to temple chanting. This was a definite departure from the Muslim practice of silent worship. Hamadani also introduced the *dua-e-subah* (morning prayer), same as the morning chanting of Buddhists. These practices were seen as an abiding example of Kashmir's famed syncretic tradition.

Hamdani, a descendant of Prophet Mohammad, was born in Hamadan in modern day Iran in 1314, and lies buried in Kulob, Tajikistan. He visited the Kashmir Valley for last time in 1384, coinciding with the siege and overrun of Central Asia by Turco-Mongol conqueror Timur. He brought about 700 people with him, including artists, craftsmen, painters, calligraphers and scholars. Hamdani, whom Kashmiris know as Amir-i-Kabir (the great leader), is credited with promoting crafts including shawl weaving, which later became a symbol of Kashmir globally. He was himself an expert needle worker.

Hamadani authored about 100 books ranging in subjects from

---

[115]'Mir Muhammad Hamadani and His Contribution towards Islamisation of Kashmir', *Kasmirisufi's Blog*, 16 August 2018, https://tinyurl.com/2n8vd3zj. Accessed on 12 September 2023.

religion to jurisprudence to politics and philosophical poetry. His work *Dhakhirat al-Mulk* was a guide to rulers on how to treat their subjects. It also called for 'equitable justice, irrespective of religious differences' of the people. Hamadani established a network of khanqahs, where people could eat and pray together—a path-breaking social change in a rigidly hierarchical society. There is a temple in Srinagar, where on the upper floor there is a mosque and on the ground floor a temple of Kali. The popular Sufism that took shape in the Valley however, made the Kashmiri Muslims more gullible and credulous.

From the Indian Islamic perspective, the eighteenth century has a great significance. The mighty Mughal Empire was on the decline, but the intellectual and social awakening was on the rise. The century produced scholars like Shah Waliullah Dehlavi, Sufis like Shah Kalimullah of Jahanabad, and Urdu poets like Rafi Sauda, Mir Taqi Mir and Mehar Chand Bahar. Shah Waliullah belonged to a prominent family of theologians and Sufis. He was educated in Delhi and later in Mecca and Medina. He has rightly been called a bridge between the medieval and modern Islam in India. He was perturbed by the religious and moral corruption in the Muslim community. He often lamented that Muslims lost interest in the command of God and the teachings of the Prophet. He was convinced that the only way to salvage the Muslims from the abyss of misguided religious innovations and moral decadence was by making them aware of the Quran and teachings of the Prophet.

Shah Waliullah's approach to Sufism was cosmopolitan. Through a Naqshbandi by initiation, he took inspiration from all the four principal Sufi orders of his time. He did not prohibit people visiting saints' graves but cautioned them against seeking material help from the dead saints. He visited the mausoleum of Prophet Mohammad in Medina and described it as an uplifting experience.

The Deoband seminary, about 150 km north of Delhi, was founded in 1866 by a group of ulamas led by Maulana Muhammad Qasim in the year 1866. Some of the founders had strong links with Sufi Islam. The founders of Deoband, in the Shah Waliullah tradition, had inherited the spiritual legacy of the four important Sufi orders, with special reference to Chishtiya and Naqshbandiyya. Scholars believed that the Deoband group was inspired by Sayyid Ahmad of Rae Bareli, who followed Naqshbandiyya order. With respect to tasawwuf or mysticism, all the founders of Deoband, and more specifically Maulana Muhammad Qasim Nanotvi and Maulana Rasheed Ahmed Gangohi, had received their broad Sufistic vision from their mentor and Sufi saint Haji Imdadullah.

The Deobandi instructions, authenticated by the Quran, the Hadith and the Sunnah were closely linked to the traditional learning and understanding of the medieval Sunni Hanafi authorities, to which the majority of Indian Muslims belonged. Moreover, the Deobandi reformist stance largely represents a modern approach towards faith, as it was linked with the doctrines of popular Sufi orders.

Deoband, from the beginning, was associated with the Indian freedom movement and religious defence. The rapid advance of Deoband in its early decade and the high prestige that it earned as an institution of religious trust and education was based largely on its liberal attitude and pluralistic approach, rather than any purist reforms institutionalized by the eighteenth-century Saudi scholar Ibn Abd al-Wahhab. Notwithstanding the good motives and moderation of its founders, the learning centre later found itself involved and implicated in some avoidable controversies. There is no denying of the fact that the guardianship of tombs of the medieval Sufi saints was characteristic of the popular Islam narratives in India. Deoband, on the other hand, practised a purer form of Sufism, devoid of customs and rituals surrounding the mausoleums in the form of Urs, sama rituals and ceremonial Milad celebrations of Prophet Mohammad. The very fact of Deoband professing and recognizing all the Sufi orders and its mild approach towards popular customs left little room for contentions and conflicts. However, before the end of the nineteenth century, Deoband came under the cloud of sectarian controversies with a group under it—Ahle Hadith—taking a radically puritanical stance against the tomb cult.

The second half of the nineteenth century witnessed Deoband and the Ahle Hadith movement falling under the influence of the Salafi movement promoted by Saudi Arabia. The sectarian stance of Ahle Hadith was more visible to the common man in its outright rejection of Sufism and its doctrines. The traditional Deobandis, however, were opposed to the radical version of reform, including the rejection of Sufism proposed by the Ahle Hadith. Deoband generally maintained a distance from the popular Sufi cults as a matter of policy and devoted itself to more 'positive' aspects of religious reform, thereafter.

The Hanafi Barelvi group that emerged at the end of the nineteenth century, however, took up the cause of popular Islam. Pitted against Deoband, it was led by Moulana Ahmed Raza Khan of Bareilly, Uttar Pradesh. He provided regional leadership and academic support to popular Islam by establishing a seminary similar to Deoband in the Bundelkhand region. The intensity of opposition reached such a level that Barelvi leadership had to obtain a fatwa against Deoband from the Muftis of Hijaz (Mecca and Medina), and even declare an upholder of belief at variance with them as a kafir. Popular Islam had never been represented and defended so strongly as it was under the leadership of the Barelvi ulemas. Unfortunately, the Sunni Indian Muslim community was divided largely into two Hanafi camps: Deobandis and Barelvis.

The spiritual mentor of Deobandi founders, Haji Imdadullah, who had migrated to Mecca, was conscious of his influence on both schools of Hanafi Muslims in India. In order to strike a conciliatory note between the rival camps, he wrote a letter to them, which was published under the title 'Faisla Haft Masala' or 'verdict concerning the seven issues'. It was a carefully worded piece of advice addressed to both the contending Hanafi groups—the reformist Deoband and the upholder of the popular Islam the Barelvi. The letter advised both groups to have a more tolerant understanding of each other's point of view.

The Sunnis of India are divided among themselves into Wahhabi–Salafi and Sufi sections. An intense struggle has been going on between the two factions for the past many decades with the powerful Saudi-supported, groups of Indian Wahhabis working overtime to convert their fellow Sufis–Sunni into their fold. It is a battle of two religious ideologies—one a moderate inclusive, the other orthodox and exclusive. The Sufis Sunnis, who are also known by two other names in India, Ahle-Sunnat and Barelvi, venerate saints and celebrate Prophet Mohammad's birthday, unlike the Wahhabis. For Sufi Sunnis, praying and paying obeisance at the saint's dargah is an uplifting experience. The Wahhabis, however, are driven by the radical ideology pushed by Saudi Arabia and believe that there is nothing between an individual Muslim and Allah and any form of intercession is akin to idolatry.

All the jihadi terrorists groups like ISIS, al-Qaeda and Taliban follow the Wahhabi ideology. Almost all the radicalized individuals in different parts of the world also belong to the Wahhabi–Salafi stream of Islam, while no significant terrorist group has ever come out from the moderate and inclusive Sufi Sunni stream of Islam. Saudi-funded Wahhabi preachers in the Indian mosques and madrasas have converted many impressionable Sufi youths into the Wahhabi fold.

Sufism in Southern India

Sufism has profoundly impacted the socio-cultural existence of the Mappila Muslim community of the Malabar region in the southern state of Kerala over a period of several centuries. In the initial years, Islam in Kerala was propagated largely by Malik-Ibn Dinar, who reached the Kerala coast with a group of people from Arabia. Dinar was a Sufi practitioner and disciple of one of the greatest Sufis of Islam, Hasan al-Basri.

In the second half of the fifteenth century, Ponnani in Kerala became a major religious and cultural centre of Mappila Muslims. The first Sheikh Makhdum Zainuddin (1467–1521) of Ponnani wrote the manual of Sufism of Malabar. Sufi Sunni Islam was widespread in Kerala during sixteenth and seventeenth centuries. In the earlier stages of its evolution, Sufism had been confined to the elite class. Later, it spread across common folks and took the shape of a popular movement. Devotion to saints through veneration at tombs, had a greater appeal among the ordinary people of Kerala as it provided them with a spiritual affinity to God. Sufi organizations like khanqahs, *jamat khana*s and *zawiya* still exist in different parts of Malabar. An equivalent of khanqah, at present, is the Ponnani Palli, the mosque in Ponnani, where students take both religious and moral training as they live together in a common facility. Emphasis is given to acquiring broad-based knowledge along with lessons in Sharia. On satisfactory completion of the course at the seminary, the students graduate and the Sheikh confers on them a title, which makes them eligible to be religious teachers.

The Sheikh Makhdum of Ponnani had been the highest ecclesiastical authority of the Muslims in the Malabar region until the spread of Wahhabi Salafism by the early twentieth century. By the end of the century, the Wahhabi influence grew significantly in Kerala society due to various reasons, including the aggressive campaigns led by the Salafi outfits funded by Saudi Arabia. Apparently, most Keralites who had joined ISIS were associated with Salafi groups. The proliferation of Salafi groups across Kerala has been damaging the communal harmony of Kerala's pluralistic society.

The group of islands off the western coast of Kerala is known as Lakshadweep. In the year 900, these islands were visited by Sheikh Jalaluddin, a Sufi saint from Bukhara. His descendants were known for their scholarship and community leadership. Syed Moula, born on the island of Kavaratti was the fifth in succession. The influence of their Sufi teachings can be seen in different parts of the west coast of Kerala, stretching from Mangalore to Travancore.

According to Syed Hussaini, trustee of Hazrat Khwaja Bande Nawaz Dargah in Gulbarga, Karnataka, there is a marked difference between Sufism and mysticism. While Sufism is a concept based purely on spiritual experience, mysticism contains philosophical ideas and concepts mixed with the spiritual experimental knowledge. Everything, he believes, has two sides, external and internal, or exoteric and esoteric. Religion is no exception. The esoteric aspect of religion is nothing but mysticism. Sufis are interpreters of Islam, who follow in the footsteps of Prophet Mohammad. Syed Hussaini also said that the teachings of twelfth century *Sharana*s and *Veerashaiva* saints were similar to the Sufi teachings. The teachings of Saint Sharanab Asaveshwara and Khwaja Bande Nawaz had glaring resemblances and a few scholars even believe that Khwaja was the originator of the Chaitanya school, which has disciples all over India. Even today, the procession of the annual Sharana Basaveshwara fair starts after the arrival of the Holy Chalice from the Khwaja Bande Nawaz dargah.

The Bhakti movement, in a way, was the direct result of the spread of Islam in India. Monotheism, equality, brotherhood, and rejection of class divisions are some of the characteristics of Islam. These Islamic ideas created a profound impact on the religious leaders of this period in India. The preaching of Sufis shaped the thinking of Bhakti reformists like Ramanand, Kabir and Nanak, who preached a non-sectarian religion based on universal love.

Sufism is a liberal movement within Islam. It has its origin in Persia, and mainly spread into India in the eleventh century. The Hindu rulers of South India needed Arab traders, extended them full facilities and treated them as equals. These early missionaries and their progress enabled the spread of Sufi Islam all over the Tamil region. The Bhakti movement, in fact, was a regional revival of Hinduism, linking it with different languages, geographies, and cultural identities through devotion of a deity or god.

According to Professor Gnanasundaram of Pondicherry University, there is no Tamil literature without Bhakti. One may look at the number of songs and the range of topics covered. Bhakti is not just about religion; it is an expression of the Tamil social history from the seventh century onwards. The first great Sufi who came to India and spent most of his life in Tamil Nadu was Nathar Wali. Born in 959, he brought the message of Islam to the Tamils and died in 1026 to be buried in Tiruchirappalli. In the views of Harbans Mukhia, professor of History at Jawaharlal Nehru University, Delhi, the Sufi and Bhakti movements are illuminating illustrations for the other ways of explaining history. History, according to him, occurs through silent corrosion of something from within, without constituting an adversarial relationship with something outside, without any traumatic events like French or Russian revolution, without any dramatic incidents taking place anywhere. The Sufi movement, even as it developed and enforced or reinforced an Islamic vision of the world, substantially differed from the vision of the rulers and the ulamas, and that is where it brought about the changes.

Dara Shikoh, one of the four sons of Emperor Shah Jahan, was a scholar and a follower of Sufism of Qadiriyya order. He had a great interest and understanding of Hinduism. He has written a fascinating book, *Majma al Bahrain*, meaning 'the confluence of two rivers', on Islam and Hinduism. He had read almost all Hindu scriptures in Sanskrit and held wide-ranging conversations with Hindu scholars of both Vaishnava and Shaiva sects. He read the Persian translations of Sanskrit works on Hindu religion, produced during the period of Emperor Akbar and Jahangir, and that probably aroused his interests in Hindu philosophy and mysticism.

The reformist influences of Shah Waliullah Dehlvi, a Sufi leader and religious scholar from Delhi, can be seen in the southern region of Tamil Nadu, where his reform movement reached through his disciples like Sheikh Makhdum, who was active in the Tirunelveli district of Tamil Nadu in nineteenth century. Nevertheless, one of the earliest Indian radicals to carry out attacks on Sufi practices and the cult of Muslim saints and their shrines was none other than Shah Abdul Aziz, son of Shah Waliullah. Taking a Wahhabi stand, he criticized the ceremonies linked with the annual festival or Urs around the shrines of Sufi saints.

The All India Ulama and Mashaikh Board (AIUMB), a body of moderate clerics and spiritual Sufi leaders in India, spoke out against the fundamentalist ways of Wahhabi Salafism. They denounced the radical doctrine funded and promoted by Saudi Arabia, which had gradually infiltrated all Sunni schools of thought across India. The board also advocated purging of madrasas and mosques from the Wahhabi educated ulamas, literature and interpretation of the Quran. The members of the board maintained that traditionally, Indian Muslims were influenced by the devotional Islam and would never accept the extremism propagated by the Wahhabi ideology. They further elaborated that the Sufi Sunni Muslims were always nationalistic and never compromised on allegiance to their motherland. After Afghanistan and Pakistan, the Wahhabists seem to have turned their attention towards radicalizing the Indian Muslim youths. Its penetration is so deep and widespread that a good percent of even the Mappila Muslims of Malabar and the Muslims of Kashmir who traditionally follow Sufi Sunni Islam, have become followers of Wahhabism.

During recent years, Sufism has come under violent attack from the followers of Wahhabi Salafism in different parts of the world. Even as it faces flak from the progressive world internationally for propagating a destructive and extremist ideology, the Wahhabists are going ahead with their hate for Sufis–Sunni and all other moderate forms of Islam across the globe. Their militants are also engaged in destroying the Sufi shrines and tombs of Sufi saints in different places. They believe that Sufism ought to be met with violence and deny its centrality within Sunni Islam. The majority of Saudi religious establishments also subscribe to this view. And this is the most important challenge Crown Prince MBS is facing in his effort to materialize the promise of 'restoring the Islam of moderation'.

The Wahhabi–Salafis, also known as Ahle Hadiths in South Asia, view Sufis as a threat to Islam and its adherents as heretics and apostates. The Islamic State targets Sufis because it believes that only the fundamentalist form of Wahhabi Sunni Islam is valid and Sufism is a deviation from the 'puritanical Islam'. According to them, Sufis and Shias are heretics and apostates, whose blood should be shed to purge Islam of the deviations. This is the religious sanction for the sectarian killings and violence unleashed by all the Sunni extremist Islamic outfits, be it ISIS, al-Qaeda or Tehrik-e-Taliban of Pakistan.

Sufi sites and worshippers have been the target of jihadis since the emergence of the Islamic terrorism. In February 2017, a bomb exploded at the tomb of the Sufi saint, Lal Shahbaz Qalandar in Pakistan, killing around 100 people and injuring many. In 2016, the Islamic State had put on YouTube the images of Sufi teachers being executed. In the same year, the Pakistani Taliban murdered the famous Sufi singer Amjad Sabri. In 2010, the tomb of the famous Sufi saint Data Ganj Bakhsh (Ali bin Usman al-Hajveri) was bombed in the city of Lahore. He was one among the first Sufi saints to travel to India and settle in Lahore. Many Muslims and non-Muslims around the globe, and particularly in Morocco, Turkey and many countries in South Asia, celebrate Sufi saints and gather in their shrines to pay their respects. It represents a millennia of peaceful, tolerant and pious Sufi Sunni Islam which is now directly under attack by the extremist puritans.

Many Muslims proudly defend Sufi customs, such as the devotion shown to the saints and their shrines, because they are so integral to their understanding of religion and spirituality. It is so not only in South Asia but also in various other regions of the world. Today, about 15 per cent of the Egyptian population belongs to one or the other Sufi orders or practice Sufi traditions. Given the popularity of Sufis and their tolerant attitude towards different faiths and other religious sects, there is no wonder why the Islamic State opposes all models of Islamic pluralism.

The Islamic terrorists, in 2003, attacked a popular restaurant in the Moroccan city of Casablanca, which was packed with French tourists at the time of the attack. This was an attempt by the Wahhabis in Morocco to scare the Western tourists and send a strong message to the king of Morocco that the Salafi and Wahhabi ideology had taken roots in the Moroccan society. The Wahhabi leaders wanted the government to move away from any support given to the traditional Sufi Sunni ways of Islam, which they label as 'shirk' or 'polytheism'. It was a direct challenge to the Moroccan king as he was revered by the Muslims there as the Emir al-Muminin. The science of Islamic spirituality or tasawwuf is taught in all the top religious institutions in the Muslim world, including Egypt's Al-Azhar University and Morocco's Quaraouiyine University, considered to be two of the oldest seats of Islamic learning.

Many scholars in the West and in rest of the Islamic world strongly argue that the propagation of Sufi Islam and its great values can counter the influence of Wahhabism and the extremism associated with it. There is a pressing need to revive Sufism, which lies deep in the Muslim societies. In Morocco, the assault against Sufism gained momentum in the late 1970s and 1980s under Hassan II, father of the current monarch, who did little to block the export of Wahhabism into the country from Saudi Arabia. But, the present king, Mohammed VI, has sought greater regulatory control over religious affairs, purging Wahhabi-leaning preachers from mosques, removing lessons against Sufism from religious curricula, revamping the training programs for Imams and promoting Sufism across the country.

According to many scholars, Islam had a central role in the development of science, education, art, literature and culture in its earlier centuries of existence. In his book titled *What Went Wrong?*, British historian Bernard Lewis has attributed the decline of Islam to its inability to develop legal, economic and political institutions capable of rivaling the ones in Europe.[116] These institutions were the hallmark of Europe's enlightenment philosophy, and, Islam, in the meanwhile, was busy dealing with its internal struggles in coping with the diverse interpretations of the Quran and the Hadith.

---

[116]Lewis, Bernard, *What Went Wrong? : The Clash between Islam and Modernity in the Middle East*, Harper Perennial, 2006.

It was only in the middle of the twentieth century that the Muslim-majority countries in the world attempted to rebuild their societies in the wake of the decolonization of their territories. To achieve this, they were more inclined towards accepting ideologically secular political systems rather than looking inwards to find its own strong points. The form of reforms adopted by Kemal Ataturk in Turkey, the pan-Arabism under the Egyptian nationalist Gamal Abdel Nasser and the secular government of the Mohammad Reza Pahlavi or even the Shia-Islamic regime of Iran, were all examples for this. None of these political forms fully appreciated the spiritual pluralism of the traditional Islamic societies. In 2011, the entire Arab world witnessed one or the other forms of revolution and counter-revolutions, and the emergence of extremist organizations like the al-Qaeda, ISIS and a short-lived 'Islamic caliphate', which drew their strength from Wahhabism.

Before the advent of colonization, the Muslim population, stretching from Saudi Arabia to Anatolia and from India to Indonesia, had opened themselves to a range of understandings of the Islamic tradition. They were based on a flexible and non-dogmatic interpretation of Islam that saw different cultural and spiritual practices getting assimilated into the Islamic mainstream, making it more organic and spiritually meaningful. Having flourished since the twentieth century, the quest of Sufism has been to uphold the inner and esoteric aspects of the Islamic thought based on its sacred texts.

Interestingly, the growth and expansion of Sufism was occurring at a time, when the Greek philosophy and scientific developments were being valued highly by Muslim societies. It coincided with their extraordinary achievements in science and literature, as many Muslim mystics produced exceptional works in philosophy, medicine, astronomy and the arts.

The Golden Age of Islam witnessed the flourishing of both the inner and outer dimensions of Islam. Both dimensions built a civilization that valued the notion of governance and law as much as it did the inner workings of philosophy, spirituality and transcendence. It helped build a diverse population, willing to inquire and express Islam through many different languages, cultures and traditions. Sadly, many of these traditional practices that were widely espoused during the Golden Age of Islam have become almost extinct in the present Muslim world, or at the very least, they have been threatened seriously as a direct consequence of the authoritarian rules and reforms that took place at the turn of the twentieth century.

Sufism was subjected to an increasingly ferocious attack by the Saudi-educated ulamas across the world in the twentieth century. In this attack, the fundamentalist forces joined hands with several other modern forces. Most important among these was the Western-inspired nationalist philosophy with its typical contempt of mysticism. South Asia had served as the focal point in the dissemination of Sufism and Sufi related ideologies during the pre-modern period. It was in the same geographical region that anti-Sufi reformist ideologies of fundamental Islam also took roots in the modern period.

Unlike other concentrations of the communities, Muslims on the Indian subcontinent were always a minority living amidst a large Hindu population. Even during the sixteenth and seventeenth centuries, the heyday of Muslim rule in India, the political culture of Mughals was based on religious coexistence.[117] Only very few like the last major Mughal emperor Aurangzeb (1657–1707) tried to reverse this trend by partially discriminating against Hindus. This, too, is attributed to the influence of Salafism as his teacher was from the Najd region of Saudi Arabia, who must have been influenced by the writings of Ibn Tamiyyah, the initial proponent of Salafism.

In the twentieth and twenty-first centuries, the anti-Sufi reform movements have put the Sufi orders, and more generally the devotional Sufi practices and understandings, into a defensive

---

[117]Ahmed, Tufail, 'Book Review: India's First Jihadi Movement, Led by Syed Ahmed Barelvi', *MEMRI*, 1 April 2016, https://tinyurl.com/3xrxzxrz. Accessed on 12 September 2023.

and apologetic mode. Nonetheless, many Muslim majority sovereign nations like Morocco and Uzbekistan are using Sufism as a distinctive counterweight to Wahhabis and the Saudi-backed fundamental Islamic outfits that campaign for the unification of Muslims throughout the world into a single caliphate. It was in the city of Bukhara in Uzbekistan that the great Sufi Bahauddin Naqsbandi was born in the fourteenth century.[118] The followers of Naqshbandiyya order are spread all over the world. The biggest Madrasa in the city of Bukhara, Mir-Arab Madrasa, has given full support to the government policy to spread Sufism in the country, as a measure to strongly counter Wahhabi Salafism that is pushed by Saudi Arabia.

In the ongoing debates over how to respond to the extremist views of Wahhabi Salafism, too little attention has gone to the vast and deep repertoire of Sufi philosophy, art, music and literature produced during the 'golden era' of Islamic civilization. The Grand Mufti of Egypt has rejected the extremist interpretations of the Quranic verses as they do not represent 'true' Islam. The potency of Sufism lies in its ability to remind the world that the holy texts of Islam have deeper and broader meanings to them beyond their literal readings and interpretations, which have been lived and experienced across different countries and cultures in the world for more than 1,400 years.

The global Muslim experience of the interconnected, technology-empowered and globalized world has been catastrophic and brutal. The Wahhabi–Salafi ideology, an extremist version of intolerant Islam, promoted and exported by Saudi Arabia, with the backing of billions of US dollars, has devastated and isolated the Muslim communities across the world. In this context, Muslims world over need to explore and revive some of its past traditions that had kept its glorious civilization intact and safe from extremism for centuries.

---

[118]Rotar, Igor, 'Uzbekistan: Government Backs Sufism to Counter Wahhabism', *Religioscope*, 26 May 2002, https://tinyurl.com/5n7asewt. Accessed on 12 September 2023.

The mystical and esoteric tradition of Islam—Sufism—is that lost heritage, the reclamation of which is the need of the hour for peace to prevail in the entire world.

CONCLUSION

The Iranian Islamic Revolution, led by Ayatollah Khomeni in 1979, resonated throughout the Middle East and beyond. Among the most concerned countries was Saudi Arabia, which found that its former ally had suddenly turned into a revolutionary Shiite regime. The ruling Saudi royal family feared that Iran's revolutionary message would trigger a competitive Islamic uprising across the Arabian Peninsula. Their suspicion turned into a nightmare when a group of Sunni Islamist insurgents, led by Juhayman al-Otaybi, sieged the Grand Mosque of Mecca on 20 November the same year, in a direct challenge to the ruling Al Saud family of the Kingdom. The insurgents were motivated to depose the House of Saud and restore Sharia rule in Saudi Arabia. Otaybi announced to the media that the Al Saud family was corrupt and dictated by the West. The group also castigated the Saudi clergy's betrayal of Islam by compromising with the ruling family.

The siege of the Grand Mosque was led by a group of insurgents—and not by the masses as was seen in Iran—to depose the Shah of Iran. To avoid further escalation of mass radicalization, the royal family quickly agreed to discussions with the insurgents and brought them to the negotiation table. In the end, a solution was hammered out and a decision was taken to strictly enforce the Wahhabi version of Islam at home besides aggressively promoting it abroad. An agreement was also reached to expand religious schools and set up a special police force to enforce Sharia law strictly on the civil society. The oil boom of the early 1970s provided the kingdom with billions of US dollars to fund charities such as the Muslim World League to invest globally among Muslim communities and propagate Wahhabism among them.

The Muslim World League played a crucial role in supporting the Islamic associations and making investment plans for the spread of Wahhabism. In addition, the Saudi Ministry of Religious Affairs initiated measures to distribute millions of copies of the Holy Quran free of cost, along with other Wahhabi–Salafi doctrinal texts, among mosques across the world. For the first time in the 1,400-year-old history of Islam, a deliberate move was made to create an identical form of Islam based on a cleric's interpretation of it and push it from one end of the world to the other. The ideology of Salafism gained traction among the Muslim societies in the Middle East during the second half of the nineteenth century, when Muslim lands were being colonized by Western countries. Salafi reformists quickly blamed the believers for the colonization, saying that it was happening unbridled as they were deviating from the fundamentals of Islam. The reformists argued that returning to the oldest and purest form of Islam was the only way out.

Salafism has sought to purify Islam of Western influences and the forms of 'digressions' such as Shiism, Sufism and even the non-Salafi forms of Sunni Islam. The core Salafi literature was based on the writings of Ibn Taymiyyah and his disciples. They emphasized on the restoration of Islamic doctrines in the 'purest' form within the framework of the Quran and the Sunnah. Salafism focussed on eliminating shirk or idolatry and affirming the oneness of God or tawheed. Salafis claim themselves as the true followers of Islam. Those who are praying at tombs of saints are considered apostates. Salafists prefer to keep women inside the four walls and deprive them of formal modern education.

The unprecedented proliferation in the number of mosques was one of the most visible changes in the landscape of the rapidly urbanizing Muslim world. The Saudi clergy who aggressively pushed Wahhabi Salafism through their different global arms during 1980s and 1990s also ridiculed the Khomeini version of Islam to underscore their sectarian differences. This strategy had a huge impact on the Muslim world and it triggered the rise of Sunni fundamentalism on a global scale.

US Support for Jihadists

The Soviet invasion of Afghanistan in December 1979 prompted the US administration under Ronald Reagan to take on the 'evil empire' of Russia by taking the help of the Islamic insurgents (mujahideen) in Afghanistan. On the strategic advice of Israel, the US also saw the utility of Saudi's religious doctrine in containing the Soviet Union and restricting the expansion of Shia Iran. Because the US financially and materially supported the mujahideen in Afghanistan under the leadership of Osama bin Laden, this weird strategy made them complicit in spreading global jihad. The CIA used these insurgent groups to fight a proxy war against its strategic and ideological enemy, the Soviet Union. The National Security team of the Reagan administration instructed CIA to bring its close allies, Saudi Arabia and Pakistan, on board. With the help of Prince Bandar bin Sultan, who was the then Saudi ambassador to the US, Saudis committed full financial support to the Afghan Islamic mujahideen. Saudi Arabia, the US and Pakistan, through their intelligence agencies, set up jihadi training camps in Pakistan and supported them with advisers, weapons and cash to fight the Soviets.

According to journalist Steve Coll, the US strategists 'looked forward to introduce advanced military technology into Afghanistan and intensified training in explosives and sabotage techniques to intensify targeted attacks on the Soviet military installations.'[119] The US Agency for International Development (USAID), spending millions of dollars, supplied textbooks on militant Islamic teachings written by Wahhabi clergy from Saudi Arabia to help the cause. Paradoxically, President Ronald Reagan even praised jihadists like Gulbaddin Hekmatyer, who had founded the extremist outfit Hizb-i-Islami. Osama bin Laden, the founder of al-Qaeda, was also praised

---

[119] Wood, Graeme, 'Review: America's Slow-Motion Military and Policy Disaster in Afghanistan and Pakistan', *Washington Post*, 4 February 2018, https://tinyurl.com/t6sxeckd. Accessed on 28 September 2023.

by the US media for fighting the Soviets. He was also close to the Saudi intelligence chief, Prince Turki al-Faisal. Strangely, the CIA glossed over their extreme radicalism and the anti-West sentiments.

The US intelligence encouraged the fanaticism driven by the Wahhabi-inspired militants to achieve their short-term goal of defeating the Soviet Union. In the process, they unwittingly created a monster, not realizing that one day it will come back to bite them with all its ferocity and destructive force.

The US, with the help of the jihadi militants, comprehensively defeated the Soviet Union and forced them to withdraw from Afghanistan. But they squarely failed to comprehend the enormous consequences of providing legitimacy to the extremist organizations like al-Qaeda and, in the process, radicalized an entire generation of Muslims. The non-partisan US strategists had cautioned the Reagan administration against supporting the Wahhabi–Salafi strain of Islam as it preached violence and hate against non-believers and Western values. By endorsing Saudi Arabia's Wahhabi brand of Islam, the US has not only compromised on its own security but also done enormous damage to the future of the Muslim community globally. After the Grand Mosque seizure of 1979, the Wahhabi clerics had received a blanket license from the Saudi government to push Wahhabism globally, with the support of successive US administrations.

After the 1989 withdrawal of the Soviet forces, the US conveniently walked away from Afghanistan, leaving behind a failed country and a network of Western-educated young men, fully charged with a jihadi ideology and readiness to sacrifice their lives under the leadership of Osama bin Laden to make Western democracies bleed. Decades later, Senator Hillary Clinton succinctly summed it up:

> The people we are fighting today, we funded and mentored years ago… it was President Regan, in partnership with the Congress, led by Democrats, who had said; 'you know what, sounds like a pretty good idea… let's go recruit these Mujahideen, let us bring

some from Saudi Arabia and other Arab countries, importing their Wahhabi brand of Islam, so that we can beat the Soviet Union.' They retreated and soon we left and asked Pakistan to deal with the stingers and the jihadi young Muslims. Now we reap what we sow.[120]

US Invasion of Iraq

The US invasion of Iraq in 2003 was the inflection point of Middle East's anger against the US and Western democracies. A group inspired from the al-Qaeda tent, led by Abu Musab al-Zarqawi, fought the US occupation forces. The US administration under President George W. Bush committed a mistake again, oblivious of the sectarian fault lines of the region, this time by giving an opportunity to the Shiite majority of Iraq to rule a major Arab country for the first time in its history.

Abu Musab al-Zarqawi was a strong follower of the Wahhabi-Salafi brand of Islam, which calls followers of Shiite Islam apostate. He was upset about the fact that the political leadership of Iraq had gone to the hands of Shias. The Iraqi Sunni Muslims felt humiliated as they were pushed out of government jobs, military positions and became second-class citizens one fine morning in the new political dispensation supported by the US. Nelson Mandela had famously said, 'There is nobody more dangerous than one who has been humiliated.' Al-Zarqawi articulated the humiliation angle of the Sunni Muslims and scaled up terrorist attacks against the US forces and the holy places of the Shiite Muslims in Iraq. He mobilized and motivated the former army officers of the Saddam regime to join ISIS as fighters. Even though he was killed in the US airstrike in 2006, his vision of establishing ISIS eventually gained traction. His main successor, Abu Bakr al-Baghdadi, established ISIS 'caliphate'

---

[120]'US Created Taliban and Abandoned Pakistan, Says Hillary', *DAWN*, 25 April 2009, https://tinyurl.com/mr3encm9. Accessed on 28 September 2023.

in 2014 in swathes of land across Iraq and Syria.

The uprising against Bashar al-Assad as part of the Arab Spring broke out in 2011. Hillary Clinton, the then Secretary of State; David Petraeus, CIA director; and many others advocated for training and arming Syrian rebels as well as creating a no-fly zone to protect civilians. President Obama rejected the proposal and argued for 'red lines' on the use of chemical weapons but failed to enforce it. He later agreed on President Putin's proposal to safely transfer the chemical weapons to Russia. It was a strategic mistake on the part of the US to accept the Russian proposal.

President Obama was squarely blamed, and rightly so, for causing over a million deaths and a huge migration of civilians out of Syria. Not all chemical weapons were shifted to Russia. A large part of it was left behind, and Bashar al-Assad used them later against civilians as well. President Obama, undoubtedly a laggard in confronting ISIS militarily in the early stages, allowed the terrorist organization to grow. Perhaps Obama had become overcautious as he entered the White House after President Bush's Iraq adventurism and, as per his wisdom, wiggled his way out of another Middle Eastern quagmire.

Flawed US Policies

In August 2014, during a media briefing, President Obama remarked that the US 'didn't have a strategy yet' for dealing with the Islamic State militants in Syria. It was not a secret that the threat of ISIS was festering for a long time and it was only growing in strength. Obama was sharply criticized for his inept handling of the growing menace of ISIS. Despite his failure in dealing with the expanding footprints of ISIS in Syria and Iraq, he finally decided in 2015 to provide air power and military advisers to help the Kurds in their battle against the Islamic State. This was indeed a game changer—the US could decimate the ISIS caliphate without putting its boots on the ground.

In 2016, President Trump inherited the policies from the Obama administration, which were effectively working both in Syria and Iraq in squeezing the geographical area of ISIS and degrading its military capabilities. The Syrian Democratic Forces (SDF), an alliance of Kurdish and Arab fighters backed by the US air cover, achieved the seemingly impossible and defeated the ISIS caliphate. At one time, it had ruled approximately 10 million people spread across major cities like Mosul and Raqqa. The fact of the matter is that the SDF fighters with the US air support recaptured almost 95 per cent of land and took thousands of Arab and foreign fighters as captives. The SDF secured all the cities and towns in the Euphrates river valley except some small pockets of ISIS. President Trump, in a pompous language, tweeted on 20 March 2018: 'We have taken back almost 100 per cent, in a very short period of time, of the land that ISIS took. And it all took place since my election.'

Senator Lindsey Graham, a high-ranking Republican, denounced President Trump's decision to pull out US troops from Syria. He described it as an impulsive, short-sighted and irresponsible decision by the President. The Kurdish fighters were totally upset that in the middle of the campaign, the US forces began to withdraw from their positions ahead of a Turkish military attack. The vacuum created by the US forces was to be filled by Russia, Iran and the Assad regime. President Erdogan always considered the Kurdish forces in Syria to be terrorists, allied with the Kurdish insurgents within his country and long threatened a military incursion into northern Syria where they dominated. President Trump flip-flopped while reacting on the Turkish president's threat to enter Syria and annihilate the Kurds who fought as American allies against ISIS.

Trump's intention was to first withdraw US troops from Syria in 2018, but he agreed to keep a residual force when his security advisers insisted that the American presence was vital to maintain peace in the region. The SDF cautioned that Turkey's planned incursion would have a major negative impact on the ISIS war and destroy the past victories. The US Defense Secretary Jim Mattis and other senior national security members of the team were upset and angry with Trump. They remarked that it would be a 'stain on America's honor to abandon the Kurds and ensure an ISIS comeback'.[121]

The senior members of the Trump administration, including his national security adviser John Bolton, have admitted that the ISIS threat would remain. This explained the contrary positions taken by the President and his national security team. The US military had decided to keep around 1,000 forces in Syria and not to follow the advice of Trump for a total withdrawal. According to Jim Jeffery, the special US envoy to Syria at the time, about 15,000 to 20,000 ISIS sleeper-cells were operating across Iraq and Syria. In eastern Syria, they popped up at night at checkpoints.

The US military has effectively decimated the terrorist groups in Afghanistan, Iraq and Syria, but it always messes up in the last leg in converting the tactical advantages into categorical and meaningful victories. The SDF is managing the former jihadi militants' camps in Syria. They house their spouses and children evacuated from ISIS-held enclaves. Their number runs into tens of thousands. Stateless, they are people who arrived from Western countries to be part of a delusional caliphate.

After the US troops withdrew from Iraq in 2011 and Bashar al-Assad survived in Syria by covert financial and military support from Iran and Hezbollah, Iran's regional influence increased exponentially. Iran and Hezbollah also supported the Zaydi Houthis in Yemen against the Saudi-led forces. It is no secret that Iran has emerged a strong regional power in the Middle East. Israel has legitimate reasons to fear Iran's influence expanding in its immediate neighbourhood, particularly in Lebanon.

President Trump withdrew from the Iran nuclear deal (JCPOA) to please his friend Netanyahu, even at the cost of annoying the five

---

[121] Cummings, William et al., '"A Stain on America's Honor": Lindsey Graham Says Trump's Syria Pullout Abandons Kurds, Helps ISIS', *USA Today*, 7 September 2019, https://tinyurl.com/5d8eudw4. Accessed on 28 September 2023.

UN Permanent Security Council members. His other personal motive was to ensure support of the Jewish lobby in the coming presidential re-election. The harsh US sanctions have shattered Iran's economy. But it managed to do business with China and a few South American countries. President Trump has nudged important Gulf countries like the UAE and Bahrain to establish a diplomatic relationship with Israel, despite the fact that the US had relocated its embassy in the disputed city of Jerusalem in a clear sign of partiality towards Israel. The UAE hopes that the ties would enable it to push Israel towards some serious peace talks with the PLO. It is a win-win for Israel as it will break Israel's regional isolation and offer an opportunity to sell arms and technology to gain economic and commercial benefits. The Gulf countries are vulnerable due to very low oil prices, popular revolts and fear of the US withdrawal of support. In the final analysis, Israel seems to have taken control of the Middle East and brought all the Arab GCC nations under its control.

According to the Trump administration officials, the easing of hostility between Israel, the UAE and Bahrain and a possible future deal between Israel and other Arab nations like Oman and Saudi Arabia are part of a larger effort to counter Iran. On a note of caution, the UAE and Bahrain have, however, decided to locate their embassies in Tel Aviv and not Jerusalem.

Iran has condemned the UAE–Israel and Bahrain–Israel agreements to start diplomatic relations. Iranian business and firms operating in the United Arab Emirates control roughly US $300 billion in assets. An estimated 600,000 Iranians live and own property in the UAE. The long-term goal of Israel's accord is to eliminate the voice of Palestinians from global platforms and project Iran as the only bad boy of the Middle East. The Middle East of the twenty-first century poses a far greater danger to the US than at any other time in the past. Martin Indyk, former US ambassador to Israel and senior fellow at Brookings, in his *Wall Street Journal* essay, argues that the oil and security of Israel are no longer important for the

US.[122] This does not mean that the US will completely withdraw from the Middle East and yield a place for China, Russia, Turkey and Iran. The US still has to maintain global economic stability by controlling oil prices and freedom of navigation through the volatile region of the Middle East.

The US has been supporting the Wahhabi–Salafi brand of radical Islam since 1979 to leverage its strategic interests in the region and, by default, strengthening the interests of the royal family of Saudi Arabia and other monarchies in the Gulf region. They were suspecting armed uprisings by the Arab civil society, inspired by the revolutionary socialist Arab nations like Shiite Iran, Baathist Iraq and nationalist Egypt and Libya. The most bizarre long-term consequence of the policy response by the US to the Soviet invasion of Afghanistan was the mobilization of the jihadist to the camps in Pakistan and Afghanistan. The CIA and ISI invited Osama bin Laden to lead the Arab and non-Arab volunteers seeking martyrdom. A large group of Western-educated young men were from the middle- and upper-class Muslim families with a strong belief in Wahhabism that has completely isolated them from mainstream European societies.

The radicalized followers of the Wahhabi–Salafi brand of Islam, in the meanwhile, became a serious threat to the US and Western democracies. The all-powerful Crown Prince MBS of Saudi Arabia initiated a series of reforms, including ordering the assertive and strident clergy to make concessions in the Wahhabi–Salafi brand of Islam domestically. Nevertheless, the larger question is how to reverse the process of radicalization that Wahhabis–Salafis carry out by training their imams and making Wahhabi literature available at their mosques and Islamic study centres across the world.

The US, as a sovereign country, had been continuously using flawed initiatives to rein in the dangerous ideology of Wahhabi–

---

[122]Indyk, Martin, 'The Middle East Isn't Worth It Anymore', *Wall Street Journal*, 17 January 2020, https://tinyurl.com/ymunme98. Accessed on 26 September 2023.

Salafism among Muslim communities spread across its states. The officials of different security agencies in charge of dealing with this challenge lacked even a basic understanding of Islamic history or the ethno-cultural and sectarian characteristics of the Muslim community. They refused to go into the layered history of Islam that provides vital clues on how an extremely peaceful and tolerant ideology of Sufi Sunni Islam was sidelined by the Saudi rulers on the advice of an eighteenth-century cleric, Muhammad ibn Abd al-Wahhab, to make an intolerant and regressive version of Islam its state religion.

The most profound failure of the US security agencies was in not understanding the Muslim millennials who were hijacked by Saudi-sponsored Wahhabi–Salafi brand of Islam. In 2004, the National Security Council conducted research on why young Muslims in American universities were attracted by the ideology of al-Qaeda. Perhaps the experts missed an important point—jihadi architecture was a built-in feature of Wahhabi Salafism, which was taught to them from an early age through Sunday schools and madrasas. What the US embassies lacked in their initiatives to reach out to the local Muslim communities was the wisdom to caution their leadership about the teachings of Wahhabi–Salafism, which has extremism and hate at its core.

After 9/11, the US had a unique opportunity, as global sympathy was with it to make an attempt to purge global Muslim communities of extremism. But it either failed to identify the dangerous implications of endorsing Wahhabi–Salafism, a limited and vicious ideology, or deliberately did nothing to ward off its spread across the world. Extremism among Muslims is not due to poverty, deprivation or any grievance against the policies of Western democracies. Neither are the Western democracies at war against Islam. The elephant in the room unfortunately is the ultra-conservative Wahhabi–Salafi Islam, which, for Saudi Arabia is the 'authentic' and 'real Islam'. They branded and sold it to the Muslim world as the strongest, vibrant and purposeful version of Islam. The majority of Sunni Muslim youths, especially in the Middle East and in the Western world, became its followers through the Internet and social media platforms.

Senior policy makers of the Obama administration believed that they could do two things at once—extend their hand in friendship to Muslims and speak honestly with them about extremism. However, they failed to name Wahhabi Salafism as the promoter of extremism and hate. The mistakes made by successive US administrations in dealing with Saudi Arabia and its extreme brand of Islam allowed the extremism to flourish. Security advisers, counter-terrorism experts and the National Security Council personnel under the Obama administration groped in the dark for vain ways to reach out to Muslim communities, analyse them and contain terrorism.

Many inter-agnecy offices across the US focussed on choking the financial sources of ISIS and other terrorist outfits. But they didn't see that the Muslims youths have been radicalized by the Wahhabi imams and other religious arms of Saudi Arabia in the last 40 years. They have not only radicalized the next generation of Muslims, but also totally changed their attitude towards Western democracies and the progressive values they represent.

The bottom line is that the US has an undeniable role and responsibility in the spread of extremism among the Muslim communities world over. The military protection to Saudi Arabia by the US superpower since 1935 gave them confidence and a level playing field to spread Wahhabism among the Muslim communities across the world. By 2030, the global Muslim population is projected to touch 2.2 billion with an overwhelming majority of Muslims following the Wahhabi–Salafi brand of extremist Islam. It is high time that the progressive forces of the world unite for the cause of peace and do something, collectively and empathetically, to stop this regressive ideology from causing further harm to the world.

The total withdrawal of the US and NATO forces from Afghanistan, by default giving political space to Taliban under the Afghan–US peace deal, was a monumental mistake with serious regional and international consequences.

If the US again installs Taliban in Afghanistan, as they intend to, the world will be on the edge once again (Taliban has announced to implement Sharia law based on Wahhabi ideology.) This will be a recipe for disaster and will give legitimacy to the Wahhabi brand of Islam that many Muslim countries (including Saudi Arabia) are now trying to marginalize or moderate.

If the US would seriously like to see any substantial change in the ultra-conservative ways of the Islamic fundamentalists, the US National Security Council and other agencies should grab the opportunity and do whatever needs to be done to change it as is done by countries like Morocco. By banning all Wahhabi literature from its mosques and Islamic study centres, Morocco as a sovereign country has initiated steps to rein in Wahhabism. The ideology has long been described as an ultra-conservative and intolerant interpretation of Islamic faith that encourages believers to commit crimes against humanity.

Way Forward for the US

The Islamic Supreme Council of America, Cordoba House and the Islamic Society of North America (ISNA) are some of the major Muslim organizations active in the US. The National Security Council and other agencies dealing with terrorism should start dialogues with these organizations to revive the concept of a more moderate form of Islam in public life. Fundamentalism means lack of tolerance, an increase in bigotry and a unilateral interpretation of faith, as represented by the Wahhabi–Salafi brand of Islam.

The ISNA, based in Plainfield, Indiana, USA, is an umbrella organization. It is perhaps, the largest Muslim organization in North America. It holds an annual convention, which is regarded as the largest annual gathering of American Muslims, to discuss their role in civil society, politics, media, education and public administration.

The US Department of Homeland Security should involve ISNA to get the Wahhabi–Salafi leadership to mend its ways and moderate its stance, with regards to its approach towards other faiths and cultures. The authorities should also urge the various Muslim communities to disconnect their ties with the Saudi charities that fund the promotion of Wahhabism, and instead start collaborating with countries like Morocco that promote a more tolerant and peaceful version of Islam, such as the Sufi Sunni Islam. The US, as a sovereign nation, has a right to ban all the Wahhabi literature from its mosques and Islamic study centres that promote hate towards other faiths and encourage jihadism. The Internet and social media platforms may also be monitored by ISNA in collaboration with American security agencies. It should warn them of punitive action against the violators. The choice is left with the US administration as it has an obligation to take leadership in constructing the architecture of peace for the US and for the rest of the world.

ACKNOWLEDGEMENTS

In 1994, I joined as Senior European Union Marie Curie Fellow at the Alpine Research Center, University of Manchester, UK. The university had a large number of Muslim students from Middle Eastern countries and South Asian students born and raised in UK. The Friday weekly prayers used to be held in the packed colonnade hall of the students union. Before the prayers, the khutba (sermon) was given by a young student who also led the prayers. By narrating stories of Muslim persecution by America and other Western powers, a young and fiery imam would argue for mandatory jihad by young Muslims.

I was taken aback by the level of anger and hatred among the youth against America and liberal British society to which their parents decided to immigrate to, for a secured future of the next generation. In subsequent years, I had an opportunity to visit Islamic centres and societies of universities across many states in the US, the UK, France, Germany and the Netherlands. Everywhere I would come across young people full of hate and anger against Western culture and their policies towards Islamic countries. In later years, many angry educated Muslim youths have been sucked up by terrorist organizations.

It is a huge challenge to write a book on the complex and layered issue of weaponization of Islam. The book narrates three pivotal events that occurred in 1979 that had a profound impact on the Western and Islamic world.

I am grateful to Jabir Mushthari, journalist and editor from Kerala, who has done an amazing job of improving the narrative of the book. He has painstakingly gone through the entire manuscript, offered advice and encouragement and demanded clarification.

On the complex issue of political Islam, I have had detailed discussions with Prof. Aftab Kamal Pasha, School of International Studies, Jawaharlal Nehru University, New Delhi. I am indebted to him for his constructive suggestions in improving the content of the book.

I am also indebted to my friend Satish Jacob, former BBC correspondent in Delhi, who encouraged me to write a book on this subject.

INDEX

9/11, xiv, xv, 11, 12, 13, 14, 38, 39, 42, 49, 51, 52, 53, 54, 55, 56, 57, 69, 73, 74, 119, 144, 151, 152, 174, 195, 210, 211, 221, 235, 273
9/11 Commission Report, 13, 14, 53
1973 Israel–Arab conflict, 36
1998 Pan-Am Lockerbie bombing disaster, 54
2007 Casablanca terror attack, 59
2019 Easter Sunday terror attacks, 57

Abbasid dynasty, 25
Abd al-Salam Faraj, Muhammad, 43
Abd al-Wahhab, Muhammad ibn, xiv, xxx, xxxi, 2, 3, 5, 16, 26, 27, 28, 29, 30, 43, 47, 65, 75, 124, 177, 188, 229, 232, 233, 245, 250, 273
Abdulazeez, Mohammad, 23
Abdullah Saleh, Ali, 86, 87
Abraham Accords, xx
Afghan Islamic mujahideen, 265
Afghanistan, viii, xi, xii, xiii, xiv, xxii, xxvii, 4, 5, 6, 7, 8, 9, 10, 11, 14, 15, 19, 20, 21, 44, 46, 49, 50, 51, 52, 60, 61, 62, 68, 71, 72, 88, 91, 93, 99, 103, 113, 118, 127, 140, 143, 152, 155, 194, 195, 197, 199, 205, 209, 215, 221, 222, 225, 239, 247, 256, 265, 266, 270, 272, 274, 275
Afghanistan–Pakistan jihadi theatre, 8
ahl al-Bida, 30
Ahmadinejad, Mahmoud, 40
Alawite, 78, 80, 82, 83, 84, 109, 110, 111, 131, 183, 206
al-Awlaki, Anwar, 151, 175
Al-Furqan, 160, 179
Al-Ghazali, 232
Al-Khansa Brigade, 184
al-Khobar, 9
All India Ulama and Mashaikh Board (AIUMB), 256
al-Nuri mosque, 18
al-Qaeda, viii, xiii, xiv, xvii, xxv, xxvi, xxvii, xxviii, 7, 8, 9, 10, 12, 14, 16, 17, 20, 21, 22, 23, 38, 39, 43, 44, 49, 51, 52, 53, 54, 55, 66, 67, 68, 69, 72, 74, 75, 76, 77, 84, 86, 88, 100, 104, 110, 120, 126, 140, 151, 152, 154, 158, 159, 161, 162, 164, 170, 171, 174, 175, 194, 195, 196, 197, 199, 200, 201, 202, 204, 205, 207, 210, 213, 214, 220, 234, 252, 257, 259, 265, 266, 267, 273

al-Qaeda in Iraq (AQI), xxviii, 171, 196, 197, 201, 202
al-Quds Mosque, 11
al-salaf al-salih, 25, 27
Al Saud family, xv, 32, 34, 43, 263
al-Shabaab, 154, 155, 191
America First, 96
Anglo-Saudi Treaty, 33, 34
Ansar al-Islam, 195
anti-American, xiii, 14, 38, 39, 51, 54, 56, 76, 203, 210
anti-Americanism, 103
anti-Iran demonstrations, xviii
anti-Semitism, 14
anti-West, xxv, 162, 266
anti-Zionism, 103
Arabian–American Oil Company (ARAMCO), 48
Arab Spring, xxi, 23, 65, 82, 84, 86, 87, 102, 107, 110, 113, 117, 119, 122, 125, 161, 177, 202, 209, 233, 268
Araji, Qasim al-, 98
Ashari, 78
ASKfm, 176
Assad, Bashar al-, xxviii, 16, 42, 57, 71, 75, 78, 82, 83, 89, 92, 93, 102, 104, 109, 111, 122, 126, 161, 204, 205, 210, 212, 220, 223, 268, 270
Assad, Hafez al-, xviii, 82, 83, 105, 210, 211
attacks on the US embassies, xiv, 10
Atta, Mohammad, 11
Auliya, Hazarat Nizamuddin, 239, 241, 242, 243
Awlaki, Anwar al-, 53, 151, 175

Aziz Ibn Abd al-Rahman, Abd al- (Ibn Saud), xiv, xv, 3, 5, 26, 29, 30, 32, 33, 34, 136, 177, 233

Baathist force, xxvii
Baath party, xxviii, 64, 98, 211
Bab-el-Mandeb Strait, xviii
Baghdadi, Abu Bakr al-, xxviii, xxix, 16, 17, 18, 19, 160, 168, 177, 188, 201, 202, 204, 205, 213, 218, 219, 222, 224, 225, 267
Baghdadi, Abu Omar al-, xxviii, 201
Baghdad Pact, 107
Bakhsh, Data Ganj, 239, 257
Basnan, Osama, 53
Battle of Karbala, xvi, 60
Beduin forces, 32
Bell, Gertrude, 63
Berbers, xxiii, 136
Bhakti movement, 244, 254
bin Abdullah, Turki, 32
bin Laden, Osama, xi, xiii, 4, 6, 7, 8, 9, 10, 11, 12, 14, 16, 39, 43, 49, 50, 51, 52, 53, 69, 154, 159, 174, 196, 197, 210, 265, 266, 272
bin Salman, Mohammad, xv, xxii, 23, 24, 74, 81, 87, 98, 101, 111, 112, 114, 115, 116, 119, 121, 124, 125, 128, 131, 132, 134, 188, 256, 272
bin Saud, Abdullah, 32
Boko Haram, viii, 69, 75, 140
Boston Marathon bombing, 57, 162

British air force, 34
Brussels airport bombing, 148
Bush, George H.W., 8, 12, 13, 50, 64, 85, 267

Camp David Accords, vii
Capitol Hill, 12, 44
Center for Strategic Counter-terrorism Communications (CSCC), 187
Central Intelligence Agency (CIA), xii, xiii, xv, 4, 7, 8, 9, 14, 53, 56, 265, 266, 268, 272
Chabahar Port, 103
Chishti, Khwaja Moinuddin, 239, 240
Chishtiya, 231, 250
Christianity, xi, xxiii, 14, 17, 137, 139, 149, 221
Christian renaissance, xxiii
Clinton, Bill, 10, 44
Clinton, Hillary, 45, 85, 266, 268
Coalition Provisional Authority (CPA), xxvii, 199, 200
Cold War, 37, 100, 110, 233
Cordoba House, 228, 275
Council on American–Islamic Relations (CAIR), xxiv, xxv, 151, 152
Council on Foreign Relations (CFR), 7
Countering Violent Extremism (CVE), 187
Counter Terrorism Internet Referral Unit (CTIRU), 173
crypto-Persians, 77
cyber armies, xxvi, 170

cyber caliphate, 173
cyber jihad, xxvi, 174
cyber-jihadists, 173

Dabiq, 171, 172, 173, 183
Daesh, 195, 224
Dahabshiil, 54
dawah, 75, 142, 154
Dawn of Glad Tidings, 179
Dehlavi, Shah Waliullah, xxxi, 230, 249, 250, 255
Deoband, 249, 250, 251
Der Spiegel, 105
Desert Islam, 13, 177
Din Muhammad, Jalal ad-, xxxi, 232, 234, 235, 240
Diriyah, xiv, 3, 29, 32
Durand Line, 4

Emilie Konig vs Ummu Tawwab, 148
Emir al-Muminin, 201, 219, 258
European Union, xix, 66, 95, 165, 170, 212, 277

fake news, 20, 163, 180
fall of Mosul, xxviii, 217
Federal Bureau of Investigation (FBI), xv, 9, 52, 53, 54, 56, 151, 168, 208
First World War, xxiii, 33, 34, 63, 144, 145
flat world, xxv, 67, 68, 157, 158, 164, 166
Foreign Affairs, 24 104
Free Syrian Army (FSA), 110, 204, 206, 210, 214

Gaza, xx, 123, 224
General People's Congress, 87
Ghawar oilfield, 36
Gilani, Abdul-Qadir, 229, 232
Gilani, Shaykh Abdul Qadir, 240
Global Center for Combating Extremist Ideology, 97
Golan Heights, xviii, 24, 36, 82, 92, 105, 213
Golden Age of Islam, 259, 260
Golden Age' of Islam, xxx
Gonzalez, Nohemi, 192
Gormez, Mehmet, 46
Gothenburg Mosque, 46
Graham, Bob, 54
Grand Mosque, 2, 12, 13, 23, 47, 48, 61, 119, 146, 263, 266
Grand Mufti, 106, 261
Gulbuddin Hekmatyar, 49
Gulf News, 1, 97
Gulf War, 8, 15, 38, 85

Hadith, xxx, xxxi, 26, 48, 156, 161, 171, 172, 175, 188, 190, 208, 226, 230, 231, 236, 237, 250, 251, 258
Haley, Nikki, xix, 90
Hamas, xx, 69, 79, 123, 224
Hamdani, Shaykh Abu Yusuf, 240
Hanafi Barelvi group, 251
Hanbali, 27, 28, 31, 71, 77, 139, 142, 231
Haq, Muhammad Zia ul-, 7
Hashemite kingdom, 35
Henning, Alan, 183
heretics, xxxi, 17, 28, 33, 56, 65, 77, 172, 201, 233, 256, 257
Hezbollah, xviii, xxii, 42, 57, 70, 76, 79, 80, 82, 83, 84, 86, 87, 88, 91, 93, 94, 98, 99, 100, 102, 104, 105, 113, 114, 115, 116, 117, 118, 120, 122, 130, 131, 132, 161, 205, 206, 223, 270
hijab, 46, 156
Hinduism, 14, 244, 254, 255
Holy Land, 9
House of Saud, xvi, 27, 64, 65, 124, 126, 263
Houthi, Abdul Malik al-, xxi
Houthi, Hussein Badreddin al-, xxi
Houthis, xviii, xix, xxii, 41, 57, 60, 70, 76, 80, 86, 87, 88, 101, 112, 113, 114, 120, 130, 131, 270
Hujwiri, Ali al-, 239, 240
hussainias, 73, 83
Hussein, Saddam, xvii, 8, 15, 16, 38, 42, 56, 64, 65, 84, 85, 109, 111, 195, 219

Iberian Peninsula, xxiii, 136
Ibn Khaldun, Abdur Rahman, vii
Ibn Saud, xiv, 3, 5, 26, 29, 30, 32, 33, 34, 177, 233
Ibn Taymiyyah, Taqi al-Din Ahmad, xiv, xxx, 2, 5, 16, 25, 26, 28, 31, 228, 229, 237, 245, 264
ijtihad, 28
Ikhwan, xv, 33, 34, 38, 48, 49
Institute for Political and International Studies, 39
International Atomic Energy Agency (IAEA), xix, 89, 90, 91, 95
International Islamic Unity Conference, 80

Inter-Services Intelligence (ISI), xii, xiii, xxviii, 4, 7, 8, 10, 11, 14, 50, 51, 76, 159, 201, 202, 203, 207, 272
interventionist policies, xviii
Iranian revolution, 61, 96
Iran–Iraq conflict, 85
Iran–Iraq war, 121
Iran Project, 39, 40
Iraqi invasion of Kuwait, 97, 107
Iraq–Syria border, xxviii, 217
IRGC Aerospace Force, 105
Islamic centres, 3, 6, 27, 74, 130, 139, 277
Islamic Revolution, viii, xi, xii, xvi, xx, 1, 38, 60, 61, 95, 96, 107, 108, 263
Islamic Revolutionary Guard Corps (IRGC), 94, 102, 103, 104, 105, 133
Islamic State Khorasan (IS-K), 19
Islamic State of Iraq and the Levant (ISIL), 189, 195, 222
Islamism, vii, 17
Ismaili, 60, 78
Ismail, Shah, xvi, 61
Israeli occupation of Palestine, xxv
Israeli–Palestinian conflict, xx, 22, 24, 128

Jaish-e-Mohammed, 7
Jamaat al-Tawhid wal-Jihad, xvii, 69, 194
Jamiyat Ihya Minhaj al-Sunnah (JIMAS), 141, 142, 143, 237
Javad Zarif, Mohammad, 95

jihadi brides, 185, 187, 225
Jihadi John, 141, 183
Joint Comprehensive Plan of Action (JCPOA), xix, 89, 120, 121, 270
Judaism, xi, 14
Justice Against Sponsors of Terrorism Act (JASTA), 55

Kabir, 244, 248, 254
Kabul bombing, 19
Kaki, Sheikh Qutbuddin, 240
Kashmiri Pandits, 7
Keyboard Warriors, 178, 180
Khalizad, Zilmay, 20
Khan, Moulana Ahmed Raza, 251
Khashoggi, Jamal, 40, 173
Khomeini, Ayatollah, 1, 23, 60, 108, 111, 133
Khusro, Hazrat Amir, 241
khutbah, xxv
King Abdullah II, xviii, 78
King Fahad Mosque, 46, 54
King Faisal Mosque, 46
King Khalid, 1, 109
King of Hijaz, 34
Kitab Al-Tawhid, 3
Knox William, 35
Konig, Emilie, 148
Kosovo Liberation Army (KLA), 8
Kreindler & Kreindler, 54
Kubrawi, Sheikh Ismail, 247
Kushner, Jared, xix, 123, 124, 126, 127, 131

Lashkar-e-Taiba, 7
Liberation Movement of Iran, 1

Line of Control (LoC), 7
lone-wolf, 55, 168

Macron, Emmanuel, xxiv
madrasas, xiii, 4, 5, 7, 27, 38, 50, 51, 74, 210, 247, 252, 256, 273
Maliki, Nouri al-, 76, 209, 217, 219, 221
martyrs virtues, 182
Masri, Abu Ayyub al-, 16, 201
mazar, 14
McCants, William, 45
McGhee, George, 35
Mecca, viii, 2, 12, 23, 26, 28, 31, 34, 47, 48, 61, 63, 107, 109, 119, 156, 172, 228, 229, 230, 249, 251, 263
Medina, 26, 28, 31, 34, 107, 109, 156, 172, 173, 228, 229, 230, 249, 251
Ministry of Islamic Affairs, Dawah, and Guidance (MOIA), xxiv
miraj, xxx, 228
Mohammad, Khalid Sheikh, 11, 151
Mossad, xx, xxii
mujahideen, xii, 4, 5, 49, 51, 205, 265
musawat, 35
Muslim Brotherhood, viii, xx, 87, 126, 132, 146, 150, 195, 213
Muslim Students Association (MSA), xxiv, 150, 151
Muslim women, 59, 165, 192
Muslim World League (MWL), xxiii, xxv, 42
mutaween, 124

Naqshbandiyya, 231, 250
Nasr, Seyyed Hossein, 39, 71
Nasser, Gamal Abdel, 105, 259
nationalism, vii, viii, xvi, xviii, 22, 63, 64, 79, 81, 95, 98, 105, 118, 133, 189
Nation of Islam (NOI), 150
Netanyahu, Benjamin, 21, 41, 92, 129, 270
New York Times, xxv, 23, 40, 45, 47, 54, 97, 134, 151, 153, 187
Nooruddin, Sheikh, 247
North Atlantic Treaty Organization (NATO), 52, 274

Obama administration, xxix, 120, 269, 274
Obama, Barack, xvii, xxix, 37, 41, 55, 66, 70, 71, 84, 85, 86, 120, 163, 187, 209, 218, 220, 268, 269, 274
Omar, Mullah, xii, xiii, 5, 7, 10, 14, 50, 51, 194
OPEC, 108, 131
Operation Cyclone, 4
Operation Desert Storm, 8
Operation Enduring Freedom (OEF), 14
Organization of Islamic Countries (OIC), 125, 129, 187
Ottoman Empire, xiv, xv, xxxi, 26, 31, 32, 33, 144, 177, 232

P5+1, xix, 81, 89
Pahlavi, Mohammad Reza, 61, 108, 110, 146, 259
Pakistan–Afghanistan

international border, 50
Pandith, Farah, 45
Panjshir valley, 52
Paris bombing, 148
Pasha, Ibrahim, xiv, 32
Pearl, Daniel, 68, 158
Pentagon, 12, 16, 44, 157, 194
Persian Gulf, 38, 73, 84, 91, 101, 103, 105, 111
petrodollar, 74, 188, 233
Prophet Mohammad, xxix, xxx, 2, 14 26, 27, 28, 31, 48, 58, 59, 60, 77, 156, 227, 228, 229, 230, 231, 243, 248, 249, 250, 252, 254
Putin, Vladimir, xix, 86, 90, 92, 122, 268

Qadiriyya, 231, 234, 255
Qalandar, Lal Shahbaz, 257
Qasim, Maulana Muhammad, 249, 250
Quran, xxx, xxxi, 1, 2, 6, 26, 27, 28, 29, 30, 43, 48, 77, 138, 142, 156, 172, 175, 188, 190, 208, 210, 226, 227, 229, 230, 232, 236, 237, 242, 245, 246, 249, 250, 256, 258, 264

rafida, 77, 198
Reagan, Ronald, 4, 49, 265
Rifaiyyah, 231
Rockefeller Brothers Fund, 39
Roosevelt administration, 35
Rouhani, Hassan, 40, 66, 75, 80, 95, 103

Saad Hariri, 99, 102, 115, 116, 129
Sabri, Amjad, 257
Sadat, Anwar, vii, 43
Sadr, Ayatollah Muhammad Sadiq al-, 64
Sadr, Muqtada al-, 98, 118
Safavid dynasty, xvi, 61, 62
sahabah, 230, 231
Sahwa, viii
Sai Baba of Shirdi, 239
San Bernardino shooting, 57
Saudi–Iran rivalry, xxi, 117, 120
Saudi–US bloc, xix, 90
Saud–Wahhab Alliance, 27
Second Gulf War, 15
Second World War, xv, 35, 135, 145, 222
September 11 attacks, xiv
Shadhiliyya, 231
Shahnameh, 95
Sharia law, xiii, xxviii, 5, 16, 18, 20, 140, 161, 184, 185, 189, 197, 201, 207, 214, 219, 221, 263, 275
Shia Crescent, xviii, 72, 80, 81, 84, 104
shirk, 26, 29, 258, 264
Society for the Revival of the Prophetic Ways, xxiv
Soleimani, Qassem, 90
Standard Oil Company, California, 36
Stinger, 4
Stockholm International Peace Research Institute, 40
Suhrawardi, Abu Najib, 240

Sulaiman Barre, Mohammad, 54
Sultan of Najd, 34
Sunnah, 3, 26, 28, 30, 77, 141, 142, 195, 230, 231, 237, 250, 264
Supreme Sacrifice, 5
Syrian Democratic Forces (SDF), xxix, 21, 91, 127, 167, 225, 269, 270
Syrian Islamic Liberation Front (SILF), 205

Tabqa Air Base, 182
Tabrizi, Sheikh Shamsuddin, 240
Taliban's cultural commission, 20
Tasawwuf, 228
tawhid, 26
Tehrik-e-Taliban, 140, 257
Telegram, 20, 159, 167, 192
The Clanging of the Sword IV, 182
The International Atomic Energy Agency (IAEA), xix, 89, 90, 91, 95
Think Again Turn Away, 181, 187
Thumairy, Fahad al-, 54
Trump, Donald, xix, xxix, 17, 18, 20, 21, 24, 37, 40, 55, 81, 82, 89, 90, 91, 92, 94, 95, 96, 97, 111, 121, 123, 124, 125, 126, 128, 129, 132, 269, 270, 271
Trump, Ivanka, 96
Twin Pillar Policy, 108
Twin Towers, 39, 44

Umm, 142, 184, 186
United Nations, xviii, 8, 20, 39, 75, 121, 134, 166
US air force housing complex, 9

USA PATRIOT Act, 52
US army Corps of Engineers, 36
US Congress, xix, xxvi, 41, 52
US intervention in Iraq, xvii
US invasion of Iraq in 2003, xviii, xxvii, 70, 81, 111, 267
US–Iran nuclear agreement, xvii
US–Islamic World Forum, 73
US National Security Council, xxvi, xxxi, 275
US–Saudi economic and military alliance, xx
USS Cole bombing, xiv
USS Quincy, 36

vehicle-borne improvised explosive devices (VBIED), 15
Velayat-e Faqih, 93, 100
Viber, 20
virtual caliphate, 68, 189, 191

Wahdat, 105, 244
West Bank, xviii, 24, 68
Westgate shopping mall attack, 191
WhatsApp, 20, 156, 174
World against Violence and Extremism (WAVE), 75
World Assembly of Muslim Youth (WAMY), xxv
World Trade Center, 10, 12, 44

Yazidi, 17, 183, 186

Zakaria, Fareed, 45
Zakariya, Sheikh Bahauddin, 242
Zar-Baksh, Zar Zari, 239
Zarqawi, Abu Musab al-, xvii,

xxvii, 16, 66, 77, 159, 171, 194, 196, 267
Zawahiri, Ayman al-, 10, 14, 43, 159, 174, 197, 204

Zaydi, xxi, 60, 78, 113, 122, 270
Zaydi Shia, xxi, 113
Zhora Foundation, 184
Zionist state, xxii

www.ingramcontent.com/pod-product-compliance
Lightning Source LLC
Chambersburg PA
CBHW031435150426
43191CB00006B/534